D1521764

EVIL AND THE MYSTICS' GOD

Evil and the Mystics' God

Towards a Mystical Theodicy

Michael Stoeber

University of Toronto Press
Toronto and Buffalo

First published in North America in 1992 by
UNIVERSITY OF TORONTO PRESS
Toronto and Buffalo

ISBN 0–8020–5000–X

Printed in Great Britain

Canadian Cataloguing in Publication Data
Stoeber, Michael F., 1958–
Evil and the mystics' God
Includes bibliographical references and index.
ISBN 0–8020–5000–X
1. Theodicy.   2. Mysticism.   3. Good and evil.
I. Title.
BT160.S76   1992 214   C91–094268–4

In memory of my father
John M. Stoeber

Contents

PART TWO   MYSTICAL THEODICY

Acknowledgements

For financial assistance I thank the School of Graduate Studies at the University of Toronto, the government of Ontario, and the Social Sciences and Humanities Research Council of Canada. Also, for their support I thank the Department of Religious Studies, University of Calgary, and the Centre for Religious Studies at the University of Toronto, especially Ms Muna Salloum. For permission to draw upon 'Personal Identity and Rebirth', I thank the University of Cambridge Press.

This book is a version of my PhD thesis. The fundamental theme of the dissertation arose in a short paper I wrote in a graduate seminar on theodicy led by Paul Gooch. He provided a great deal of encouragement and direction throughout my PhD programme, as well as extensive comments and criticisms on the drafts of the book. I appreciate his support very much. Also in this seminar I met Michael Latzer and Frank Gonzales, both of whom read and commented on various chapters of the manuscript. Along with R. Z. Friedman, who also read earlier drafts, I thank them for their helpful comments.

Donald Evans supervised the thesis. He recognised immediately the possibilities of drawing the topic out in such an extended context, and his insightful advice very much influenced the research process. His academic scope and practical mystical experience made him an excellent supervisor of the topic, and his prompt and extensive responses to the various drafts was quite astonishing given his many other interests and commitments. I consider myself very lucky indeed to have fallen upon such a knowledgeable and conscientious supervisor.

Finally, I acknowledge the love of my wife, Lois, and my children, Thomas and Anne, who have so patiently endured the many negative side-effects of graduate student life. Without their encouragement and support, this book would not be.

MFS

Introduction

> That both philosophy and theology encounter evil as a *challenge* unlike any other, the greatest thinkers in both these disciplines are willing to admit. What is important is the way in which this challenge, or this failure, is received: do we find an invitation to think less about the problem or a provocation to think more, or to think differently about it?[1]

Theodicies are not usually associated with mysticism. The general perception is that mystics do not even respond to the challenge of evil, let alone invite one to think more or differently about it. Indeed, there has always been great concern about the mystic denial of evil and the moral consequences of such a perspective. In these instances mystics are denounced for becoming so enraptured in the isolated pursuit of their experiences that they do not recognise or care about the force and reality of evil.

It is true that at one point or another all mystics stress a withdrawal from the natural and social realities with which evil is associated. The evil that obtains in this realm is left behind, so to speak, in the other-worldly pursuit beyond. But certain mystics not only respond to the problem of evil, they do so in uniquely 'mystical' ways. These mystics provide a variety of responses to the challenge of evil, answers which are associated with their mystical experiences. These solutions, then, differ from traditional theodicies in certain significant ways. Together these various responses form a unified 'mystical' theodicy.

What I hope to do in this book is to draw the structure of this mystical theodicy together, to provoke not only further thought concerning the challenge of evil, but also to bring to light features of theodicy that have gone unnoticed or been neglected by major figures in the field. This mystical theodicy provides a number of provocative responses to the problem of evil, solutions which not only go much further than traditional theodicies, but which also overcome many of their associated problems. Thus it offers a more coherent and cogent response to the challenge of evil than do traditional non-mystical theodicies.

This reflection on mystical theodicy arose in encounter with the thought of a variety of both non-mystical and mystical philosophers and theologians. Perhaps the most significant influences on this work are John Hick's *Evil and the God of Love*, and Fyodor Dostoevsky's *The Brothers Karamazov*. Professor Hick provides one of the most complete and plausible systematic theodicies, and Dostoevsky gives an outline of mystical theodicy and offers one of the best accounts of the problem. These two books provide important reference points through which I draw my argument together.

The argument itself is divided into two distinct parts: non-mystical theodicy and mystical theodicy. The first part of the book is an examination of traditional non-mystical theodicies. I begin by defining theodicy, proposing a 'positive' or 'affirmative' aspect of theodicy. This is a response which affirms the active beneficence of the Divine, thereby giving some positive account of *specific* experienced evils and providing some comforting force for those suffering through evil. This aspect is often neglected in the emphasis of traditional theodicy upon the 'defensive' component of theodicy. Theodicy is generally perceived as a defence against those who charge that the reality of evil shows religious beliefs to be false. Though such a defence is necessary to theodicy, a more effective response to the challenge of evil will include also a positive or affirmative consolatory thrust.

Following this discussion in Chapter 1 of the role and function of theodicy, I briefly turn to the traditional responses to the challenge. These can be distinguished in terms of four major themes: retributive, free-will, aesthetic, and the teleological. Evil is explained either as a *retribution* for wrong-doing; as a possibility which could not be excluded if human beings are to be *free*; as a constituent in an overall good which can be discerned *aesthetically*; or as a necessary context for some divine *telos* or purpose. I argue that the teleological theme is the only coherent move for theodicy; the retributive, free-will and aesthetic themes are only effective when subordinated to the teleological theme. For the most satisfactory response to evil we must look to that which attempts to explain or justify evil in terms of some future good to which it is ordered.

But before examining traditional teleological theodicies, I examine the nature of the problem. In Chapter 2 I illustrate the problem of

evil through Dostoevsky's *The Brothers Karamazov*. Though Dostoevsky recognises human freedom and an essential human good–evil
polarity as necessary elements in his religious teleology, he nevertheless doubts theodicy in the face of the many dysteleological evils
of the world. Through Ivan Karamazov he raises the major criticisms
for teleological theodicy in a very moving and practical manner.

Returning, then, to the response to evil in teleological theodicy, I
examine the systematic development of Gottfried Leibniz's optimistic perspective. He provides one of the clearer and more systematic
teleological theodicies, emphasising the free-will theme in distancing
God's responsibility from the reality of evil. He distinguishes
between the antecedent will and the consequent will of God,
arguing that the latter is that which harmoniously synthesises the
many diverse goods of God's antecedent will. Evil is necessary to
this best of all possible worlds; though it does not exist in terms of
the antecedent will it occurs in the context of the consequent, and
solely for the purpose of manifesting and communicating divine
perfections.

Now Leibniz's theodicy fails on a number of counts: he does not
detail the nature of the telos, does not effectively relate the present
state of affairs with the telos, does not give evidence to justify his
view, and he gives no indication of active divine beneficence. In
Chapter 4 we move to a more effective development. John Hick's
famous soul-making theodicy overcomes in many respects the difficulties of Leibniz's response. Professor Hick lucidly outlines the
teleology in terms of an autonomous growth to divine likeness that
involves personal relationship and participation in a divine life. The
ideal is made intelligible and the process is plausible; the telos is
coherently connected to our present situation and the necessity of
personal freedom justifies evil and removes God from direct responsibility of evil. Nevertheless, there are four major difficulties for his
view: though he speaks of a future other-worldly eschaton that
verifies soul-making theodicy, he does not give sufficient evidence
in support of the telos; he takes a rather ambiguous stance regarding
the consolatory force of his theodicy, treating the affirmative aspect
of theodicy rather indirectly and incompletely; he does not explain
the depth, scope and impulse to evil; he does not adequately account
for the many dysteleological evils of the world.

These difficulties are the subject of Chapter 5. The first problem
is raised most effectively by Immanuel Kant. Kant gives both a
practical and a theoretical critique of theodicy, showing that there

is insufficient evidence to justify teleological theodicy. Though Hick gives some evidence in support of his theodicy, Kant is right to point out that the hypothesis cannot be empirically verified. Hick can only point vaguely to a future eschatological experience to justify his view. Mystical theodicies, on the other hand, claim possible verification here and now, a mystical experience of God's purposes that Kant himself points towards. In Chapter 7 I will develop this approach as it occurs in the thought of Meister Eckhart. He espouses a mystical path which, he claims, gives rise to evidence confirming teleology. I will examine the various issues surrounding such a claim – its nature, implications, significance and plausibility – and I will argue that this feature of mystical theodicy offers much more than Hick's theodicy possibly can.

The second problem discussed in Chapter 5 surrounds the issue of the positive/affirmative aspect of theodicy. Professor Hick depicts God in rather impassible and transcendent terms, while at the same time insisting upon a divine presence open to the human being. The issues of active divine beneficence and consolatory force in the encounter of evil are treated by him rather briefly and ambiguously. This is in contrast to those mystical theodicies which stress very much the consolatory power of mystical experience and the passibility of God. In Chapter 8 I will return to the thought of Eckhart who, following the tradition of Plotinus and Pseudo-Dionysius, speaks of evil as 'nothing' and stresses the tremendous consolatory power of mystical experience. But he does not thereby deny the negative force of evil; he reconciles mystical consolation with the active response to the problem. In this context I also develop Dostoevsky's positive view of theodicy. This involves active love and compassion as vehicles in religious transformation, a transformation that involves experiences of consolation and of evidence verifying theodicy. Mystical theodicies such as those of Dostoevsky and Eckhart offer a practical consolation and a rational response to the sceptic which are much stronger than we find in non-mystical theodicies.

The third problem developed in Chapter 5 is that of the depth and scope of evil and the human impulse to evil. Though Kant provides the structure within which we might understand the incentives to evil, neither he nor Hick explains the apparent teleological *necessity* for these incentives, nor do they sufficiently distance this darker side of human nature from God. In Chapter 9 we will turn to Jacob Boehme's mystical response to this issue. He provides a theogony that explains the human impulse to evil in terms of the first principle of the Divine Essence. This is the *Ungrund*, that which depends upon the second principle for its existence, and without which God cannot create. It is the hidden principle of dynamism, that through which God is personal and active, and that which the human being actualises in choosing against the second principle of the Divine Essence. But in God this principle is eternally transformed; it has no existence apart from God. So Boehme explains the darker side of human nature while at the same time distancing it from God. Created in an image of the three principles of the Divine Essence, the human being is involved in autonomous growth to the divine life. So human beings fulfil the Divine Essence. The human impulse to evil resides in the *Ungrund*, that which is necessary to the dynamic creative world of human teleology, but which the human being must overcome and transform in spiritual progression.

The final problem discussed in Chapter 5 is the issue of dysteleological evils. These evils are those unjustified by any future good that we can imagine, those that do not contribute to the supposed teleology. Hick suggests future realms of soul-making in the attempt to explain the failure of soul-making teleology in this world. In Chapter 10 I will develop this possibility as it is conceived in the hypotheses of probationary purgatory and the doctrine of rebirth. In examination of two major views of rebirth, I will argue that if the hypothesis is dissociated in certain respects from a retributive theme, it provides a much stronger response to the issue of dysteleological evils than does the hypothesis of probationary purgatory. As it is espoused by Aurobindo Ghose, the idea of rebirth maintains the notion of this world as essential to spiritual teleology. This is a fundamental premise for teleological theodicies, one that cannot be upheld in the hypothesis of probationary purgatory because it implies that another world is a better context for soul-making than this world is.

To summarise, Part I consists of an examination of non-mystical theodicies that possess a teleological emphasis. After exploring arguments in Leibniz, Hick, Kant and Hume, I note in Chapter 5 the four main problems that face such theodicies. In Part II I show how these problems are dealt with more adequately in a mystical theodicy. The problems are considered successively in Chapters 7, 8, 9 and 10, where I refer to ideas in Eckhart, Dostoevsky, Boehme and Aurobindo. My main other mystical source is Evelyn Underhill, whose account of teleological mysticism I present at the beginning of Part II, in Chapter 6. Drawing on these five mystical thinkers I propose a coherent and cogent mystical theodicy. Though mystical theodicy does not *solve* the challenge of evil, it resolves many of the issues in a manner more effective than that of non-mystical theodicy. Of course it does not resolve them all, nor do I fully treat all the related questions surrounding these responses to the challenge. Nevertheless, I hope this book can induce the kind of positive response to the challenge of evil that Paul Ricoeur expresses in our opening quotation. Clearly some mystics do find in the challenge an invitation to think more and differently about the problem; I hope their responses in turn provoke the reader in a similar manner.

PART I

Non-mystical Theodicy

1
Defining Theodicy

NEGATIVE AND AFFIRMATIVE THEODICY

Theodicy is the religious response to the problem of pain and suffering. It has been defined by John Hick as 'an attempt to reconcile the unlimited goodness of an all-powerful God with the reality of evil'.[1] In such a view the function of the theodicist is to show that these attributes of the Divine are consistent with the reality and experience of evil. In this regard theodicy is usually considered a defensive affair: the role of the theodicist is to defend religious beliefs against those who argue they are contradictory or implausible in the face of evil. The theodicist usually *responds* to attacks pertaining to evil that are raised against religious beliefs by the atheologian or religious sceptic. This fact about theodicy has led many to perceive theodicy as an exclusively defensive activity.

This assumption about the nature of theodicy is not surprising. Well developed and systematic theodicies grew in large part out of forces that questioned the rationality of religious belief. Religious thinkers were pressured to carefully think out and clarify the problem of evil in response to those who claimed it to be inconsistent with their view of God. A case in point that will become clear in Chapter 3 is the Pierre Bayle–Gottfried Leibniz debate which issued forth in Leibniz's famous *Theodicy*. This in turn had an effect upon others, for example, the scepticism of Voltaire (Chapter 3) and Hume (Chapter 1), and the later practical theodical stance of Kant (Chapter 5). Clearly, theodicy has been clarified and refined in the context of the dialogue between the religious sceptic and the religious believer.

This historical development has contributed to the general present-day stress on theodicy as a defence against those who claim that religious beliefs are contradicted by the reality of evil. And this emphasis has, I think, led some theodicists to maintain a rather narrow conception of the nature and role of theodicy. An influential account of this point of view is expressed by Alvin Plantinga in *God,*

Freedom and Evil. In this book Plantinga formulates a version of the
free-will defence that shows the divine attributes and the reality of
evil to be an implicitly consistent set. In specifying a state of affairs
where God might have good reason for creating and permitting evil
in the context of free-will, Professor Plantinga successfully defends
theism against the attack of inconsistency raised by atheologians
such as J. L. Mackie. Indeed, though his defence does not give
evidence justifying the *truth* of the proposed state of affairs, it is
enough to show that the theist's set (divine attributes and evil) is
not logically inconsistent. A theodicy, he claims, would show the
state of affairs to be true, but such is not necessary; the free-will
defence is a sufficient response to the sceptic.

Certainly Plantinga is correct about the charge of inconsistency,
and he is right to distinguish a free-will defence from a free-will
theodicy. Nevertheless, he goes on to imply a rather restrictive definition of theodicy, as if a theodicy was but a special kind of defence
against the sceptic's attack. I quote him at length to illustrate the
point:

> Neither a defense or a theodicy, of course, gives any hint as to
> what God's reason for some *specific* evil – the death or suffering
> of someone close to you, for example – might be. And, there is
> still another function – a sort of pastoral function – in the neigh-
> bourhood that neither serves. Confronted with evil in his own life
> or suddenly coming to realize more clearly than before the *extent*
> and *magnitude* of evil, a believer may undergo a crisis of faith. He
> may be tempted to follow the advice of Job's 'friends'; he may be
> tempted to 'curse God and die.' Neither a Free Will Defense nor
> a Free Will Theodicy is designed to be of much help or comfort to
> one suffering from such a storm in the soul (although in a specific
> case, of course, one or the other could prove useful). Neither is
> to be thought of first of all as a means of pastoral counselling.
> Probably neither will enable someone to find peace with himself
> and with God in the face of the evil the world contains. But then,
> of course, neither is intended for that purpose.[2]

Plantinga's position on these issues is not well clarified in the
quotation in question: he does not specify the purpose of theodicy
nor does he explain how a theodicy or free-will defence might, in the
specific cases he has in mind, prove useful as pastoral counselling.
But here he stimulates a number of questions about the nature and

role of theodicy. Considered as a religious response to the problem of evil one would naturally think that a theodicy might provide justification for specific evils and serve a pastoral function. Should a theodicy function in this manner? Does *no* theodicy provide even a hint of the reason for a specific evil? Does *no* theodicy carry consolatory force for the believer? Is theodicy intended for such purposes? Plantinga replies firmly in the negative to this final question; he seems a bit uncertain about the others. He appears to assume that the only purpose of theodicy is to answer the religious sceptic's charge of formal inconsistency. If theodicy is intended solely for this purpose then perhaps one would be correct in ruling out the pastoral function and its practical explanation of specific evils. But surely the response to the sceptic is only one aspect of theodicy, albeit perhaps the most significant and common. More generally, as I noted above, theodicy is a response to the problem of pain and suffering. Why should such a response to this problem exclude specific evils and the pastoral function, or treat these aspects of the problem only accidentally and indirectly? Are these roles ruled out by the very nature of theodicy? Let us examine the meaning of theodicy more carefully.

Theodicy is formally defined as the 'vindication of divine providence in view of the existence of evil'.[3] Providence here is the 'beneficent care of God'.[4] Theodicy then is the vindication of the beneficent care of God in the context of the reality of evil. In such a view one would expect an effective theodicy to give evidence indicating the active beneficence of the Divine. Though it is sometimes elucidated in a context of the defence of the consistency of the theistic propositions, this evidence goes beyond such a defence, introducing what might be called a positive or affirmative aspect of theodicy. The defensive aspect is necessary to an effective theodicy: theodicy should address the issues arising from the queries of the religious sceptic. But a more satisfactory theodicy will go beyond the defence, including in the response to evil some indication of the nature and extent of divine goodness, and, if not justifying a specific evil through this positive account, at least pointing the way towards such reconciliation.

But there is a danger in this aspect of the response, a threat that perhaps has influenced Plantinga, and others, to neglect this positive aspect of theodicy. This danger surfaces in the question of what constitutes a successful theodicy. As I will illustrate in a moment, the most effective theodicies tend to justify evil in terms of the realisation of a greater good that necessitates the possibility of evil. These are what I will call teleological theodicies, themes that do not reconcile evil in the present context, but look to the future for such justification. Indeed, later I will show that all theodical themes only cohere in a teleological context. The teleological theme attempts to explain or justify evil in terms of some future good to which evil is ordered. Evil, then, or the possibility of evil, is considered a necessary component in the movement or transformation of present circumstances to some future, better, state of affairs. Evil is a necessary ingredient to the fulfilment of some higher ideal, a goal which can involve either an individual or a cosmic–communal emphasis. That is, the telos can be understood to be finally realised in an individual's growth or transformation to the good, or in the universal realisation of the end-goal.

But this teleological move can give rise to a number of serious problems. It can espouse a means–end justification of dubious moral character – where divine morality is perched above and against human morality – and it can diminish the obligation to moral activity. In 'Evil and Moral Agency', R. Z. Friedman raises these issues of theodicy. On the first point he argues that in considering the experience of evil as the means to a good end that justifies the means, the human being is granting a dual moral standard of unacceptable double-dealing. Religious imperatives demand that human beings be regarded as ends in themselves; this theodicy sees them as means of bringing good into the world. The means–end proposition, says Friedman, 'forces a certain hypocrisy on the moral agent – he must judge his actions according to one principle and God's according to another'.[5]

Closely related to this problem is the question of moral agency. If evil is but for the good, then why actively strive against it? Professor Friedman asks:

> Might the agent not wonder whether by doing good he actually inhibits the greater good that God might realise in the world had he chosen to do evil? Indeed the agent might lose hold of his moral understanding altogether, for it might prove to be an inadequate guide to conduct.[6]

But these issues of the status of morality and of moral agency point to a more fundamental problem. In illustrating the beneficence of the Divine the theodicist might do away with the problem of evil altogether. The possibility exists, in this positive aspect of theodicy, of transforming the power of evil into good. By depicting evil as but a means or an aspect of the good it serves, one altogether eliminates its negative force. In this regard, Friedman asks:

> From this point of view the agent is not to shun evil but to appreciate that evil is the chrysalis out of which good comes, that the isolated individual with his moral complaint about evil in the world is himself but a moment, an element, through which good is realized. But is evil so conceived evil?[7]

So Friedman aptly perceives very serious moral implications in this radical form of teleological theodicy. Friedman goes on in his essay to develop these issues as they pertain both to theodicists and anti-theodicists, and he suggests that Job's recognition of the problem of evil together with his rejection of solutions can be interpreted as a defence of moral agency. But it is important here for us to note that radical teleological theodicies answer the problem of evil by declaring it no problem at all, a solution which is ineffective. For where evil is perceived as solely good, theodicy becomes self-defeating; it denies the terms of the problem with which it begins. Later in Chapter 8 I will examine this move in more detail as it arises in mystical theodicy. In certain mystical experiences evil is realised as beneficent; indeed, all is pictured as a harmonised good, eliminating the problem of evil and the obligations of social morality. Though this problem is not exclusive to mysticism, it is most common and pronounced in this type of mystical theodicy.

However, the important point here is to illustrate the danger and weaknesses of this extreme positive/affirmative aspect of theodicy. In its most radical form it can eliminate the negative power of evil and thereby de-legitimise moral effort to combat evil. Such a theodicy twists our moral sensibility and espouses a dubious notion of divine beneficence. The problem of evil here begins as fundamentally a moral problem – an issue that arises from our moral 'dis-ease' – and it ends by denying the very moral premises with which it begins. In this sense it is self-defeating. It does not justify evil as we understand and perceive it, but simply denies it in transforming it to good. So it fails. An effective theodicy must maintain the sense of evil as a negative force and include within itself justification for reducing the pain and suffering of others.

To summarise, then, theodicy is defined as the vindication of the beneficent care of God in the context of the existence of evil. A coherent theodicy is a consistent, unified and systematic formulation. An effective theodicy will involve the reconciliation of the divine attributes and evil – what can be understood as its defensive aspect. But it will also include evidence illustrating the active beneficence of the Divine, while at the same time maintaining the negative reality of evil and the obligations of social morality. But more than this, as I briefly mentioned earlier in this section, an effective theodicy will involve a teleological theme. I will now turn to examine the significant themes present in traditional theodicies, drawing out the weaknesses of non-teleological themes and clarifying the necessary association of these themes with teleology.

THE MOVEMENT TO TELEOLOGICAL THEODICY

Systematising the various themes of theodicy is a common practice in academic studies. Though these systems are sometimes refined in great detail, I distinguish between only four theodical themes, traditional themes within which the various strands of theodicy might be included.[8] I have already mentioned the teleological. The other three might be called non-teleological themes of theodicy. But though they can be formulated in non-teleological terms, they are only given coherence through the move to teleological theodicy. These themes are the retributive, the free-will and the aesthetic themes.

I begin with the retributive. This theme is most commonly associated with the Judeo-Christian traditions. Here we find the emphasis upon the concepts of original sin and individual sin as they arise in the interpretation of the myth of the fall of the first creatures. The source of original sin is in the fall of Adam and Eve. As a result of their disobedience to God's commands they are expelled from paradise and pass this original depravity on to their descendants. Natural evils, that is the pain and suffering associated with the natural deficiencies common to this realm of non-paradise, are considered the consequence of the original fall. Moral evils arise through individual sin. Through pride and selfish desire human beings choose and act against God. This further compounds the reality of evil.

Evil, then, is considered either as retributive punishment for sin, where God inflicts it upon his creatures, or as the consequence of sin, where God permits its actualisation. But both cases involve serious moral difficulties. For one essential element of retributive theory is that a person not be punished unless he or she has committed a crime. This retributive theme would have all of humanity paying the price for the misdeeds of their ancestors, a price compounded in its seeming disproportion to the original wrong-doing.[9] Moreover, fairness in distribution and proportionate punishment for wrong-doing are also key elements in retributive punishment. But pain and suffering arising from moral and natural evils is from our perspective often allocated arbitrarily and unfairly; the unjust often do not suffer and the just often do.[10] So, in light of these difficulties for the retributive theme, it would appear that even if, as some theorists hold, 'the application to the offender of the pain of punishment is itself a thing of value',[11] some teleological point seems also to be required when retribution is advanced as theodicy. A 'backward-looking' retributive theodicy must give way in some respects to a 'forward-looking' theme, one that will perhaps draw on elements such as education, reform or deterrence.[12] In these cases certain moral and natural evils are justified as instrumental in achieving some future good.

So the retributive theme must be supplemented with a teleological explanation. Often this move will involve some reference to free-will, where sin is understood as the consequence of the free choice of human beings. This free-will defence is perhaps the most significant theodical theme. Many thinkers consider it a sufficient response to the problem of moral evil. Moral evil arises in the misuse of human freedom. The greater part of pain and suffering is caused by creatures who freely choose against God. Moral evil, then, is explained through human freedom. However, even this move, in itself, is not complete; it calls for teleological reference. For the moral evil arising in freedom must be justified. We must ask, why freedom when it involves such an incredible amount of moral evil?[13] In answer the theodicist will incorporate some kind of teleological reference, where freedom will be seen in its role in bringing about some future good.

On the other hand, natural evil, the evil arising in the processes of the natural world, is not usually justified in terms of a free-will defence.[14] Often such justification involves some reference to the aesthetic theme, a very common theme in mystical theodicy. Evil in this view is considered but an aspect of our narrow and limited human perspective; though parts of the universe are imperfect or

defective, even the most negative features contribute to the goodness and perfection of the universe on the whole. From an overall
perspective that arises in certain mystical experiences of aesthetic
wisdom, the world is perfect and good.

In so far as the theme maintains the present state of affairs to be
perfectly good *as it is*, however, it denies the terms of the problem
it begins with. In such a perspective evil has no negative power or
reality, and theodicy fails, as Friedman has pointed out. For some
mystics, however, the consolation that issues forth from aesthetic-
wisdom experiences is combined with a teleological eschatology
that consists of the experience of a personal and active benevolent
Divine. Though the effects of evil are profoundly reduced for the
mystic in experiences of divine presence in the natural world, this
consolation is combined with a participation in a personal divine
concern to reduce or transform the negative force of evil in oneself and in the world. As we will see, for certain mystics aesthetic
wisdom is not realised as a static, isolated and final event; it is
only properly fulfilled when there is a universal and communal
realisation involving a personal, dynamic and benevolent God.[15]

So the aesthetic theme, like the free-will and retributive themes,
calls for teleological reference in order to cohere. There remains,
however, the issue of other themes of theodicy. Though I have
not shown how the many various themes of theodicy fit within the
framework of the four themes which I consider major, I have made
the stronger claim that *all* theodical themes are only coherent when
subordinated to a teleological perspective. So, for a more general
argument that shows that all theodical themes *must* be related to a
teleological theme, we turn now to certain criticisms raised by David
Hume regarding the problem of evil.

DAVID HUME: A BETTER WORLD

In Part XI of the *Dialogues Concerning Natural Religion*, David Hume
discusses four circumstances upon which he considers evil to
depend. Three of the four can be adapted to illustrate the necessity
and significance of teleological theodicy. I begin with his fourth
circumstance of evil.

Though admitting the particular purposefulness and general harmony of the principles of the natural world, Philo, the character who
develops these circumstances of evil, points out their tendency to

extreme and excess. Wind, rain, heat and human passions often exceed their efficacious bounds with disastrous consequences:

> none of these parts or principles, however useful, are so accurately adjusted as to keep precisely within those bounds in which their utility consists; but they are, all of them, apt, on every occasion, to run into one extreme or the other. . . . There is nothing so advantageous in the universe but what frequently becomes pernicious, by its excess or defect; nor has nature guarded, with the requisite accuracy, against all disorder or confusion.[16]

Philo goes on to imagine the better condition of the world should these springs and principles be checked in moderation. But this tendency to excess and defect is not the only the problem he perceives in the natural principles of the world. The third circumstance of evil proposed by Philo contrasts the tendency to extremes. These are the seeming limitations of creatures, particularly human beings, whose natural capacities might have received a greater expansion or extension. Philo suggests a moral analogy of parental concern for children in his illustration of these human weaknesses. He says:

> In short, nature seems to have formed an exact calculation of the necessities of her creatures, and, like a *rigid master*, has afforded them little more powers or endowments than what are strictly sufficient to supply those necessities. An *indulgent parent* would have bestowed a large stock in order to guard against accidents, and secure the happiness and welfare of the creature in the most unfortunate concurrence of circumstances.[17]

Now Philo's second circumstance of evil ties the argument together by stressing the ability of a perfect being to make better the many evil conditions without thereby overthrowing the habitual and regulative principles of general laws. Through particular volitions God might intervene upon the evils arising in these general laws of the world, and lessen, indeed, even eliminate, their force:

> In short, might not the Deity exterminate all ill, wherever it were to be found, and produce all good, without any preparation or long progress of causes and effects? . . . A being, therefore, who knows the secret springs of the universe might easily, by particular volitions, turn all these accidents to the good of mankind and

render the whole world happy, without discovering himself in any operation.[18]

So God, acting upon the natural processes, might eliminate the tendency to excess and destruction characteristic of the fourth circumstance of evil without revealing himself. Moreover, He might have better endowed and empowered His creatures against that of the third circumstance of evil. Indeed, God might eliminate all ill; in His omnipotence He could secure a hedonistic paradise of temporal delight.

Such a suggestion implies a view of human nature radically different from that which we presently understand. Theologians have responded to this conception by pointing to its negative implications. John Hick argues that the human 'race would consist of feckless Adams and Eves, harmless and innocent, but devoid of positive character and without the dignity of real responsibilities, tasks, and achievements'.[19] Similarly, St Thomas Aquinas recognises good that arises only from particular defects. He says:

Since God, then, provides universally for all being, it belongs to His providence to permit certain defects in particular effects, that the perfect good of the universe may not be hindered; for if all evil were prevented, much good would be absent from the universe. A lion would cease to live, if there were no slaying of animals; and there would be no patience of martyrs if there were no tyrannical persecution.[20]

So Thomas and Hick suggest that to propose the elimination of all evils is to conceive a world absent of many of the goods we presently know. Still, despite these responses, Hume's criticism holds force. For he need not ask so much. He suggests that there might be 'very little ill in comparison of what we feel at present,'[21] that, given the omnipotent nature of God, the suffering and pain present to the world might be lessened, that the world might be made better. The force of the criticism thus rests on the nature of God. Thomas, though arguing that a better world would be a different world, nevertheless stresses the omnipotence of God in this regard. He says, 'God could make other things, or add something to the present creation; and then there would be another and a better universe'.[22] The universe, though good as an expression of

God, could nevertheless be made different and better. But to this view Philo responds with the questions 'why didn't He and why doesn't He'?

To such questions both Thomas and Hick offer a variety of theodical replies, of course, but the significant point is that their theodicies, if they are to cohere, *demand* a response, a reply that involves some teleological reference. This can be drawn out more clearly by noting the two senses of a good world that are at play here. Because God could do better the world cannot be understood as *intrinsically* good. Though Thomas speaks of the world as wholly good this cannot mean absolutely good, the world as good in and of itself. Indeed, in and of itself it is defective, possessing weaknesses arising in its secondary and contingent nature. Thus the goodness of the universe is qualified in terms of something other and external to it. Stress on the omnipotence and freedom of God regarding the creative process results in the conceptions of other, better, possible worlds.[23]

But here 'better' is qualified; it is understood as a world less defective and less painful, as a world containing less particular evil. When pressed for a reason for this universe as opposed to another, better universe, theodicy must deal with this qualification of the goodness of the universe. And this qualification will involve elucidation of the appropriateness of this universe in achieving this or that particular end.

Is this the *best* of all possible worlds? Clearly we can conceive of a world in which there was less evil, that is, less suffering and less human wrong-doing. So why didn't God, who is omnipotent and good, create such a world? Any theodicy must provide an answer to this question. And the only feasible answer seems to be: 'because this world provides the best context for the eventual fulfilment of some ultimate end'. That is, this world is not intrinsically the best of all possible worlds, but it is so instrumentally. If theodicy does not bring in a teleological reference, it breaks down in the face of Philo's questions.

So coherent and effective theodicy always takes the teleological form where evil, or the possibility of evil, is justified in terms of its necessary role in fulfilling some future state of affairs. Naturally, then, this theme is present in some form in most traditional theodicies. However, often in these instances the teleological theme does not clearly predominate in any clear systematic manner. Perhaps the earliest theodicy where the teleological theme is clearly presented as the main element is that of Gottfried Leibniz. In the *Theodicy* he effectively clarifies and systematises teleological theodicy. Indeed, Leibniz, who is famous for his depiction of this world as the best of all possible worlds, provides one of the more coherent teleological theodicies. But before turning to the theodicy of Leibniz we should introduce the significant problems of the traditional themes of retribution, free-will and aesthetics, as they occur in the context of a teleological theodicy. So we will consider Fyodor Dostoevsky's insightful version and attack of these themes in *The Brothers Karamazov*. Then, with these problems in mind, we can critically examine Leibniz's systematic teleological theodicy.

2
Dostoevsky's Critique of Theodicy

In the previous chapter I showed the failure of traditional themes of theodicy to resolve, in themselves, the problem of evil. In theodical dialogue the themes of aesthetics, retribution and free-will beg for teleological support; traditional theodicy always moves to teleology. But in so doing I did not illustrate the problems that arise in this natural teleological movement. The purpose of this chapter is to examine in a practical and relevant manner the issues connected with these traditional themes, before turning to the more abstract developments that we find in systematic teleological theodicies.

Perhaps no one has illustrated more provocatively the practical implications of the problem of evil than Fyodor Dostoevsky. Indeed, the problem of pain and suffering dominates the many religious and philosophical themes he develops in his literary endeavours.[1] In *The Brothers Karamazov* the theme is present more directly and fully than in Dostoevsky's other works, and here it is accentuated by his literary genius; the book is considered his greatest story.

In this novel Dostoevsky treats the traditional theodical themes of aesthetic harmony, retribution and free-will in a teleological context. That is to say, he develops and examines the attempt to justify evil in terms of some future good to which these three themes are ordered. Evil, or the possibility of evil, is thought to arise as a requisite component: (1) in its minor contribution to the greater aesthetic picture that is good on the whole, (2) as punishment in retribution, or (3) in free-will. But the necessity of these conditions is found in their role in the movement or transformation of present circumstances to some future, better, state of affairs. Now Dostoevsky *denies* these teleological moves to justify evil; he adamantly rejects the teleological theodicy he so vividly portrays. Yet, in striking contradistinction he does move towards a particular theodical resolution, one which stresses very strongly the necessity of freedom for human dignity, and the importance of active compassion and personal love that leads to and arises from mystical experience. So he proposes a mystical theodicy, a theodical resolution which, despite the serious moral problems associated with traditional theodicy, nevertheless occurs in mystical experience.

In Chapter 8, I will develop this mystical theodicy and evaluate Dostoevsky's theodical antithesis, but for now it is important only to note that this antithesis is presented as a tension in theodicy, a conflict between the rejection of traditional theodicy on rational, moral grounds, and the acceptance of mystical theodicy. This tension is never fully resolved in *The Brothers Karamazov*.[2] It is illustrated through the contrasting characters of Ivan Karamazov on the one hand and Alyosha Karamazov and Father Zosima on the other. Ivan represents the negative pole of Dostoevsky's theodicy, a figure set in opposition to Alyosha and Zosima, characters who point the way towards the acceptance of theodicy. While Alyosha and Zosima express the positive religious consciousness of Dostoevsky, it is in Ivan that the problems of evil are elucidated and shaped, and theodicy rejected.

IVAN

The general plot of the story is simple: three brothers return to their neglectful father, Fyodor Karamazov, where they become involved in romantic intrigue. The plot culminates in the murder of the father by the illegitimate son, Smerdyakov, and the trial and unjust conviction of the elder brother, Dmitri. But around this main plot circles a great complexity of subplots. Ivan is the second son, the first of two boys born from Fyodor's second marriage. In many senses, Alyosha, the youngest son of this second marriage and the positive hero of the story, is the opposite of Ivan, who has been aptly characterised as the negative hero. Henry Troyat describes him as 'an irritable intellectual with a tormented and destructive mind – a hero and martyr of negation'.[3] He is bright, self-reliant and independent, an intellectual who borders upon atheism and nihilism. His role in the plot is significant. The dialectic he propounds becomes the theoretical underpinning for the parricide; his 'everything is lawful' pronouncement inspires Smerdyakov to the murder of Fyodor. Ivan's indirect role in this crime is further compounded in his abandonment of Dmitri. He claims not to be his brother's keeper. Furthermore, it is only in his absence that the murder can occur; his presence at his father's house insures his father's safety, and his hasty departure opens the door for the crime.

But the major role of Ivan lies not in his position in the story's plot, which itself is subordinate to the ideas that Dostoevsky propounds in the book. Ivan expresses most powerfully the problems of evil; he is the negative of Dostoevsky's religious consciousness, giving expression to the 'purging flame of doubts'[4] that haunted Dostoevsky's religious vision. Through Ivan, Dostoevsky gives voice to his religious scepticism. As Troyat says, 'Ivan's blasphemous negations are Dostoevsky's own negations in his moments of doubt'.[5] Similarly, D.H. Lawrence describes him as 'the thinking mind of the human being in rebellion, thinking the whole thing out to the bitter end',[6] and Richard Peace pictures Ivan's intellectual disposition as that of an 'inverted theologian',[7] stressing the deep passion and indignation that Ivan brings to his scepticism.

Three chapters in particular express Ivan's contribution to the issue of theodicy: 'Rebellion', 'The Grand Inquisitor' and 'The devil. Ivan Fyodorovich's Nightmare'. 'Rebellion' sets forth the problems in the context of innocent and unjustified suffering. Therein Dostoevsky touches upon the aesthetic and retributive themes of theodicy, using them to introduce and outline what he takes to be the more significant theodical response, that of free-will. In 'The Grand Inquisitor' he examines the implications of the move to justify evil in terms of freedom, developing the key related problem of the weakness of human nature. In 'The devil', this issue of human nature is given depth and scope, illustrating Dostoevsky's view of the impulse to evil in human nature. I begin with 'Rebellion'.

'Rebellion'

Interestingly enough, Ivan prefaces his rebellion by formulating a theodicy that he claims to believe but cannot accept. The theodicy involves the aesthetic theme in a teleological version that sees evil resolved in a future eternal harmony. Just prior to 'Rebellion', he says:

> I believe like a child that suffering will be healed and made up for, that all the humiliating absurdity of human contradictions

will vanish like a pitiful mirage, . . . that in the world's finale, at the moment of eternal harmony, something so precious will come to pass that it will suffice for all hearts, for the comforting of all resentments, for the atonement of all the crimes of humanity, of all the blood they've shed; that it will make it not only possible to forgive but to justify all that has happened with men – but though all that may come to pass, I don't accept it. I won't accept it. (pp. 216–17)[8]

So Ivan introduces his rebellion. Though he understands the justification of suffering in terms of a future good whereupon the divine wisdom and purpose will become clear in a higher justification that is presently unintelligible, he refuses to accept it, refuses to accept the suffering of this world as moral justification of this higher future vision. Alyosha, audience to this monologue, urges Ivan to explain his reasons, and so 'Rebellion' begins with a statement that, though provocative, seems out of place in his present thesis: Ivan says 'Christ-like love for men is a miracle impossible on earth' (p. 218). One can love one's neighbours in the abstract but not in person. This point, I think, is very significant to Dostoevsky's view, but must be set aside for a moment.

Ivan then develops the main premise of his argument: one cannot reasonably justify the suffering of the morally innocent. To illustrate his point he concentrates upon the suffering of children. Indeed, to the morally sensitive mind he need introduce no other examples to make his case. Children, for the most part, are not morally culpable beings and they are the most defenceless in these matters. He makes the point clear in his description of the merciless beating of a five-year-old girl by her parents, who go on to imprison her in a freezing outhouse, forcefully feeding and smearing her with excrement. He asks:

Do you understand why this rigmarole must be and is permitted? Without it, I am told, man could not have existed on earth, for he could not have known good and evil. Why should he know that diabolical good and evil when it costs so much? Why, the whole world of knowledge is not worth that child's prayer to "dear, kind God" . . . (p. 223)

Its not worth the tears of that one tortured child who beat itself on the breast with its little fist and prayed in its stinking outhouse, with its unexpiated tears to "dear, kind God!" . . . Its not worth it because those tears are unatoned for. (p. 225)

Another example that Ivan vividly explores is the case of the serf-boy who accidentally stones the general's favourite hound. As punishment the boy is stripped naked and forced to become victim in the most sadistic of fox-hunts:

> He shivers, numb with terror, not daring to cry. . . . "Make him run", commands the general. "Run! run!" shout the dog-boys. The boy runs. . . . "At him!" yells the general, and he sets the whole pack of hounds on the child. The hounds catch him, and tear him to pieces before his mother's eyes! (p. 224)

Dostoevsky here de-intellectualises the issue; he 'sticks to the facts', bringing the problem from the abstract to the concrete, thereby giving tremendous force to his argument. He outlines three levels of the problem. Knowledge of good and evil leads to suffering that seems from the standpoint of the human mind a very steep price indeed. Ivan insists that the price of harmony is too high: 'it's beyond our means to pay so much to enter on it' (p. 226). Furthermore he argues that no individual has the right to forgive for others those who have caused them immoral suffering: 'I don't want the mother to embrace the oppressor who threw her son to the dogs! She dare not forgive him! . . . the sufferings of her tortured child she has no right to forgive' (p. 226). Because no one can forgive the sins that are inflicted upon another, there will be unexpiated suffering and evil. But more than this, certain suffering apparently involves no atonement, no expiation of the suffering *for the sufferer him- or herself*, and thus runs against the grain of our moral sense of justice. In this regard Ivan asks if this suffering could be retributive, but gives the hypothesis very short shrift indeed:

> Listen! If all must suffer to pay for the eternal harmony, what have children to do with it, tell me, please? Its beyond all comprehension why they should suffer, and why they should pay for the harmony. (p. 225)

The child does not know sin. But are the children perhaps suffering for original sin, must they 'share responsibility for all their father's crimes?' To this Ivan replies 'such a truth is not of this world and beyond my comprehension' (p. 225). So where is the justice? Will later punishment of the torturer somehow even things out? But Ivan rejects also the notion of hell for the torturer: 'What good can hell do, since those children have already been tortured?' (p. 226). How can the further suffering of the criminal expiate the suffering of the child? And furthermore, asks Ivan, how is the notion of hell to be reconciled with the aesthetic teleology: 'what becomes of harmony, if there is hell?' (p. 226).

So Ivan poses the famous question to Alyosha: would you create a world with the object of happiness in harmony, knowing that the process would involve the torture of even one innocent child? Would you 'found that edifice on its unavenged tears?' (p. 226). Could the participants of such a process 'accept their happiness on the foundation of the unexpiated blood of a little victim?' (p. 226). To this Alyosha replies softly with his simple 'no'. He too agrees that the price seems too steep, and that the unexpiated suffering of the morally innocent is not justified in rational terms and by human conceptions. Ivan demands an immediate and intelligible explanation, one that he can witness and comprehend in the here and now, on earth, not in a religious future that is shrouded in non-rational mysteries. At this point Alyosha brings the Christ figure into the discussion in his attempt to check Ivan's point regarding the inability of an individual to forgive for another somebody's sins. But Ivan himself recognises that this theodicy is not yet complete, and senses the attempt to justify this suffering in terms of human freedom necessary to the religious process. So he gives his story of 'The Grand Inquisitor', wherein he examines the nature of Christian freedom.

'The Grand Inquisitor'

The setting for Ivan's story is the time of the Inquisition in Spain. It consists of a reproach by the Cardinal, the Grand Inquisitor, of Jesus, who has reappeared on the scene for the moment. Consistent with the theme of the monologue, Jesus is immediately silenced by the Inquisitor who says,

> Thou mayest not add to what has been said of old, and mayest not take from men the freedom which thou didst exalt when thou wast on earth. Whatsoever Thou revealest anew will encroach on men's freedom of faith; for it will be manifest as a miracle, and

the freedom of their faith was dearer to Thee than anything in those days fifteen hundred years ago. (p. 232)

So begins Ivan's highly original and unusual approach in examining the theme of freedom in theodicy. Rather than raising questions about the origin, necessity or significance of freedom in justifying moral evil, he examines its implications and consequences.

In rejecting the three temptations in the wilderness Jesus secured for human beings a moral and religious autonomy and independence. Through his interpretation of the Gospel wilderness scene, the Inquisitor argues that Jesus has not given to human beings that which they desire   indeed which they need – that is, mystery, authority and miracles, features that would have set a reasonable limit upon human freedom. In his negative responses to the Devil, Jesus has set before the human being a profound but hard and heavy freedom. Henry Troyat makes the point:

> "I want to make you free", Jesus had said. But by proclaiming the freedom of choice between good and evil, Jesus proclaimed man's responsibility, condemned man to the torments of his conscience, and made him the object of a whole machinery of suffering, in which remorse, temptation and hope are inextricably mixed. Freedom is inconceivable without suffering.[9]

This is the problem. Human nature is such that this freedom is generally unbearable; the human being has not the strength to appropriately apply it. The Inquisitor describes the human being as a rebel who seeks before all else direction, assurance and stability – a submission to moral and spiritual authority that will alone bring peace from the difficulties of moral and religious conscience. The Inquisitor says,

> There are three powers, three powers alone, able to conquer and hold captive for ever the conscience of these impotent rebels for their happiness – those forces are miracle, mystery and authority. (p. 236)

The Inquisitor is one of the very few of the elite strong enough to accept this hard autonomy of Jesus' teachings: 'I too have been in the wilderness, I too have lived on roots and locusts, I too prized the freedom from which Thou hast blessed men' (p. 240). But the Inquisitor's intense love for humanity, his recognition of the apparent weakness of the many, led to the non-acceptance that Ivan develops in his 'Rebellion': 'And we who have taken their sins upon us for their happiness will stand up before them and say: Judge us if Thou canst and darest' (p. 240). Out of his moral sense of love and justice the Inquisitor takes up the position of religious authority and removes the hard freedom so problematic to the masses. Jesus' teachings are practicable only to a few; freedom has proved too much for the majority who, obviously incapable of such responsibility, crumble under the heavy yoke. Ivan makes his argument against freedom plain:

> But yet all his life [the Grand Inquisitor] loved humanity, and suddenly his eyes were opened, and he saw that it is no great moral blessedness to attain perfection and freedom, if at the same time one gains the conviction that millions of God's creatures have been created as a mockery, that they will never be capable of using their freedom, that these poor rebels can never turn into giants to complete the tower, that it was not for such geese that the great idealist dreamt his dream of harmony. (p. 242)

So the Inquisitor, out of compassion for humanity, takes it upon himself to secure peace and happiness for the many. He shoulders their freedom, and guides them morally and spiritually through this temporal wilderness. Such a noble undertaking can move the reader to forget that this Cardinal, this old man, is himself the *Grand Inquisitor* and thus associated by Ivan with the terrible reality of that horrible movement. D. H. Lawrence recognises this seeming incongruity and observes that Dostoevsky has depicted a character of such noble depth and moral sensitivity that it is absurd to connect him to the Inquisition. He argues:

> The Spanish Inquisition was diabolic. It could not have produced a Grand Inquisitor who put Dostoevsky's sad question to Jesus. And the man who put those sad questions to Jesus could not possibly have burn't a hundred people in an *auto-da-fé*. He would have been too wise and far-seeing.[10]

But, contrary to Lawrence's view, such an association on Dostoevsky's part is not to be attributed to his 'epileptic and slightly criminal perversity'.[11] For it is clearly consistent with the theme. Recognising the far-reaching effects that an opposing religious perspective would have upon the masses, the Cardinal takes upon himself the Inquisitor's cassock. The danger he perceives is the eventuality of the people thinking and judging, forced to choose between spiritual alternatives and, in the option, perhaps even beginning to recognise the weaknesses of the Inquisitor's structural dogma. No, what the Inquisitor desires and pursues in his love for humanity is the elimination of freedom for the people, their submission to his humanitarian elitism, a herd mentality, a manner of utter subservience that is justified by any means whatsoever.

Thus Dostoevsky, through Ivan, gives a subtle counter-example to those who criticise the freedom that free-will theodicy entails. To deny the freedom in the manner of the Grand Inquisitor is to eliminate the dignity and the lovability of the individual person. Like Ivan, the Inquisitor loves *humanity* but not the *person*; his concern is to control and manipulate in order to secure against the unjustified suffering of the many that Christian freedom entails. In contrast, love of the person requires respect for his or her individual dignity which in turn rests on their autonomy. Such a love gives freedom rein. Thus the point of the inability to love one's neighbour which Ivan raises early in his rebellion surfaces in 'The Grand Inquisitor' and is vividly highlighted in the departing kiss Jesus gives to the Inquisitor, the kiss that 'glows in his heart' though 'the old man adheres to his idea' (p. 243). Nevertheless, despite this theme of 'active love' present in Dostoevsky's theodical view, a theme which we will return to later, the criticism Ivan raises against the free-will theodicy maintains its force. Freedom seems unjustified in the wake of the weaknesses of human nature. This objection to free-will theodicy is further compounded in Dostoevsky's treatment of the impulse to evil in human nature, a view that is expressed in 'The devil. Ivan Fyodorovich's Nightmare'.

'The devil. Ivan Fyodorovich's Nightmare'

In 'Rebellion' Ivan foretells his encounter with the Devil when he says, 'I think if the devil doesn't exist, but man has created him, he has created him in his own image and likeness' (p. 220). This later dialogue consists of Ivan wrestling with his darker side, and illustrates Dostoevsky's view of the impulse to evil in human nature. Indeed, this chapter is not to be read simply as an illustration of

Ivan's 'destructive self-mockery',[12] nor merely as Ivan's discovery
of 'the reasons for his own atheism',[13] but as Dostoevsky's exposition of the dark impulses he saw at work in human nature.

The Devil is Ivan's dark side, the negative aspects of his being:
'You are the incarnation of myself, but only of one side of me . . . of
my thoughts and feelings, but only the nastiest and stupidest of
them' (p. 604). The Devil agrees and describes himself as fallen
(though perhaps not an angel), as the dark dreams of human
beings – their nightmares – and as one that can take on fleshly
form. The Devil here is not to be understood simply as an illusion
of brain fever, nor as exclusive to Ivan. He does embody the intellectual scepticism that Ivan struggles with throughout the novel; he
maintains the same philosophy, he says. More than this, though,
he instigates the inner conflict that Ivan undergoes and symbolises
the darker side of human nature in general. This is his role, and in
this sense Dostoevsky would seem to ascribe ontological reality to
him, over and apart from human beings. But, be that as it may, he
is the dark doubt that Alyosha experienced over Father Zosima's
quick decay (p. 604), he is the tempter in the wilderness (p. 612),
the impetus behind suicide (p. 613), the impulse to sexual infidelity
(pp. 613–14), the 'nastiness' in human nature (p. 614). He is the
negative principle of the individual, the basic 'demonic stuff', we
might say, that in freedom the human being works out.

Yet he disdains this negative role. He claims to love human kind
(p. 605) and the truth, and to 'genuinely desire good' (p. 614). He
describes his witness of the resurrection scene, his urge to rejoice
with the angels in their ecstasy of 'hosannah', but the obligations
that held him back:

> The word [hosannah] had almost escaped me, had almost broke
> from my lips . . . you know how susceptible and aesthetically
> impressionable I am. But common sense – oh a most unhappy
> trait in my character – kept me in due bounds and I let the
> moment pass! For what would have happened, I reflected, what
> would have happened after my hosannah? Everything on earth
> would have extinguished at once and no events could have
> occurred. (p. 614)

So the Devil symbolises the evil impulses of human nature, and
through him Dostoevsky explains his theodicy. As Troyat says,
this 'devil knows God, yet rejects Him'.[14] But more than this,

the important point for Dostoevsky's theodicy is that the Devil cannot *but* reject God. Though he wishes to incarnate irrevocably 'the form of some merchant's wife weighing two hundred fifty pounds, and of believing all she believes . . . to go to church and offer a candle in simple-hearted faith' (p. 605), it is quite impossible. Without this darker irrational side of human nature no events would occur and history would cease:

> No, live, I am told, for there'd be nothing without you. If every-thing in the universe were sensible, nothing would happen. There would be no events without you, and there must be events. So against the grain I serve to produce events and do what's irrational because that is what I am commanded to do. (p. 609)

So Dostoevsky recognises an impulse to evil in human nature that is somehow necessary to active, dynamic existence. But he is not fully satisfied with this explanation. He asks for the meaning of these events, questions the justification of the evil that arises from this darker side. The theodicy is clear: like the doubting philosopher who walked a quadrillion kilometres in the dark despite himself, who in the end falls in ecstasy to his knees singing 'hosannah', human beings must suffer in their freedom this minus side of themselves and others, they must experience the Devil in the image and likeness of man, in order that in the end they can experience this mysterious 'hosannah'. But the rational and moral justification of this theodicy remains dubious. Dostoevsky makes this point in the Devil's irony:

> But till that happens I am sulking and fulfil my destiny though it is against the grain – that is, to ruin thousands for the sake of one. How many souls have had to be ruined and how many honourable reputations destroyed for the sake of that one right-eous man, Job, over whom they made such a fool of me in the old days. (p. 615)

The logic of this theodicy is morally reprehensible. Perhaps human nature does have a dark side that can be actualised through indi-vidual autonomy, a minus sign necessary to spiritual development. But if this is the case then Dostoevsky questions the apparent spiritual elitism; many destroy themselves through their natural minus sign and carry with them the souls of many others. How can this insensitivity to human suffering, this neglect of the innocent, be justified in the name of the few that are strong enough to survive and realise the higher secret?

DOSTOEVSKY'S CRITIQUE

The three chapters examined illustrate, in the context of the theodical themes of aesthetics, retribution and free-will, Dostoevsky's view of the evil inherent to human nature, the role of freedom in his religious ideal, and the evil and suffering that is actualised in this process. The emphasis has been on the negative features of Dostoevsky's anthropology. However, as Zenkovsky points out, Dostoevsky 'exhibits *no less profoundly* the impulses toward justice and good in the human soul, the "angelic" principle in man'.[15] Indeed, most of Dostoevsky's characters exhibit a good–evil polarity, a tension he considered *essential* to human nature. The substance of being is potentially good and evil – impulses to *both* lie below the surface of personality. As Berdyaev recognises, for Dostoevsky 'the battle between the divine and hellish elements is carried on deep down in the spirit of man: he finds the antagonism of the two principles in the very essence of being'.[16] Continuing on this theme Berdyaev makes the further comment that if Dostoevsky had developed this view 'to its necessary conclusion he would have had to acknowledge an antinomy in the nature even of God, to have in him a chasm of darkness, thus approximating to Jacob Boehme's theory of the *Ungrund*'.[17]

Berdyaev is quite correct on this point; particularly in 'The devil. Ivan Fyodorovich's Nightmare' Dostoevsky clearly implies a thearchy like Boehme's, in the light of which this chapter of *The Brothers Karamazov* can be given its fullest and most coherent interpretation. Moreover, it is in such a view of human nature that we find an account of evil more satisfactory than that of traditional theodicies, as I will show later in Chapter 9 when I expound Boehme's mystical theodicy. In this regard, Zenkovsky, consistent with Berdyaev, emphasises the fact that Dostoevsky recognises no morally neutral realm. The active human being is either good or evil, always involved in 'a dilemma *from which he can never retreat*. The man who fails to take the path of good necessarily places himself on the path of evil'.[18] The instrument of struggle between this essential moral realm is freedom, an autonomy that Dostoevsky considered necessary to his religious ideal. As we will see in Chapters 3 and 4, the free-will theme is an essential aspect of teleological theodicy, a feature by which moral evil finds its justification. Dostoevsky expresses this opinion most poignantly in 'The Grand Inquisitor', though also illustrating the negative side to this freedom. Berdyaev sums it up when he says that Dostoevsky could 'acknowledge neither a paradise wherein this liberty was not yet possible, nor one wherein – as it seemed to him – it had ceased to exist'.[19] As Zenkovsky puts it, freedom is that through which human beings tend toward 'Godmanhood'.[20]

Human beings are morally autonomous; thus the necessity of understanding in their essence the potential to both good and evil. But, importantly, though one might freely choose evil, one thereby renounces freedom. Choosing evil inhibits freedom. Berdyaev notes how Dostoevsky's characters show 'freedom deteriorating into self-will and a defiant self-affirmation to be thenceforward ineffectual, worthless, and a drain on the individual'.[21] We saw this clearly in the case of Ivan's destructive scepticism. But Berdyaev also recognises the other side of freedom that Dostoevsky develops. The human being is not to be coerced into good without the loss of his freedom. This is the main point of 'The Grand Inquisitor'. Freedom, then, has a peculiar logic. In freely choosing evil this freedom gradually dissolves into a limiting, destructive self-avowal. But in choosing the good one can never have the assurance of overwhelming evidence in support of the move. As we witnessed in 'The Grand Inquisitor', Dostoevsky thought such evidence favouring the good was not given by Christ, and, anyway, such would amount to coercion into the good; freedom would prove a sham. Thus for Dostoevsky, freedom – real freedom – means no absolute assurances in the move towards the religious good. It will *always* involve some element of doubt.

Given this logic of freedom, and the fundamental nature of human beings, life will always involve suffering, the kind of terrible 'events' that are illustrated in 'Rebellion' and 'The Grand Inquisitor'. Not surprisingly, Dostoevsky recognises an antithesis in this suffering. Berdyaev recognises its positive aspect, the fact that Dostoevsky perceives suffering as an enriching and ennobling experience. He comments: 'The idea that suffering raises man to his highest level is essential in Dostoevsky's anthropology; suffering is the index of man's depth'.[22] But Dostoevsky, we have seen, is also very cognisant of the negative aspects of suffering, the fact that it does not raise all, does not dignify all, but very often merely crushes the fragile human character, punishes without justification, and tortures the weak and the innocent. Thus he saw that this theodicy that justifies freedom, human nature and its consequent evils in terms of a future 'harmony', 'hosannah' or 'secret', is not intelligible in the here and now, and, in the case of unexpiated suffering, contrary to human reason and morality. Dostoevsky thought that none of the themes of aesthetics, retribution, or free-will, provided effective justifications of the problem of evil. So, consistent with his notion of freedom, Dostoevsky doubted traditional teleological theodicy. But despite this doubt, he offered a certain amount of consolation to those tormented by the problem of evil, a solace in his mysticism and his view of 'active love' as presented in the characters of Alyosha and Father Zosima, as we shall see in Chapter 8. But for now we should turn to examine certain systematic non-mystical theodicies, to determine their effectiveness in the face of these and other criticisms that might be raised against them.

3

Leibniz's Teleological Theodicy

Theodicy derives from the Greek *theos* (God) and *dike* (justice), meaning 'the vindication of the divine attributes'.[1] G. W. Leibniz (1646–1716) is famous for introducing this term to the problem; he titles his essays on the goodness of God, human freedom, and the origin of evil, *Theodicy*.[2] But his work provides much more than an appellation for the problem of evil. Leibniz provides one of the earliest formal and systematic teleological theodicies. In the defence of the consistency of the divine attributes with evil, he examines the theoretical issues underlying the challenge of evil. In Dostoevsky we saw theodicy developed and its problems discussed in a very vivid, practical manner, which culminated in negative conclusions. Leibniz contrasts this approach in emphasising 'the more speculative and metaphysical difficulties' (p. 135:20),[3] and in maintaining a positive view about the success of the defence. In this chapter I will draw out the key features of Leibniz's treatment of the problem of evil and discuss its strengths and weaknesses through the criticisms raised against it, directly by Voltaire and John Hick, and indirectly by Dostoevsky. Though Leibniz's theodicy fails on a number of significant points, it does provide the basic teleological structure necessary to effective theodicy.

REASON AND THEODICY

Leibniz begins the *Theodicy* with his essay the 'Preliminary Dissertation on the Conformity of Faith with Reason'. In this essay he attempts to reconcile the facets of faith and reason that some theologians past and contemporary to him had sought to pull apart. In so doing he effectively clarifies the role of reason in coherent theodicy, specifying the framework necessary to the theodical defence against the religious sceptic.

This development comes in response to Pierre Bayle (1647–1706), who in his *Reply to the Questions of a Provincial* argues that reason destroys the religious sense that faith induces. Indeed, the *Theodicy* is structured around the argument on the problem of evil that Bayle develops, and it well illustrates the dialogic role of the religious sceptic in the development of theodicy. Austin Farrer notes that Bayle, though not a sceptic in the true sense of the word, provides an effective foil for Leibniz's development. In his introduction to the *Theodicy*, Farrer says Bayle 'was a scholar, a wit, and a philosophical sparring-partner of so perfectly convenient a kind that if we had not evidence of his historical reality, we might have suspected Leibniz of inventing him'.[4]

Bayle is an extreme fideist. He thinks that religious truths, what Leibniz refers to as 'Mysteries', are such that they contradict propositions that are 'probable, plausible, or even possible on rational or reasonable standards'.[5] Against Bayle, Leibniz argues that faith is not at all incompatible with reason, that if certain articles *are* contradicted by reason they must be rejected. Simply put, Leibniz believes that a truth of any kind cannot be contradicted by reason. He says: 'But a truth can never be contrary to reason, and once a dogma has been disputed and refuted by reason, instead of it being incomprehensible, one may say that nothing is easier to understand, nor more obvious, than its absurdity' (p. 88:23).

In so arguing Leibniz secures against the criticism of relativism that Bayle opens up for himself in his position on faith and reason. Leibniz distinguishes between two types of truths of reason. One is the 'eternal verities', the necessary truths of metaphysics, logic and geometry, the truth of which cannot be denied without contradiction. The other is positive truths, the laws of nature, contingent facts whose truth depends only upon the moral necessity of divine freedom. The objection or disruption of these latter truths does not imply contradiction, but at best can only make a probable case against them. Mysteries of faith are of this second type of truth. Reason is very important in terms of determining the truth of articles of faith. He defines reason simply as the 'inviolable linking together of truths' (p. 88:23). Reason will not provide proof or comprehension of the Mysteries of faith. In this regard Leibniz proves himself to be a moderate fideist, but he tempers this view of the importance of faith by stressing the significance of reason as a mode of critical analysis that holds sway even in the realm of faith. For he argues that Mysteries must be *explained* to some degree to justify belief – they cannot remain utterly vacuous (p. 103:54), and, further, we must be able to *uphold* them against objections. He says 'Without that our belief in them would have no firm foundation; for all that which can be refuted in a sound and conclusive manner cannot but be false' (p. 76:5).

He goes on to distinguish between truths that are *above* reason and truths that are *against* reason (p. 88:23). The Mysteries are those that are above reason; though they stand against the truth of common experience and understanding they do not stand against reason. If they did they would prove to be falsehoods, and not truths at all. In regard to the Mysteries, then, one must answer the objections raised against their truth. This act of rebuttal is necessary and sufficient to the *maintenance* of the truth of the Mysteries.

Leibniz formulates an assumption common to all coherent theodicy: one can and should reasonably answer the objections that are raised against a theological system in and from the encounter with evil. Should reason be found to be incapable of bolstering such a defence, theodicy breaks down. Reason is an essential tool in setting one theodicy off against another, and in clarifying dogma pertinent to the problem of evil, despite whatever limitations it might have as vehicle of proof and comprehension of religious truth.

LEIBNIZ'S THEODICY[6]

In his preliminary essay on the conformity of faith with reason Leibniz briefly states the problems for theodicy:

> There remains, then, the question of natural theology, how a sole Principle, all-good, all-wise, and all-powerful, has been able to admit evil, and especially to permit sin, and how it could resolve to make the wicked often happy and the good unhappy (p. 98:43).

In his 'Essay on the Justice of God and the Freedom of Man in the Origin of Evil' he goes into the problem in more detail. The points he considers major are: that divine grace is limited to a few, and Jesus Christ is known to but a relative minority – the majority are damned; that this eschatological fact hinges on a temptation of which the negative results were foreknown by God; and human beings are encumbered by an original sin for which they are not responsible (p. 126:5). These problems appear to indicate that God permits, cooperates with, and even promotes sin and misery.

Leibniz approaches the problems directly and theoretically, attempting, as we saw in the case of Alvin Plantinga (see Chapter 1), to show that the reality of evil does not contradict the conceptions of Christian theism. In so doing he generally neglects the positive/affirmative aspects of theodicy. As we shall see, this is a limitation of his presentation that is illustrated very vividly by Voltaire in *Candide*.

Leibniz asks where evil is derived. He says, evil 'must be sought in the ideal nature of the creature, in so far as this nature is contained in the eternal verities which are in the understanding of God, independently of his will' (p. 135:20). Leibniz here distinguishes between divine understanding and divine will. As we will see in a moment, divine will is also very important to Leibniz's theodicy, but divine understanding, the region of the eternal verities, 'is the ideal cause of evil (as it were) as well as of good' (p. 136:20). This is not to attribute substantive form to the evil that arises through the action of God, for evil is understood as the privation or deficiency of good, lacking an efficient cause. Metaphysical evil is understood as the imperfect nature of this world, and indeed of all possible worlds, in so far as they fall short of perfect being. Yet metaphysical evil can be viewed as instrumental evil which contributes to good.

God is seen by Leibniz as willing the best in terms of what he calls the *consequent will*, which is the overriding synthesis of the many particular goods of God's *antecedent will*, which 'considers each good separately in the capacity of a good' (p. 136:22).[7] The antecedent will is the many diverse good purposes which God brings to the world. As examples Leibniz cites God's earnest disposition 'to sanctify and to save all men, to exclude sin, and to prevent damnation' (p. 136:22), as well as to ensure the freedom of imperfect but intelligent creatures (p. 164:78). This latter good, of course, will inhibit the full success of the former examples given, and illustrates the manner in which the goods of the antecedent will can impinge upon each other. As Leibniz says, 'these acts of antecedent will are not called decrees, since they are not yet inevitable, the outcome depending on the total result' (p. 168:84). The individual and separate purposes interrelate and combine in the greater picture of existence, to contribute to the overall end or completion of the many diverse goods. As Leibniz puts it:

> Now this consequent will, final and decisive, results from the conflict of all the antecedent wills, of those which tend toward good, even as those which repel evil; and from the concurrence of all these particular wills comes the total will. (p. 137:22)

To illustrate his point Leibniz gives an analogy of a moving body consisting of a number of distinctive movements of the parts which, though moving in various directions, together contribute to the singular movement of the total body (p. 137:22). Similarly, the different goods of the antecedent will together contribute to the overriding synthetic realisation of the consequent will. So Leibniz concludes, 'Thence it follows that God wills *antecedently* the good and *consequently* the best' (p. 137:23).

Yet the antecedent goods and the consequent best only arise in the context of imperfection. The nature of the physical world and human beings is necessarily imperfect:

> The imperfections, on the other hand, and the defects in operations spring from the original limitations that the creature could not but receive with the first beginning of its being, through the ideal reasons which restrict it. For God could not give the creature all without making of it a God; therefore there must needs be different degrees in the perfection of things, and limitations also of every kind. (pp. 141–2:31)

As contingent and secondary, the world and human beings could not but be imperfect. Because of this essential weakness arising in the creative act itself, the creature 'cannot know all, and . . . it can deceive itself and commit other errors' (p. 135:20). Nevertheless, the imperfect world and imperfect creatures, that is, 'the whole succession and the whole agglomeration of all existent things' (p. 128:8), are to be regarded as the best. Key to Leibniz's theodicy is the argument that God in His wisdom, power and goodness would create only the best of an infinity of possible worlds, that is, a world which antecedently is directed to many goods which consequently result in the best harmonious synthesis of these diverse intentions. Despite the fact that not all the goods of the antecedent will find their realisation, the world, taken as a whole as witnessed from the omniscient standpoint of God, is the best. This is the aesthetic emphasis of Leibniz's theodicy. God's consequent will is the overriding synthesis of the many particular goods of God's antecedent will. Leibniz says, 'This total decree comprises equally all the particular decrees, without setting one of them before or after another' (p. 168:84). And, included in this total decree, is the necessity of evil. Though evil is not a feature of the antecedent will, it is an aspect of the consequent. Evil is a necessary feature of this best of all possible worlds, and Leibniz concludes that 'if the smallest evil that comes to pass in the world were missing in it, it would no longer be this world; which, with nothing omitted and all allowance made, was found the best by the creator who made it' (pp. 128–9:9).

So God has determined this world, which contains a significant amount of pain and suffering, to be the best possible. But this world is not unqualifiedly the best. Rather, it is the world by which God can best manifest Himself to His creatures; it is the most appropriate vehicle of divine epiphany. Leibniz describes his teleology as follows:

> In truth God, in designing to create the world, purposed solely to manifest and communicate his perfections in the way that was most efficacious, and most worthy of his greatness, his wisdom and his goodness. But that very purpose pledged him to consider all the actions of creatures while still in the state of pure possibility, that he might form the most fitting plan. (p. 164:78)

God, in surveying the various compossible goods of the antecedent will, took all the factors into consideration and chose to create this world, recognising it as the best in regard to His telos. In terms of the consequent will – the harmonious synthesis of all antecedent goods – the world is the best suited for the purpose of manifesting and communicating God's perfections. But of course this fact – this 'bestness' of the world in manifesting and communicating the divine attributes – is well beyond human comprehension. Such knowledge requires omniscience. However, these ideal reasons will, presumably, become clear as the human being comes in the future divine life to see the overall plan of the divine consequent will. The appropriateness of this world to the fulfilment of the telos, that is to say, the bestness of this world in manifesting and communicating the divine perfections, will be realised in the future divine life.

Leibniz's Teleological Theodicy 41

Within this concept of creation as the manifestation and communication of divine perfections, Leibniz considers human autonomy one of the most valuable goods of the antecedent will. Freedom, however, in conjunction with human imperfections, inevitably leads to the problem of evil. To distance God's responsibility for evil Leibniz relies heavily upon the free-will theme. Human freedom is fundamental to his theodicy. He considers the misappropriation of freedom to result in the fall of the Devil and human beings, and to justify eternal damnation, as well as the human situation. All evil he considers justified in this fact of free-will:

> Now since it is henceforth permitted to have recourse to the misuse of free will, in order to account for other evils, since the divine permission of this misuse is justified, the ordinary system of the theologian meets with justification at the same time. Now we can seek with confidence *the origin of evil in the freedom of creatures.* (pp. 294–5:273)

The evil of the world is of two types: physical and moral. Leibniz justifies physical evil by reference to the retributive theme and by arguing that it is never willed by God absolutely; it exists only either as a penalty owing to moral guilt or as a means 'to prevent greater evils or to obtain greater good' (p. 137:23), and cannot be understood as arising without such justification. Physical evil is deemed necessary as a means in the realisation of the consequent will, but itself only arises in the prior problem of moral evil. Physical evil is a kind of counterbalance against the effects of moral evil. Moral evil, on the other hand, is not willed by God at all. This evil is sin, and it can lead, as Leibniz points out, to much greater physical evils than does natural evil. God's participation in this kind of evil is only in terms of permission. Leibniz says 'the *consequent will* of God, which has sin for its object, is only *permissive*' (p. 138:25). For the sake of the telos He allows the actualisation of human sin. But God's distance from direct responsibility of sin is secured by human freedom, an autonomy of will that is 'admitted or *permitted* in so far as it is considered to be a certain consequence of an indispensable duty' (p. 137:25). So Leibniz concludes:

> God wills all good *in himself antecedently,* that he wills the best *consequently* as an *end,* that he wills what is indifferent, and physical evil, sometimes as a *means,* but that he will only permit

moral evil as the *sine quo non* or as a hypothetical necessity which connects it with the best. (p. 138:25)

Freedom, considered necessary in this best of all possible worlds, gives rise to the many terrible evils that human beings encounter. God cannot be responsible for these evils; freedom places the direct responsibility of moral evil upon the creature. Though God allows sin, He is not the doer – He commits no moral improprieties that would contradict His goodness. Further, He could have created a world where there is no human freedom, and consequently no moral evil, but such would not have been the best possible world to manifest and communicate His attributes. So there is no contradiction of His omnipotence. However, it is in His omniscience that the matter of the justification of evil is complicated, for God in His foreknowledge knows the soteriological picture clearly and in complete detail. This would seem to impinge upon human freedom, for it appears that human destiny is determined beforehand in the foresight of the consequent will. Indeed, though perhaps God is not the determinative efficient cause of moral evil or good, His foreknowledge implies that such a cause exists quite apart from the agent himself. Certain knowledge of a *future* action undermines the sense of freedom in human consciousness, proving freedom to be a sham. However, Leibniz thinks that omniscience does not contradict freedom.

Leibniz recognises an element of determinancy in human action that arises in the passion and reason of human beings. He argues that there is in will a direction to which a human being is predisposed. Such a predisposition is not final and absolutely determinative, however, for it is accompanied by the faculty of judgement. Freedom, Leibniz argues, does not mean an 'indifference of equipoise', nor can it involve a determinative efficient cause. It is rather a combination of historical factors, involving passion and will, which secure against staticity, and judgement, which secures the element of choice. He says, 'when there is no judgement in him who acts there is no *freedom*. And if we had judgement not accompanied by an inclination to act, our soul would be understanding without will' (p. 143:34).

So long as these conditions obtain there can be action that is contingent, action that is effected by free choice. Now for an action to be necessary and not free requires that the contrary be impossible or that it implies contradiction. Such a state of affairs Leibniz terms an absolute necessity, as distinguished from a hypothetical necessity. He considers the latter to hold in the case of God's foreknowledge. He says, 'it is very easily seen that foreknowledge in itself adds nothing to the determination of the truth of contingent futurities, save that this determination is known' (p. 144:37). He thinks that though God might foresee an event, so long as judgement exists the event will not be determined. This is because divine omniscience includes not only the particular event of this actualised world, but also the 'infinitude of possible worlds . . . where all conditional futurities must be comprised' (p. 146:42). God sees not only the actual but also the possible, that which in judgement the human being visualises as possible states of affairs. Because God sees all possible futurities, human action is a hypothetical necessity rather than an absolute necessity.

Without going into detail, I would like to note briefly that I think Leibniz's attempted reconciliation of free actions and omniscience fails. In the context of Leibniz's assumptions there is the possibility of a free creature choosing other than that which God knows, and thereby falsifying God's knowledge (– a contradiction).[8] Thus, in conjunction with omniscience human action is an absolute rather than a hypothetical necessity. So God cannot know free actions. But clarifying this logical limitation of omniscience does not rule omniscience out altogether, nor does it mean that God cannot foresee that which is likely, given His knowledge of conditions and influences. Moreover, such a move does not undermine the general structure and content of Leibniz's theodicy, which can be summarised as follows.

Key to its structure are the notions of the best possible world, metaphysical evil, physical evil, moral evil and human freedom. Moral and physical evils arise in part from the metaphysical, which is the limitations or natural imperfections of creatures. Evil does not have substantive form but is the privation of the good in both human beings and the natural world. In the context of Leibniz's notion of physical evil we can draw out a conception of natural evil. These are evils in the natural world quite distinct from those that occur in human action. Justification of these evils is possible in the view that they arise in the ideal conditions or imperfections necessary to the overall plan of God. The idea is that these evils lead to the greater good, and their necessity arises ultimately from moral evil. Moral evil arises in the misappropriation of human freedom. Human beings are understood as responsible for the moral evil

arising in their free choice. God does not create the moral evil
of this world; his responsibility for its actualisation is limited to
the status of permissibility. And this authorisation is justified by
its role in the realisation of the teleological ideal. Presumably,
human freedom is an aspect of the antecedent will that intensifies
and enhances the manifestation and communication of the divine
perfections. But the evils arising from human freedom are finally
justified only in the future divine life. The ideal reasons justifying
evil will become clear only in a glimpse of the consequent will of
God. This world, then, with all its physical and moral evils, is
nevertheless understood as the best of all possible worlds in the
context of the overall picture as it occurs in the consequent will
of God. The consequent will, the harmonious synthesis of all the
particular goods of the antecedent will, is that state of affairs that
illuminates the appropriateness of this world in manifesting and
communicating the divine attributes.

So Leibniz develops his teleological theodicy around the conceptions of human freedom, the best possible world and the consequent will of God. His view is intelligible and optimistic, but not
without problems. To evaluate his theodicy it is perhaps most
appropriate to begin with the criticisms directed against it by his
historical antagonist, François-Marie Arouet – better known by his
pen name, Voltaire (1694–1778). Voltaire was a deist who denied
divine goodness and providence; he is famous for his novel *Candide*,
a provocative satire of the theodicy of Leibniz. Though not always
accurately interpreting Leibniz's thought, Voltaire does begin, in a
very entertaining manner, to effectively draw out the significant
weaknesses of Leibniz's view.[9]

CANDIDE: PROBLEMS OF LEIBNIZ'S THEODICY

Candide is a rather difficult story to précis; it possesses a fantastic
and absurd plot of a most convoluted nature. Its main purpose is
to satirise Leibniz's theodicy, and the plot is well suited to such
an effect. As his name signifies, Candide is an innocently candid
character of a virtuous and sincere, if not a somewhat simple,
disposition – not wholly unlike prince Myshkin of Dostoevsky's
The Idiot. The story is an account of the incredible misfortunes
experienced by Candide and his companions. It begins at the
castle of Baron Thunder-ten-Tronckh, where the bastard nephew

Candide encounters the philosophy of Leibniz in the form of the tutor, Master Pangloss. But Candide finds himself seduced by the Baron's beautiful daughter, Cunegonde, and, caught in the act, is banished from the castle. He is conscripted into the Bulgarian army, escapes only after considerable misfortune, is reunited with Pangloss, shipwrecked, and finds himself amidst the Lisbon earthquake and the Inquisition. Here he miraculously discovers his love, Cunegonde, previously thought dead, travels to the New World, experiences further horrors and sufferings, loses her again, makes his way to the imaginary Eldorado where he secures a great treasure, and returns to Europe in search of his love. Thence to Constantinople, where he ransoms out of slavery all of the characters he had, in his and their misfortunes, repeatedly lost and found. Settling down on a small property the group resigns itself to refrain from the metaphysical reflections that had disturbed them throughout their misadventures, and to concentrate their efforts productively at work upon the farm.

   The story, then, expresses a highly pessimistic view of human nature and the human situation. The characters experience deceit, treachery, extortion, enslavement, rape, torture and disease, all within the brutal setting of earthquakes, inquisitions and wars. Except for Candide, any character showing some degree of sincere human compassion and moral integrity is given very short shrift by Voltaire, and remains undeveloped and insignificant to the story. And none achieves any semblance of happiness and contentment, except the idyllic people of Eldorado who exist in seclusion, independent of the corrupting influences of the real world. This is in stark contrast to the optimism offered by Leibniz who in his positive view argues that there is much more good than evil in the world. Against the kind of negative perspective of Voltaire, Leibniz argues that the human body is very enduring, that most people would choose to live again in the context of similar past experienced evils, that the negative aspects of the world highlight and give relief to the positive, and, that in any case, good outweighs evil in the universe as a whole.[10] But this positive view can be effectively countered by the Voltairian perspective, in the emphasis on the great physical deficiencies of the human body, the incredible natural evils of the world, the fact that a great many people die unhappy and unsatisfied, that the negative aspects of the world sometimes possess no apparent point and give no relief to anything, and with the question of what other more fortunate inhabitants of the universe might have to do with the evil conditions of *our* world.

Voltaire paints a very dark picture indeed of Leibniz's 'best of all possible worlds'. His attack occurs throughout the story, as the characters, in their misfortune and misery, are pressed again and again to give reason against the theodicy of Professor Pangloss. The general type of attack is illustrated in what is perhaps the book's most famous passage, where Pangloss offers evidence that everything is for the best:

> "It is demonstrable", said he, "that things cannot be otherwise than they are: for all things having been made for some end, they must necessarily be for the best end. Observe well, that the nose has been made for carrying spectacles; therefore we have spectacles".[11]

But there are other good examples. For instance, though wasting away from venereal disease, Pangloss refers to it as a good thing, as 'a thing indispensable; a necessary ingredient in the best of worlds'.[12] And regarding the Lisbon earthquake he argues in a bizarrely circular manner that 'all this must necessarily be for the best. As this volcano is at Lisbon, it could not be elsewhere; as it is impossible that things should not be what they are, as all is good'.[13] Or again, but this time from Candide, under the tutelage of Pangloss:

> all is necessarily linked, and ordered for the best. A necessity banished me from Miss Cunegonde; a necessity forced me to run the gauntlet; another necessity makes me beg for bread, till I can get into some business by which to earn it. All this could not be otherwise.[14]

It soon becomes obvious that Voltaire is not interested in giving a carefully reasoned and systematic argument against Leibniz's metaphysical view. Rather he points out the overwhelming reality of evil that is downplayed in Leibniz's metaphysical picture of evil. He illustrates that Leibniz's abstract theory of the best possible world offers no consolation to the suffering human being. The stubborn insistence of Pangloss that the incredible misfortunes experienced by Candide and his companions are for the best displays but a cold insensitivity to the human predicament, and tends to undermine the hard reality of the experience. Voltaire very effectively brings out the fact that Leibniz's theodicy possesses no conciliatory force; and an effective theodicy ought at least point the way towards mollifying the effects of experienced evil.

More than this, though, Voltaire shows the very shallow and unjustified optimism that Leibniz exudes. John Hick concurs with Voltaire on this point but argues further that this optimism can be read as an extreme form of pessimistic fatalism. He says, 'If this is the best *possible* world, there can be no hope either for its improvement or for an eventual translation to a better, and a despair or resignation could well be the appropriate reaction'.[15] In this context Hick also sees in Leibniz a denial of the infinite power of God. In the divine understanding–divine will distinction mentioned earlier, Hick reads the dependence of the will upon the eternal verities as a slight upon divine omnipotence. In the necessary conformity of the will to the 'eternal compossibilities', God is powerless to make a better world.[16]

But to argue in this fashion is to ignore the teleological perspective of Leibniz's thesis. Leibniz does not consider this world the best without qualification. In the infinity of possibilities of worlds there are, to Leibniz's thinking, many which contain more evil and many which contain less, though none better suited to manifest the divine perfections. If anything, Leibniz's thesis stresses the omnipotence and goodness of God in picturing God as willing and able to create a world where human beings can best come to communicate with and know God. And regarding the criticism about the inherent pessimistic fatalism of Leibniz's view, I read nothing in his theodicy to support the claim. Leibniz says nothing which would rule out the possibility of improving the world, of making it better. The 'best' world is not, in this teleological perspective, necessarily a morally immutable world nor is there anything restricting human beings from overcoming natural and moral evils. On the contrary, by referring to moral freedom as an 'indispensable duty' and by emphasising it in a Christian context, Leibniz espouses a moral imperative and implies a progressive moral movement on the part of human beings. He says, 'we must do our duty, according to the reason God has given us and according to the rules he has prescribed for us' (p. 154:58). Leibniz's theodicy presses human moral responsibility and it possesses a moral imperative. Still, Leibniz does not explicitly connect this facet to his teleology; he does not elaborate upon why such moral development might be necessary, or how it might contribute to the realisation of the teleological goal. And, given the affiliation of evil with moral freedom, we might expect such an explanation, indeed, we must demand one.

This weakness is enough to lend credence to Voltaire's original criticism about Leibniz's shallow optimism. Voltaire illustrates the deficiencies of Leibniz's theodicy through satirical counter-example, by showing that the hypothesis that this world is the best possible seems a rather bizarre proposition given the facts of the matter. Indeed, the present state of affairs would appear to count *against* Leibniz's view that the world is the best in manifesting and communicating the divine attributes. Human beings suffer from the harshest physical deficiencies, and they are up against the greatest odds in overcoming their own moral weaknesses and natural dispositions, to say nothing of those of their fellow creatures. This picture reinforces the hard reality of evil that we have already made clear in Dostoevsky's insightful development in Chapter 2. Is this reality justified in Leibniz's teleological perspective? Are these evils really necessary or helpful and suitable to the realisation of his Christian ideal? How are we to judge their teleological status?

Dostoevsky has pointed out that the suffering arising through the experience of evil often crushes the human character, punishes without justification and tortures the weak and the innocent. Leibniz, as Voltaire so effectively points out, nevertheless insists that these evils are for the best, that they somehow contribute to the greater good of communication and relationship with God. But how they contribute cannot become clear until the ideal nature of the creature is given some intelligibility. Perhaps evil is justified in terms of the telos, but until the end-goal is clarified and shown to be coherently related to the present state of affairs, the hard reality of evil can only count against teleology. One is reminded of the indignant response of Cleanthes to Demea when he proposes a teleological explanation much in the manner of Leibniz's:

> No! replied Cleanthes, no! These arbitrary suppositions can never be admitted, contrary to matter of fact, visible and uncontroverted. Whence can any cause be known but from its effects? Whence can any hypothesis be proved but from the apparent phenomena?[17]

In the face of these questions Leibniz's theodicy fails.

So, like Plantinga, Leibniz has shown that evil is not *necessarily* incompatible with the divine nature; he successfully answers the criticisms raised by Pierre Bayle, which is the primary objective of the *Theodicy*. But more than Plantinga, he points the way to coherent theodicy in his outline of the structure of systematic teleology. Evil is explained and justified in terms of the overall purpose that orients, directs and relates the various forces at play in this world. Natural evils are the physical conditions necessary to the realisation of the telos. Moral evils arise in human freedom, which is also deemed necessary. In such a teleological structure God's omnipotence is limited but not slighted. Though unable to communicate and manifest His perfections effectively without the actualisation of evil, God is able and willing to instantiate the conditions most suitable to such a realisation, thus confirming his power and goodness.

However, although Leibniz has shown that the reality of evil is not necessarily incompatible with the divine nature, he has not effectively addressed the objections related to the *plausibility* of his teleological theodicy that arise in terms of the critiques of Voltaire and Dostoevsky. For he has not provided evidence in support of the truth of this teleological structure. The telos inherent to theodicy must be elucidated more clearly, evidence justifying the truth of the teleological movement must be provided, and in this process some indication of the active beneficence of the Divine must be given. The ideal reasons justifying moral and natural evils need further development and support if teleological theodicy is to achieve a reasonable cogency. To this end we should move to examine the teleological theodicy of John Hick. For in his development of a soul-making theology he offers an effective clarification of this kind of teleological perspective, and thereby provides some answers to the difficulties of Leibniz's theodicy.

4

John Hick's
'Soul-Making' Theodicy

In *Evil and the God of Love* Professor Hick provides perhaps the most comprehensive and insightful philosophical examination of theodicy in contemporary time.[1] In the book he addresses a variety of philosophical issues in an extensive development and discussion of Christian theology as it is relevant to theodicy. But he is also sensitive to current views in biology and evolutionism, and takes these theories into account in his theodical development. As the title suggests, Hick attempts to reconcile 'sin and suffering to the perfect love of an omnipotent Creator' (p. 297).[2] In Parts I to III he discusses a variety of theodical themes in examination of a wide selection of Christian theodical literature. He rejects non-teleological theodicies, and proposes in Part IV a rather original theodicy that involves a teleological move not unlike that which we saw in Leibniz's *Theodicy*. A future-looking view, he thinks, is key to coherent theodicy: 'instead of looking to the past for its clue to the mystery of evil, it looks to the future, and indeed to that ultimate future to which only faith can look' (p. 297). Yet in his development of teleological theodicy he goes beyond that of Leibniz, clarifying and stressing a 'soul-making' theology in his teleological perspective.

THE FALL MYTH AND TELEOLOGICAL THEODICY

Professor Hick recognises the importance of myths as practical responses to the problem of evil. He sees the general function of myth to be 'to illumine by means of unforgettable imagery the religious significance of some present or remembered fact of experience' (p. 285). So, for example, the myth of the fall presents the mystery of evil to the believer in a religious context,

50

thus illuminating it in a religiously significant way. But this does not solve the mystery; only in the interpretation of the myth can the problem move towards resolution. And, Hick argues further, when people have regarded this mythic story as the solution to a particular problem, 'the "solution" has suffered from profound incoherences and contradictions' (p. 285).

On this point Wendy Doniger O'Flaherty interprets Hick as offering an 'antimythological argument' which she criticises.[3] She points out that this illumination of the mystery of evil is 'psychologically satisfactory' to the believer. But, further, she implies that such illumination is sufficient to theodicy because, as she says in passing, theodicy is 'inherently contradictory'. So she argues that the 'irrational resolution' of myth offers much more than philosophical theodicy, and implies that Hick ought to be satisfied with that.

However, Plantinga and Leibniz, as we have seen in Chapters 1 and 3, show O'Flaherty's claim about the inherently contradictory status of philosophical theodicy to be quite unjustified. But more than this, philosophical interpretation of myth is legitimate. At a kind of pre-interpretive stage I think O'Flaherty is correct; myth satisfies some deep inner need that philosophy cannot. But myth is usually theologically and philosophically interpreted in a variety of ways, and related to other myths and ideas; indeed, O'Flaherty herself is deeply involved in this very process in her own book! Philosophical interpretation is important and carries with it its own psychological satisfaction. Moreover, it has significant psychological and social repercussions that history well documents. For example, the Augustinian interpretation of the myth of the fall has far reaching theodical implications in terms of its portrayal of women, men, human teleology, guilt, punishment and the response to evil. That is to say, myth interpretation in a theodical context profoundly *influences* various human attitudes and actions. But, furthermore, as we saw in the problems Friedman raises for radical teleological theodicy in Chapter 1, certain theodicies *advocate* particular moral perspectives, views that cry out for ethical scrutiny. In so far as these perspectives arise from the interpretation of myth, it is essential to evaluate myth interpretation critically.

Hick examines the Augustinian interpretation of the myth of the fall. This interpretation of the fall myth attempts to shift the origin of evil away from God in ascribing responsibility to the first human beings. Adam and Eve, though possessing infallible moral insight, control over their bodily passions and a love and enjoyment for God, nevertheless choose against God in sin. Hick recognises the self-contradiction in this Augustinian interpretation. He says:

> The notion that man was at first spiritually and morally good, oriented in love towards his Maker, and free to express his flawless nature without even the hindrance of contrary temptations, and yet that he preferred to be evil and miserable, cannot be saved from the charge of self-contradiction and absurdity. (p. 75)

Indeed, there does seem to be something odd about suggesting rebellion on the part of good creatures who are in close relationship to an infinitely good and loving Creator. Even if we explain this weakness in terms of imperfection of the creature the problem remains. For example, Leibniz argues that creatures as secondary and contingent are necessarily imperfect; they do not know all so they can make mistakes. Nevertheless one wonders how even non-omniscient creatures can *turn away* in error in the face of divine perfections. In order for creatures to fall, Hick argues, 'there must be either in them or in their environment, some flaw which produces temptation and leads to sin' (p. 289).[4] Imperfection in Leibniz's sense will not suffice to explain the rebellion, and Hick rightly rejects the notion of original sin on the part of good creatures in relationship with God.

In this light, Hick reads the myth of the fall in an untraditional manner, in '"the minority report" of the Irenaean tradition' (p. 289),[5] as he calls it. Hick rejects the view of the fall as a movement of weakness on the part of creatures in close relationship with God, and rather views it as the mythic portrayaal of humankind's present circumstances *en route* to perfection. He proposes a two step 'image'-'likeness' process to human development. Referring to Irenaeus, he describes it as follows:

> His view was that man as a personal and moral being already exists in the image, but has not yet been formed into the likeness of God. By this "likeness" Irenaeus means something more than personal existence as such; he means a certain valuable quality of personal life which reflects finitely the divine life. (p. 290)

The first step, then, is the creation of human beings in the image of God where our present state as personal and moral beings is viewed in terms of evolutionary progression out of organic life. This sets the stage for the second step, to become the likeness of God. Hick characterises this likeness as the finite participation in eternal life, where human beings become children of God as exemplified in the Christ figure. It involves fellowship with others and with God; the ideal is an enhancement and intensification of the positive moral and personal features presently in process, within the centring focus of God's infinite goodness and love. As Hick describes it:

> The ideal relationship of a human person with God would con-sist in a vivid awareness of Him, at once joyous and awesome, and a consequent wholehearted worship of the infinite Good-ness and Love by obedient service to His purposes within the creaturely realm. (p. 298)

So in Hick's view the fall myth does not involve a fall from perfection at all, but speaks of human beings created in God's image and estab-lished in an environment suitable for their development towards this eschatalogical perfection. But this end is such that it requires a preliminary distance between human beings and God. For the telos involves an autonomous response on the part of creatures to God, a 'response consisting in an uncompelled interpretive activity whereby we experience the world as mediating the divine presence' (p. 317).

The importance of freedom, which I will discuss in more detail in a moment, necessitates a preliminary distance between God and human beings. Hick calls this distance epistemic, a lack of cognitive awareness of God's presence in the world. In image human beings are epistemically distanced from God, separated from the divine presence and love. The teleological point, then, is to grow in likeness, to overcome the epistemic distance separating one from God. But this epistemic distance entails an inherent self-interest, a prior regard for self rather than a concern for God. Hick says, 'man's spiritual location at an epistemic distance from God makes it virtually inevitable that man will organise his life apart from God and in self-centred competitiveness with his fellows' (p. 322). The point of the teleology is to overcome this inherent self-interest, recognise the latent 'moral demand and holy claim' of God upon us, and through faith to perceive 'all around us the signs of a divine presence and activity' (pp. 318, 322). And in this teleological move from self-orientation in image to relationship in likeness we find the underlying necessity of freedom; for the teleology of perfect being requires 'a hazardous adventure in individual freedom' (p. 292).

Hick argues that personal life, by its very nature, entails an autonomy in human activity; growth to divine likeness is not something to be coerced by divine might. He says:

> personal life is essentially free and self-directing. It cannot be perfected by divine fiat, but only through the uncompelled responses and willing co-operation of human individuals in their actions and reactions in the world in which God has placed them. (p. 291)

Though Hick thinks that God, in His omnipotence, could have created autonomous creatures such that they would always do right, he notes that, as Ninian Smart argues, this conception entails a radical rethinking of our moral notions. If true, we could not possess positive goodness because we would be morally untemptable beings; though we would always innocently do the right thing, we could not 'justifiably be praised as being morally good' (p. 307). But more importantly for Hick, virtues of a *genuine* and *authentic* nature could not arise out of such a condition. Creatures restricted to only freely choosing the good are but moral puppets. Though they might, for example, come to love and trust God, and themselves consider these virtues to be genuine, such virtues would in God's eyes be inferior. Authentic trust and love require the real possibility of their refusal; creatures formed such that they could not but positively relate to their Creator could not participate in a fully personal relationship. Analogous to our moral sense in this regard, God values an autonomy that involves the possibility of creatures rejecting His relationship. One is reminded on this point of Dostoevsky's 'The Grand Inquisitor'. As we saw in Chapter 2, Dostoevsky thought that personal love required respect for the dignity of the individual. But dignity, in turn, rests on the moral autonomy of the person. Thus Dostoevsky confirms Hick's view in this regard, arguing that personal active love can only exist under conditions of personal moral freedom. Personal freedom is an essential element of teleological theodicy.

So the possibility of moral evil in Hick's scheme is a necessary feature. Creatures restricted from moral transgression could never participate in a relation of likeness with God in any authentic manner. Hick says that autonomy makes one 'good in a richer and more valuable sense than would be one created *ab initio* in a state either of innocence or of virtue' (p. 291). Soul-making is an autonomous affair. Thus moral evil is justified in Hick's theology in a free-will defence. Natural evil can be considered in terms of response to the natural obstacles conducive to soul-making. In the encounter of the challenges of natural evils human beings are pushed forward in the soul-making endeavour. The natural and social world is seen as the stage of the soul-making drama, as the ideal environment for one to grow in likeness to God, and the human life is understood in terms of a teleological narrative.

Evil, then, is understood as a necessary means of the soul-making drama. But although they are a means toward bringing about a greater good, evils are nevertheless negative and real; Hick says they 'threaten us with ultimate destruction' (p. 399). Yet at the same time he aptly rules out the notion of hell because it is immoral: 'The sufferings of the damned in hell, since they are interminable, can never lead to any constructive end beyond themselves, and are thus the very type of ultimately wasted and pointless anguish' (p. 377). Furthermore, he denies the possibility even of 'the divine annihilation or the dwindling out of existence of the finally lost' (p. 378), because he considers these to contradict God's good purpose. So he argues that in the end there will be 'no personal life that is unperfected and no suffering that has not eventually become a phase in the fulfilment of God's good purpose' (p. 376).

WEAKNESSES AND STRENGTHS IN HICK'S THEODICY

We can begin to evaluate Professor Hick's theodicy in reference to his view of universal salvation. How, in a conception of universal salvation can Hick consistently speak about evil as the threat of ultimate destruction? And does this view not undermine the autonomy he so forcefully emphasised against those who argue that God could create an autonomous creature that only chooses the right? Hick admits the logical possibility that God's purpose of universal salvation might be frustrated by autonomous human beings, but he considers the power and grace of God sufficient to establish the practical certainty that such will not occur. Yet this contradicts his stress on the necessity of the non-coercion of God in ensuring an authentic and genuine relationship in likeness. The

possibility that human beings might forever choose to substitute a
telos of their own making for that which is appropriate to them,
or that they might deny teleology altogether, must be practically
actualisable in order to ensure the kind of authentic and genuine
moral and personal relationship Hick espouses as the teleological
goal. But more important, unless the possibility of non-existence
or divine annihilation exists, Hick cannot properly speak of evil
as a threat of *ultimate* destruction. This runs against our intuitive
response to evil by lessening the negative force and reality of it,
and the view can be used to justify a moral callousness. In so far
as we reduce the sense of the destructive power of evil, we move
towards the problems that Friedman poses for radical teleological
theodicy, as we saw in Chapter 1.

But I do not think the possibility of non-existence contradicts
either the power or the goodness of God. In fact the movement
to non-being is quite consistent with the teleological structure that
Hick has in mind. Autonomy and the potential to divinity of human
beings are key to the teleology; the actualisation of divine beings
existing in an authentic and genuine relationship with their creator
is a difficult and hazardous undertaking that is beyond the power
of God alone, but nevertheless not unrealisable. Also required is
the power of the autonomous creature who must bear a great
deal of the responsibility and effort in his moral and spiritual
transformation to divine likeness in God. The neglect of this burden
leads to the frustration of the telos, culminating in the downfall
and non-existence of the autonomous creature. But against Hick's
view, evil does not, in the downfall, win out over good; rather,
evil disappears as human beings tragically, but responsibly and
wilfully, fail to achieve their appropriate telos.[6] God does not
cause this downfall, though he *permits* it. And His good purpose,
the actualisation of autonomously perfected divine beings is not
defeated by the downfall of some. Despite this possibility and
in light of no other way, God deems the actualisation of human
beings in divine likeness to justify the tragedy of fallen creatures,
and does everything in His power, short of coercion, to help avert
the downfall.

Such a view does qualify God's omnipotence, but no more than
we saw in Leibniz's teleological picture. And Hick's view is very
much like Leibniz's on a number of significant points. Like Leibniz,
Hick espouses a doctrine of the best possible world and stresses the
free-will defence; the world is the ideal environment in achieving

the teleological goal, and freedom is a vital aspect in such a realisation. Also, like Leibniz, Hick distances God's responsibility for evil by accentuating his role in permitting it. However, Hick's theodical view is more effective than Leibniz's; it overcomes many of the difficulties facing Leibniz's account. Though Hick's teleological goal is not unlike that which Leibniz proposes, Hick stresses the role of the human being in a future goal of personal *relationship* with God and *participation* in the divine life in contrast to Leibniz who emphasises God's revelation and communication of the divine perfections and who does not explicitly incorporate a future reference in his theodicy. Hick's theology is structured around an eschatology that involves a developmental framework which justifies freedom. Moral freedom is necessary to the moral and personal development of human beings in likeness to God. So Hick goes further than Leibniz, illustrating how freedom, which is so closely connected to evil, contributes to the teleological goal. Moral and personal beings epistemically distanced from God have been established in an environment conducive to their autonomous growth to likeness of finite divine nature where they will participate in a beatific relationship with their Creator. So the ideal nature of human beings is made intelligible in Hick's teleology, and it is coherently related to the present state of affairs.

Analogous to our understanding of personal growth in knowledge, emotion and virtue from child through adolescent to mature adult, Hick offers a religious teleology that shifts this perception of growth-advancement by including a spiritual component and depicting a future divine relationship with God. The picture is plausible, offering a cogent world view that is consistent with many of the common-sense teleological perspectives and goals generally held.

Of course, those who deny moral, emotional and intellectual teleology will remain sceptical of Hick's soul-making analogue. However, Hick does give an intelligible and plausible account that is consistent and related to his teleological goal. Evil is a necessary feature of such a teleological picture. Natural evils result from the obstacles set forth in physical nature from which human beings are pushed forward in their development. Moral evil is a consequence of the autonomy necessary for such spiritual development. Both, then, contribute to the actualisation of the teleology, and will be justified in the eschaton envisioned in Hick's theology. He says:

Given the conception of a divine intention working in and through human time towards a fulfilment that lies in its completeness beyond human time, our theodicy must find the meaning of evil in the part that it is made to play in the eventual outworking of that purpose; and must find the justification of the whole process in the magnitude of the good to which it leads. (p. 297)

So Hick justifies the existence of evil in terms of the greater good to which it is ordered. His theodicy is thus given coherence in his teleological perspective. This theodicy, however, like Leibniz's effort, is without immediate justification. Such is quite beyond present human conception; the theodicy will be validated only in the spiritual eschaton experienced at some future time.

Thus many strengths of soul-making theodicy surface when considered against traditional non-teleological themes and in contrast to Leibniz's teleological theodicy. In Hick's account we find the most satisfactory traditional theodicy. However, I consider there to be four significant weaknesses of Hick's teleological theodicy, difficulties which I will examine in the next Chapter. First, although Hick provides more evidence in support of his teleological theodicy than Leibniz does, the evidence nevertheless is insufficient. This problem will be illustrated in reference to Immanuel Kant's views on theodicy. Second, although Hick's theodicy has positive/affirmative elements and a pastoral thrust, the development of this aspect of theodicy is rather weak. Indeed, because the justification of theodicy lies for Hick in a distant eschatological future, little of this consolation can be experienced in this life. Third, his theodicy explains neither the depth and scope of evil nor the apparent impulse to evil. And finally, as Hick himself admits, his teleological theodicy cannot account for the many seemingly dysteleological evils, such as were discussed earlier in our development of Dostoevsky's theodicy.

These difficulties are significant because they apply to non-mystical teleological theodicy in general, and are, for the most part, overcome in certain mystical teleological theodicies. As such, they provide the background to the second section of this work. Since they will be used to structure the development of mystical teleological theodicy to come, they will be examined separately and, where necessary, in some detail.

5

Problems and Issues
in Traditional Theodicy

The basic structure of coherent teleological theodicy as it surfaces in the view of Leibniz and Hick is as follows: The telos is personal and moral relationship with God in participation in a divine life that is analogous in certain respects to this life. Freedom is necessary to the moral and personal development of humanity in an environment suitable to the realisation of divine likeness. Evil arises as negative side-effect of human autonomy and in terms of obstacles in the natural world, and its justification will become clear in the future eschaton.

Such a theodicy is intelligible and can be given some plausibility in common moral and personal teleological analogies. I consider it to be the most satisfactory traditional theodicy. However, as I briefly mentioned at the close of the last chapter, it gives rise to serious problems and issues that are more effectively addressed in mystical theodicy. Let us now examine these difficulties in detail, with some brief reference to their resolution in mystical theodicy.

THE PROBLEM OF EVIDENCE: THE KANTIAN CRITIQUE

From his historical position (1724–1804) Kant surveyed well the general dialectical development of philosophical theodicy, and contributed his own view to the theodical dialogue, a view that has received little scholarly attention. In 1791 he wrote *On the Failure of All Attempted Philosophical Theodicies*,[1] a short but significant essay that clearly shows his familiarity with past and current theodical thought. He was familiar with the scepticism of Pierre Bayle and the countering optimism of Leibniz's *Theodicy*, and his concern with

59

the work of David Hume is well documented. He was for some time genuinely sympathetic to the attempts at philosophical theodicy, especially Leibniz's work in this regard. Ann Loades comments that his

> 1759 lecture announcement *Some Reflections on Optimism* indicates how Kant would have replied to *Candide*. In itself the announcement restated the Leibnizian position, . . . [that the] deity chose what was most worth the choosing in the light of his assessment of his objective . . .[2]

However, as will soon become evident, Kant later significantly revised his views in this regard.[3]

Teleology was a major concern of his as well. That Kant recognised the necessary movement to teleology in theodicy is evident in his definition of theodicy as defences of the *wisdom* of God, rather than that of God's goodness. Perhaps the stress on teleology in Leibniz accounts for Kant's early favour towards Leibniz's position. Be that as it may, Kant recognised the importance of teleology in the theodicies of the day, and adapted his analysis of teleological judgement to the question of theodicy. In so doing, he penetrated deeply into the nature and limitation of philosophical teleological theodicies, formulating the analysis in his essay on theodicy in indirect reference to the 'Methodology of the Teleological Judgement'.[4]

Kant defines theodicies as 'defences of the highest wisdom of the Creator against the complaints which reason makes by pointing to the existence of things in the world which contradict the wise purpose'.[5] He qualifies this definition immediately, however, stating that this is not a plea for God's cause, as is normally presumed, but rather a plea for reason which, in theodicy, oversteps its bounds. For, he says, though we 'cannot demonstrate with certainty that reason is completely powerless when it comes to determining the *relationship between this world as we know it through experience* and *the supreme wisdom*',[6] we nevertheless have not demonstrated that reason has any force in this regard. Further, he says, until we do establish the ability of reason in ascertaining divine wisdom we ought to abandon attempts at philosophical or speculative theodicy.

This view of reason is clarified in Kant's distinction between artistic wisdom (divine purpose in natural phenomena) and moral

wisdom (divine purpose in moral freedom). Teleological theodicies espouse a divine purpose which lacks sufficient evidence; the
notion of this world as best in terms of God's telos requires 'a unity
and agreement between artistic and moral wisdom in a world of
experience'[7] that is unobtainable. This point is key to Kant's view of
theodicy, but not clearly nor fully developed in *On the Failure of All
Attempted Theodicies*. I will begin, however, by outlining the practical
significance of Kant's view as it is expressed in this essay, before
developing the notions of artistic and moral wisdom as they are
presented in the 'Methodology of the Teleological Judgement'.

The Practical Application of Kant's View

The defence of the wisdom of God, argues Kant, must take the
form of one of three proofs:[8] (a) one can show that evidence
that seems to contradict divine purposefulness in fact does not
– the contradiction is merely apparent; (b) one can argue that that
which contradicts this purposefulness is a necessary consequence
of the nature of things, hence but an inevitable contradiction; (c)
one can prove that that which contradicts divine purposefulness
arises not from God but from other responsible creatures. Concerning each of these proofs there are three different kinds of
counter-evidence, that is, evidence which contradicts, or seems
to contradict, divine purposefulness: (1) moral evil (sin), which
Kant considers absolutely contrary to God's purposefulness, either
as ends or means; (2) pain and suffering, that which can be justified
as means but not as ends of purposefulness; (3) disproportion of
crime and punishment, the injustice in the retribution of moral
evil. Kant considers all three proofs in relation to each kind of
counter-evidence in turn.

I will begin by examining (1), the move to justify moral evil. In
terms of (a), where the contradiction between fact and purposefulness is argued to be only apparent, Kant maintains that even
if we argue that our ways are not God's ways we still have to
say that the view that moral evil (sin) can accomplish His purpose runs against our moral sense. Further, (b) if we argue that
moral evil arises from necessary human limitations (for example,
imperfections in the contingent and secondary nature of human
beings) then human beings cannot be understood as guilty, hence
never morally evil. And finally we have (c), where the person is
understood as shouldering the responsibility of evil, which limits

God's participation in moral evil to permission and justifies it as necessary for higher moral ends. But against this Kant argues:

> since it was impossible for God to prevent this [moral] evil without contradicting higher moral ends, the ground for this misfortune (for this is how it must be called) must be sought in the nature of things, in the necessary limits of humanity as finite being, and thereby mankind cannot really be made responsible for it.[9]

Kant thinks the counter for (b) similarly applies to (c): as a consequence of the necessary limitations of humanity, moral evil is not ultimately dependent upon human beings. However, as we will see later in this chapter, Kant himself provides the framework within which human beings can be regarded as responsible, in their autonomy, for moral evil. And, as we have already seen, the supposition for Plantinga, Leibniz and Hick, is that God cannot will a human being to choose *freely* only the good and at the same time actualise His teleology. Nevertheless, God does not in the creative process thereby will that human beings do evil. Rather, He wills the *possibility* that they might choose evil. This perspective takes the force from Kant's counters; evil does not accomplish God's purpose, freedom does, and the human being is not conceived of as 'limited in misfortune', as Kant would phrase it, but rather as 'dignified in autonomy' even though he or she is responsible for the moral evils committed. Still, such qualifications require some account of how and why freedom is necessary to teleology. Pain and suffering, point (2), begin to show the difficulties in this regard.

Towards justifying the pain and suffering of this world one might argue (a) that this contradiction of wisdom is but apparent, by proposing that there is not really more suffering than happiness in the world. Though the defender might bizarrely suggest that even suicide does not illustrate the excess of suffering in the world, Kant points out that any wise person who has lived a long life would, if she or he could, choose better conditions for another earthly life. To argue (b) that pain is inevitable because human beings are natural creatures is to beg the question; why create human beings if life is so painful? And to propose (c) that pain and suffering are necessary trials of worthiness, that they are 'considered by the supreme wisdom as the absolute condition of the joy to come',[10] is to propose a view that can be formulated but not rendered intelligible. Kant says it does not untie the knot of theodicy but simply cuts it: though it can be stated, it does not provide the content that a theodicy sets out to give.

Now this last rejoinder is open to some doubt in light of the evidence we saw in Hick's teleological picture. There are, indeed, certain moral problems in proposing that this world is a moral testing-ground, a place where God might determine which creatures are the most obedient and resilient in the face of adversity. However, these problems are circumvented in the notion of this world as a necessary realm of growth to divinity, where one comes to divine relationship with God in the best manner possible. Thus the terms of the problem are, again, transformed. The evils of the world and those that arise in the misuse of freedom, that is, the necessary conditions of a realm of soul-making, are here more aptly described as the 'conditions for divinity' rather than by, in Kant's words, 'trials of worthiness', and this explanation gives some content to the theodical position. Nevertheless Kant's rejoinder is significant to the question of divine justice in point (3), and might be further clarified.

Against those who hold (a) that the disproportion between crime and punishment is only apparent – pointing to the fact that the unjust are punished by their conscience – Kant argues simply that they are mistaken. The radically evil are generally without conscience. To argue (b) that moral injustice is necessary to the nature of things does not take away the sense of injustice, and to propose that retribution will occur in another world does not bring satisfaction to the present sense of injustice. When we propose a future life where such reconciliation might occur, such 'in no way amounts to a *justification* of providence; it is rather a sovereign sentence passed by rational moral faith which can advise patience to the doubter but does not give him satisfaction'.[11] Furthermore, to propose (c) that there will occur a final reckoning in this future life according to one's moral worth of the present is an unwarranted hypothesis; we cannot expect an order of affairs in the future world different from that which we presently experience. As Kant asks: 'What guide can be used by reason in its theoretical capacity except the law of nature?'.[12]

This last point is vital to Kant's argument. Though the doubts raised by the theodical sceptic cannot disprove the claim of divine moral wisdom, reason can tell us nothing regarding the content of such wisdom. So theodicy can never justify this wisdom through philosophical teleology. Kant's schematic bears this out well. The notion of a future bliss or a future world of a higher order that reconciles present evils is a stateable hypothesis but not justifiable by reason. Evidence of such a future is not to be found in the realm of experience. In so far as this future good is not an experienced reality, it is not justified, and we cannot effectively justify moral evil, pain, injustice or freedom in terms of it. Or, to state it in Kant's theoretical terminology, so long as there is no notion in a world of experience that unites the concept of artistic wisdom with that of moral wisdom, speculative theodicies are doomed to failure.[13] Let us now clarify this fundamental point.

The Theoretical Justification of Kant's View

On the one hand we have artistic wisdom, the notion of the purposefulness in the things of the natural world, by which speculative reason can develop a physical theology. Physical, or natural, theology 'is the endeavour of reason to infer the supreme cause of nature and its properties from the *purposes* of nature (which can only be empirically known)'.[14] We can indeed reasonably ascribe purposefulness to nature, the view that all things are good for something, and because of this assumption of the efficacy of things we are led to hypothesise an intelligent Author of this world. But this is only as far as experience can take us; we cannot, by empirical experience, give content to the architectonic understanding at the bottom of things. Kant says:

> But because the data, and so the principles, for *determining* that concept of an intelligent world cause (as highest artist) are merely empirical, they do not enable us to infer any of its properties beyond those which experience reveals in its effects.[15]

Required for the determination of the nature of this first cause is more than empirical data can offer. Complete knowledge of its effects would alone allow us to ascribe properties to this primary intelligence. But nature offers us no knowledge of the purposefulness of this Author of nature, which could indeed be simply the 'mere necessity of its nature to produce certain forms . . . without it being necessary to ascribe to it even wisdom, much less the highest wisdom combined with all the properties requisite for the perfection of its product'.[16]

The purposes of nature allow us to infer the existence of a primary intelligence behind the empirical world, but give us no evidence to infer a final purpose for creation. One cannot claim this world to be the best of all possible worlds on the evidence of the purposefulness of things of nature. Rather, what is required for such judgement is omniscience, the ability 'to see into the purposes in nature in their whole connection', and the ability to conceive all possible plans in order to ensure that this is the best.[17] So it is that Kant characterises natural theology as really only physical teleology, which cannot give us a final purpose of nature nor provide us with religious conceptions of Deity.

Moral teleology, on the other hand, is that which provides a religious theology. Moral teleology is the attempt of reason to determine the ultimate cause and its properties from the moral purpose of human beings. The structure of this moral teleology begins with that which can establish a final purpose of human beings. Final purpose, of course, is a groundless purpose that depends upon no other purpose. Kant argues quite convincingly that it is only in the faculty of desire that we uncover a final purpose, but not in a desire that would see human beings dependent on anything other than themselves; such would prove itself not to be a *final* purpose. Independent desire is the final purpose, and this is a good will. He says, 'a good will is that whereby alone [man's] being can have an absolute worth and in reference to which the being of the world can have a *final purpose*'.[18] Final worth, then, 'is that worth which [man] alone can give to himself and consists in what he does, how and according to what principles he acts, and that not as a link in nature's chain, but in the *freedom* of his faculty of desire'.[19]

Freedom of moral choice is the final purpose of human beings and it gives them intrinsic worth. This worth, this final purpose of human beings, establishes them as the final purpose of creation, as that upon which nature is ordinated. It is the ground that connects and justifies the whole system of purposes that arise in the context of human beings and nature. So it is through Kant's moral teleology that teleological content is given to nature. But this moral teleology also gives content to theology; the intelligent source of nature established in physical teleology can be described in terms of the final purpose of moral teleology. This position is clearly developed already in the *Critique of Practical Reason*. There Kant describes the inferences about God's nature arising from practical reason:

> This being must be omniscient, in order to be able to know my conduct even to the most intimate parts of my intention in all possible cases and in the entire future. In order to allot fitting consequences to it, He must be omnipotent, and similarly omnipresent, eternal, etc. Thus the moral law by the concept of the highest good as the object of a pure practical reason, defines the concept of the First Being as that of a Supreme being.[20]

If the human being as moral being has as his or her ultimate purpose moral activity in freedom then he or she must conceive the source of self and nature to be the highest good; and as sovereign good to rational moral beings and as the impetus behind moral law, this Deity must be considered omniscient; and as nature is to be understood in this conception as in accordance with moral purpose, this primary intelligence is to be conceived of as omnipotent.[21] But Kant qualifies this theology by noting that it is only a practical proof. It is thought *a priori*, and is consequently a mere 'thing of faith'.[22] This moral proof of God has no objective reality and is not theoretically valid:

> The concept of this cannot be established as regards its objective reality in any experience possible for us, and thus adequately for the theoretical use of reason, but its use is commanded by practical pure reason . . . .[23]

Furthermore, we can think these properties of God in moral theology only by analogy; we cannot cognise God.[24] Indeed, all this proof expresses is the *relationship* of God 'to the objects of *our* practical reason';[25] the effects cannot express the properties of the cause, which, to be conceived would require experience of similar causes. So moral teleology provides a concept of final purpose that is without cognitive content and not an objective proof. Yet it has an objective reality for us in terms of practical reference, moral teleology is 'a thing of faith of the pure reason, along with God and immortality'.[26]

Although physical teleology is not necessary to moral theology, it does provide evidence that confirms this moral argument. This is important, for if it provided only evidence against the argument, then validity of the proof would be highly dubious. Physical teleology could, furthermore, give objective character to the proof, if it provided some empirical account of the nature of Deity. Kant says:[27]

> If we were able also with some plausibility to base upon the purposes of nature, which physical teleology presents to us in such rich abundance, a *determinate* concept of an intelligent world cause, then the existence [*Dasein*] of this Being would not be a thing of faith.[27]

Such empirical effects, however, cannot tell the nature of this uncaused cause. It is empirical effects that constitute evidence for what, in *On the Failure of All Attempted Theodicies*, Kant calls artistic wisdom, the notion that the world in its laws and order is a creation of perfection, 'a divine manifestation of the *intentions* of [God's] will'.[28] Theodicies based on artistic wisdom are what Kant calls doctrinal theodicies, theodicies set forth by speculative reason. They are doomed to failure because we cannot draw from empirical experience any final purpose. That is to say, artistic wisdom is a conception that is not sufficiently justified by empirical observation. We can deduce an intelligent source of nature from empirical phenomena but we cannot ascribe an ultimate purpose to this source. The arrangement and workings of the world do not justify any purpose more than the mere production of forms. To grasp the truth of artistic wisdom requires omniscience, the ability to see the teleological ends of the natural world and all other possible plans of arrangement.

In contrast with doctrinal theodicies based on artistic wisdom, Kant proposes an authentic theodicy based on the moral wisdom of practical reason which recognises the primary purpose as moral freedom. This moral ideal of practical reason is that which allows one to reject 'all reproaches addressed to divine wisdom'.[29] It is not a philosophical theodicy at all, but a practical stance that moral teleology allows one to take against those who deny the wisdom of the divine that is assumed in the context of moral theology. To become a theodicy proper, that is, to be a defence of the highest wisdom of God, would require its unification with artistic wisdom. Such would give one 'a knowledge of the super-sensible (intelligible) world . . . how this world lies at the basis of world experience'.[30] Indeed, such an experience Kant considers necessary to theodicy proper, an experience that he regards as impossible for human beings to realise. He says: 'On this knowledge only can be based the proof of the moral wisdom of the Creator of the world – no mortal man however can attain to this knowledge'.[31]

The Kantian Critique of Hick's Theodicy

Against Hick's view, then, Kant argues that there is no empirical evidence to justify soul-making theodicy. I think this is true. The positive evidence Hick proposes is of a moral nature, requiring an affirmation of moral and personal teleology that does not derive from empirical evidence. Though empirical evidence does not contradict his theodicy, neither does it give it sufficient positive support. Indeed, this problem of evidence becomes even more poignant later in this chapter, when we examine the great depth and scope of evil, and dysteleological evils. For certain evils 'are destructive, run against all purposes, and do not seem to agree with the idea of a plan established with wisdom and goodness'.[32] This fact has led some thinkers to consider this world as more of a penal colony than a soul-making realm. For example, contrary to Hick's perspective, Arthur Schopenhauer argues plausibly that the evidence speaks in favour of the Augustinian version of the myth of the fall, where our existence is considered but a punishment for misdeeds past. He goes on to say,

> As a reliable compass for orienting yourself in life nothing is more useful than to accustom yourself to regarding this world as a place of atonement, a sort of penal colony. . . . This outlook will enable us to view the so-called imperfections of the majority of men, *i.e.* their moral and intellectual shortcomings and the facial appearance resulting therefrom, without surprise and certainly without indignation: for we shall always bear in mind where we are and consequently regard every man first and foremost as a being who exists only as a consequence of his culpability and whose life is an expiation of the crime of being born.[33]

Against soul-making teleology one can quite plausibly propose a penal-colony teleology in the provocative manner of Schopenhauer. Artistic wisdom only is sufficient to validate the teleological perspective, and such is quite beyond Hick's theodical means.

Kant's theodical position is reminiscent of Dostoevsky's view developed in Chapter 2. For Dostoevsky real freedom means that faith in theodicy comes with no absolute assurances; it will always involve doubt. For Kant, intellectual integrity requires that one honestly face up to the hard reality of evil, and recognise that faith rests upon mere moral wisdom. He says 'only the uprightness of the heart, not the merit of one's insights, the sincere and undisguised confessions of one's doubts, and the avoidance of feigned convictions which one does not really feel',[34] are the appropriate theodical stances. Thus Kant refers to 'authentic' theodicy. To illustrate the practical theodical position he holds, Kant turns to the *Book of Job*. Kant pictures the friends of Job as offering a speculative theodicy in their attempt to account for the terrible trial Job undergoes. These efforts, Kant argues, are not only reasonably futile but also heretical. Job recognises their mistakes in this regard, the horrible realities of the empirical world that cannot but contradict the divine wisdom from the perspective of reason. Nevertheless, he stands the tenuous ground offered by moral teleology and refuses to speak about that of which he has no understanding. Such is the appropriate stance of authentic theodicy offered by Kant.

But Kant goes further than this, and proposes a possibility that seems quite out of sorts with his general view of spiritual matters. He says that Job in his righteousness received a profound religious experience *wherein he realises artistic wisdom*! He says:

> This denouement authenticates this last statement of Job's; for God honoured Job by showing him the wisdom of his creation and its unfathomable nature. He let him see the beautiful side of creation, where man can see an indubitable light (and understand) the purposes of the Creator and his wise providence.[35]

Here I think Kant points the way to theodicies that can be distinguished from the philosophical teleological theodicies that Kant criticises, towards mystical theodicies that, in their emphasis upon mystical experiences of the Divine, provide a defence of divine wisdom that is much more cogent than their non-mystical counterparts. That is, evidence that verifies the truth of the theodicy is realised in mystical experience. Later in Chapter 7 I will examine this view more fully and directly, as it arises in the mysticism of Meister Eckhart. But indeed, this point is not unrelated to the issues arising in positive/affirmative theodicy, issues which we should turn to now.

ISSUES IN POSITIVE/AFFIRMATIVE THEODICY

The notion of epistemic distance implies that human beings are generally unaware of the divine presence in and about the world. I think Hick would agree with this: for the most part human beings do not achieve the kind of vivid, joyous and awesome awareness of God that Hick depicts as the finite teleological ideal of his theodicy. Rather, they begin and often remain in a 'surrounding, and chronic, human self-centeredness'[36] which Hick thinks accompanies the non-awareness of the divine presence. In this regard he stresses the 'creatureliness' of human beings, their limited power and worth in comparison to the infinite mind and will of God, who has a 'moral demand and holy claim' upon them which they ought to serve and obey.[37] But where, in this picture, do we find illustration of the beneficent care of God?

Hick says we should expect the reality of God to become evident to men in so far as they are willing to live as creatures in the presence of an infinitely perfect being whose very existence sets them under a sovereign claim of worship and obedience.[38] In the volitional component of religious faith – that is, the willingness to worship and obey God – the signs of divine presence and activity in the world become evident. The world mediates the divine presence for those who have, in faith, freely committed themselves to God. So in Hick's theodicy we find a positive/affirmative aspect in the ideal relationship of God and the person who has achieved the human ideal of the teleology. No doubt this kind of feature is implicit in Leibniz' Christian view, but in Hick it is clearly maintained in his theodical context. Those who achieve the finite aspect of the teleological goal in their submission to God, gain a sense of His presence in the world, and the positive affective experience that accompanies this awareness, an awareness that issues forth in a kind of future-oriented patience and perseverance in the face of evil. He says: 'This awareness of the divine presence does not negate our agonizing human experience of evil but sets it within the context of God's purpose of good and under the assurance of the ultimate triumph of that purpose'.[39]

But as I have pointed out, even those who achieve the finite teleological goal of Hick's theodicy will not find the confirmation of the theodicy he propounds. Only in a future eschaton will epistemic distance be fully eliminated and God's goodness verified. In contrast, some mystical theodicies claim the abrogation of the divine–human distance to be possible in the present world. As I briefly mentioned earlier, certain mystics think theodical verification to be within the immediate grasp of some people. This is a cogent view, and if the mystics in question can be regarded as authoritative, it offers the believer a much more optimistic and hopeful position in the face of evil than Hick's rather meagre future-looking, other-worldly, perspective. It also means that divine participation in suffering can be experienced right now.

This last point is stressed in mystical theodicies; in Hick it is left ambiguous. Hick, generally stressing the transcendent rather than the immanent nature of the Divine, refers to God as 'but an occasional visitor'[40] to this soul-making environment, yet at the same time he claims there to be some kind of divine presence which the human being might become aware of. So the nature of God's participatory role in the human experience of evil is left unclear. And here Hick seems to imply that God is impassible in this regard,[41] and, further, he appears to downplay the relative necessity, value, power and significance of human beings in the face of God. On the other hand, mystical theodicies stress the importance and value of the human being, their potential divinity and their significance to God – their role, even, in the fulfilment of God. They also, in their emphasis on immanence as opposed to transcendence, stress the passibility of God, his active suffering for and with the human being.

As we will see in Chapter 8, mystical theodicies offer a much stronger assurance and immediacy of the ultimate triumph of God's purpose than Hick's non-mystical teleological theodicy, and they possess a good deal more consolatory force in their stress on the divine immanence and passibility, than the kind of patience and perseverance in the face of evil espoused in Hick's theodicy.

THE DEPTH AND SCOPE OF EVIL, AND THE IMPULSE TO EVIL

As we have seen, Hick locates the origin of evil in his notion of epistemic distance. He says that an individual's cognitive distance from God will entail a self-centredness, one moreover that will involve the person in competitive activity against others, a kind of egotism in relation to one's neighbour. So the origin of evil is found in the necessary epistemic distance which secures a preliminary self-centredness in relation to God and an egoistic stance in relation to other human beings. This stance gives rise to moral evil. There is, says Hick, a 'surrounding, and chronic, human self-centredness from which have flowed so many forms of man-made evil'.[42]

But the question of personal culpability arises in Hick's view.[43] Indeed, on the other hand and in tension with chronic self-centredness, Hick is adamant in his maintenance of the innocence, in immaturity, of the human creature. The creature does not wilfully fall from perfection; she or he is not originally morally defective, but rather unimputably morally ignorant. The image is one of youth, immaturity and unblameable innocence, in a condition of preliminary self-orientation. How, then, are human beings to be blamed for their moral impropriety? How, in their immature condition, can human beings be responsible for their moral lapses. To this Hick would no doubt respond that in immaturity the creature nevertheless 'immediately begins to feel, in a dim sense of moral demand and holy claim, the pressure upon his spirit of his unseen Creator'.[44] Still, the question remains as to how, in so far as the moral obligations are dim and faint, and the self-centredness is *necessary* to the teleology, the creature is to be held responsible. This is very much like the criticism that Kant raises about attributing culpability to creatures who are hindered by certain necessary limitations, as we discussed earlier in this chapter. And on the other side of the coin there arises a second question: if one moves to the proposition of a brighter and clearer understanding of the moral law on the part of human beings then how could anyone go wrong? Why would they choose against God?

Obviously some clarification is called for here. Neither self-centredness nor attraction to the good can be necessitated if the origin of evil is to be explained theodically. Also, if human beings are to be held responsible for their actions it does not make sense to consider them as originally morally immature with the potentiality for both good and evil, depending upon the various conditions and influences. No, something must be built into the conception in order to allow for human responsibility (and thereby distance God's responsibility) while at the same time explaining the deep human tendency to evil. For this we can return for a moment to the thought of Immanuel Kant; we find just such an attempt in Book One of Kant's *Religion Within the Limits of Reason Alone*.[45] He says, 'the source of evil cannot lie in an object *determining* the will through inclination, nor yet in a natural impulse; it can lie only in a rule made by the will for the use of its freedom, that is, in a maxim'.[46]

Kant sees an inherent propensity to evil in humankind; an inclination to choose the maxim against the good. Human beings are endowed with certain natural incentives or predispositions, all of which do not, in themselves, oppose the moral law. For so long as 'they enjoin the observance of the law',[47] they are directed towards the good. He describes these as predispositions to animality, to humanity and to personality. The first is 'physical and purely *mechanical* self-love'.[48] This involves concern for survival, propagation and social community. The second incorporates practical reason in an element of comparative judgement with regard to physical self-love, beginning simply as the desire for equality. One determines one's status in reference to others, from which can spring a number of cultural vices such as jealousy, rivalry and envy. In these two incentives, then, we locate the potential to evil in predispositions of self-centredness, not unlike what Hick proposes. However, there is a third incentive in Kant's framework. This is the predisposition 'to personality in man, taken as a rational and at the same time an *accountable* being'.[49] It is simply 'the capacity for respect for the moral law as *in itself a sufficient incentive of the will*'.[50] But more than the incentives to self-centredness, this predisposition to personality has the potential to be the appropriate moral telos of human beings. If it becomes the impetus of the will, if 'the free will incorporates such moral feeling into its maxim',[51] then this predisposition becomes the appropriate moral end of a human being.

Without getting into the intricacies of Kant's moral philosophy, it is helpful to outline the structure of his view in order to begin to illustrate how we can allow for human moral responsibility while at the same time explaining the impulse to evil. In the context of the natural incentives outlined above, Kant describes the location and responsibility for moral evil:

Consequently man (even the best) is evil only in that he reverses the moral order of the incentives when he adopts them into his maxim. He adopts, indeed, thee moral law along with the law of self-love; yet when he becomes aware that they cannot remain on a par with each other but that one must be subordinated to the other as its supreme condition, he makes the incentive of self-love and its inclinations the conditions of obedience to the moral law; whereas, on the contrary, the latter, as the *supreme condition* of the satisfaction of the former, ought to have been adopted into the universal maxim of the will as the sole incentive.[52]

Because human beings have within themselves an inclination to ordinate the incentive to animality and humanity over and above that to personality, there 'is in man a natural propensity to evil'.[53] The appropriate move is the subordination of the sensuous incentives to that of an intrinsic respect for the moral law. But both moves occur in freedom. So Kant thinks it accurate to speak of a radical and innate evil in human nature which human beings are nonetheless responsible for. Thus we find a structure for the origin of evil that goes further than we saw in Hick's theodicy, a structure very much like that which we drew from Dostoevsky. Like Hick, Kant stresses that human beings, to be regarded as blameworthy, must begin in a state of innocence. However, the conditions of evil are not to be found in immaturity, in ignorance or solely in a distance from God. Like Dostoevsky, Kant views the potential or 'ground antecedent' of good and evil, which rest in the predispositions or incentives, to be innate to humankind, inclinations which are equally attractive and pulling.[54] Yet the proper source of good and evil rests in the autonomy of the individual; only in the choice of the guiding maxim that subordinates one or another incentive is the person good or evil. Also, like Kant, Dostoevsky considers there to be no morally neutral realm; human beings are fundamentally moral beings, and their actions are always morally relevant. And, finally, for both there seems to be something necessary about the potentially evil lower incentives. Given his criticisms of speculative theodicy, it is not surprising that Kant generally ignores this question. While Dostoevsky suggests that these lower incentives are necessary to activities, events and life, he does not fully develop the view, and rejects it as a theodical justification anyway, as we saw in Chapter 2. These questions regarding the origin, nature and rationale for evil in human nature are very important, yet they are usually neglected in traditional theodicies. What is the point of these potentially evil lower incentives that human beings, in their autonomy, must so carefully play out? Could God have created without them? Are they necessary to a particular teleology? If so how? Hick's soul-making theodicy does not adequately address these questions. In Chapter 9 I will examine Jacob Boehme's mystical teleological theodicy in this regard, as his view of the *Ungrund* is particularly insightful and relevant to these questions.

THE PROBLEM OF DYSTELEOLOGICAL EVIL

In *The Brothers Karamazov* Dostoevsky emphasises the problem of moral evil more than that of natural evil. He notices particularly how certain moral evils crush what seems to be a very fragile human character, and give rise to a great deal of seemingly unexpiated suffering. He asks about the possible teleological point to these evils, the good that might arise in and through them, but finds no satisfactory answer. These evils remain dysteleological, unjustified by any future-looking good that we can imagine. Hick recognises this apparent failure of soul-making teleology in this world, and refers to 'further scenes of "soul making"',[55] and a future eschaton where one experiences 'an infinite good that would render worthwhile *any* finite suffering endured in the course of attaining it'.[56] So he implies a future purgatorial state where soul-making activities might continue, and he proposes a future experience of such profundity that it justifies all suffering. However, as we have seen, Dostoevsky rightly questions the morality of justifying dysteleological evils in terms of the future 'hosanna' and he does not attempt to draw these evils into a teleological context through the hypothesis of purgatory. Indeed, the problem is in our inability to conceive of any useful function that certain experienced atrocities might serve.

Nevertheless, there is a theodical usefulness that the conception of future purgatory might serve if it is understood as another soul-making realm. As I will argue in Chapter 10, certain evils may be understood as purposeless, as never being expiated, yet nevertheless as necessary brute facts of the soul-making realm arising in the misuse of freedom. Though they go unjustified, the individual is thought to continue the soul-making journey, and not to experience a final, and therefore, ultimately tragic and meaningless death by them. Though such is not a justification of evil, it is a morally sound explanation of certain dysteleological miseries. But purgatory is not a sufficient conception in this regard; rather, what is called for is a belief in rebirth or transmigration, where the soul returns to *this* soul-making realm in order to continue his or her spiritual journey to divinity. The conception of purgatory involves the difficulties of relating and connecting two diverse orders of soul-making existence and it does not explain or provide the significance of the point of a very brief life in this world. For these reasons, I shall argue, the notion of rebirth more effectively acccounts for moral dysteleological evil in teleological theodicy, so long as it is disassociated in certain respects from its traditional retributive emphasis.

But the dysteleological evils arising in natural evils such as earthquakes and diseases are more difficult to explain. In Hick's case, for example, it is very hard to justify the tendency to excess of the principles of the natural world that Hume develops in his *Dialogues*, as I mentioned in Chapter 1. Hick himself recognises the problem and asks: 'Need the world contain the more extreme and crushing evils which it in fact contains? Are not life's challenges often so severe as to be self-defeating when considered as soul-making influences'.[57] He answers that such suffering remains unjustified in his soul-making theodicy, but quickly moves to qualify his view in the appeal to the efficacy of mystery, which challenges the Christian's faith while at the same time pushing him or her to empathy, compassion and self-sacrifice. Natural evils, then, are perhaps the most difficult problem for all theodicies, and will provide us with a reference point by which to draw together in conclusion the unresolved issues of mystical theodicy, and evaluate the success of mystical theodicy relative to traditional teleological theodicy. We must turn, then, to the nature of mystical theodicy. We begin with the general question of the nature of mysticism, defining it in the teleological theodical context, in reference to Evelyn Underhill.

PART II

Mystical Theodicy

6

Defining Teleological Mysticism

A PRELIMINARY DEFINITION

Mysticism is a nebulous concept; defining it is difficult and in many respects an ongoing affair.[1] The problem can begin to be seen in its great scope of application. For instance, mysticism has been distinguished in terms of religious, non-religious, moral and amoral types. Although mysticism is traditionally associated with religion, the term has become something of a catch-all word that is used (and misused) to denote all manner of esoteric or exceptional experiences. Indeed, mysticism is often associated with artistic genius and aesthetic experience, even in cases where these are seemingly disconnected from formal religious themes and mediums, and it has been aligned with clearly immoral and anti-religious characters and practices.[2]

The issues of definition are not only found in the questions concerning non-religious and amoral mysticisms, however. Religious pluralism is the main basis of debate, for there are Shamans and Hindu mystics, Taoists and neo-Taoists, Indian and Chinese Buddhists, Christians and Kabalists, Gnostics and Sufis and the host of other individuals throughout religious history that have been rightly (or wrongly) characterised as mystical.[3] And even within the individual cultural-religious traditions, there are mystics of very diverse temperament and outlook, and a veritable kaleidoscope of varying emphases in practice, belief and attitude.

To begin to define mysticism one must significantly limit this vast field. For my purposes the focus can begin to be delimited in terms of the questions and issues of theodicy that were raised in Part I. But more than this, given the esoteric nature of the subject, we can assume that in any significant attempt at definition one must look to those who call themselves mystics, and to

79

those mystics who have recounted their experiences with relative clarity and detail. According to these criteria, the field can be narrowed down to two important features. First, the definition must be restricted to those mysticisms that involve beliefs about the nature of the Divine and of evil; the domain of examination is thus limited to religious mysticisms that espouse theodicies. Second, in this context mysticisms that possess well-developed mystical perspectives will be most helpful. Now in this regard we must further distinguish in religious mysticisms between the 'casual' mystic who treats the experiences relatively insignificantly and the 'serious' mystic who is involved in a mystical life, ever seeking mystical realisations. So we have what might be called the 'mystical dilettante', who experiences features of mysticism but who does not establish mysticism as his or her ultimate purpose, and the 'authentic' mystic, who grants the experiences extraordinary status as a central premise of his or her life.[4] In the latter case, since it offers us a structure and a direction that is absent in the mystical dilettante, systematic reflection concerning the mystical path to which a mystic is committed can be related to issues pertaining to the theodicy of mysticism.

The domain of examination is thus reduced to authentic religious mysticisms that are concerned with the problem of evil. Still, we are left with the hard question of which religious traditions to choose, and the problem of the great variety and complexity within particular traditions. Moreover, I am not in a position here to survey the many mystical perspectives in even a specific tradition. These considerations force us to compromise; we must look to a reliable source that has sensitively examined and systematised the diverse domain.

For this we can turn to one of the earliest and most outstanding survey analyses of mysticism. Recognised as a classic, Evelyn Underhill's *Mysticism* provides a vast study of the nature and history of mysticism in the Christian West. Moreover, she herself is a mystic, and thus brings her own personal experiences in analysing and systematising the subject. However, there are certain drawbacks in relying on Underhill's presentation, for she reveals a strong Christian bias and emphasis in her exposition and there are some obscurities and confusions in her systematisation and exposition. Moreover, her illustrations are for the most part limited to Christian mystics. Nevertheless, against these weaknesses we should note that she does incorporate a great variety of authentic mystic source material to highlight and justify her thesis, and where necessary we can look for clarification to the more simplified and practical version of the phases and steps of the mystical way in her *Practical Mysticism*. Also, her view is general enough to include mystics of other traditions, and, anyway, this limitation is not vital to us. In our examination of mysticism we are attempting to uncover a cogent and coherent mystical theodicy rather than to formulate an all-embracing mystical typology.

Through Underhill, then, we can draw out a basic and general definition of mysticism. Her exposition, as we shall see, is an ideal vehicle in illustrating the problems and issues in the area of the theodicy of mysticism. And, more importantly, she provides a preliminary framework for teleological mysticism. This is very important given our emphasis on teleological theodicy, for it is in a teleological theology that we uncover a teleological theodicy.

Underhill assumes there to be an inherent teleology to mysticism. Earlier I distinguished between the mystical life, what Donald Evans calls authentic mysticism, and the mystical dilettante. Authentic mysticism always involves some teleology. But Underhill sees this authentic mysticism as only properly theistic, involving a number of successive experiences of *progressive value*, and culminating in a final phase or stage. Her scheme is thus highly evaluative in her theistic teleology. She proposes the 'unitary life' as the appropriate goal for all *healthy* mysticisms, and says that focusing upon and stressing other experiences as ends in themselves is mistaken and dangerous. So she criticises the quietism of mystics who rest satisfied in the early stages of illumination; she refers to these as mere states of subconscious meditation 'which might provoke the laughter of the saints' (p. 324),[5] and claims that the contemplative experience of immanence is 'apt to degenerate into pantheism' or claims of 'deification' (p. 99) if the mystic does not interpret the experience in the context of her proposed mystical teleology.

Although, as we will see, Underhill is not alone in this view, she emphasises mysticism as it is reported by some mystics and rejects the claims of other mystics, without providing a criterion for determining the efficacy of one over the other. That some sort of teleology is a key feature of mysticism is plausible, even *prima facie* likely, given the apparent developmental structure of authentic mysticisms. But in this regard there is disagreement between mystics about the relative status of experiences; authentic religious mystics differ in their views of their importance. Nevertheless, it will begin to become clear in this chapter that some kind of theistic teleology is essential to an effective mystical theodicy. The nature of this theistic teleology will be given further expansion as we examine the mystical theodicies of Meister Eckhart and Dostoevsky (Chapters 7 and 8). Moreover, it will become apparent that this mystical theodicy is most effective if it also involves a pretheistic theogony (Chapter 9), and that it only properly coheres if it espouses a belief in rebirth (Chapter 10).

These aspects of mystical theodicy constitute its fundamental structure, a structure which we will outline in the context of this introduction of mysticism. But before proceeding in detail it will be helpful to provide a preliminary and general definition of mysticism. Underhill outlines five phases of mysticism: Awakening, Discipline, Enlightenment, Self-surrender and Union (p. 446). In relation to each phase there is a corresponding mystical process and a corresponding mystical experience. A mystical process is a set of physical, psychological, moral and spiritual disciplines that facilitate corresponding mystical experiences.[6] A selflessness is deemed necessary, a state that requires the disciplining of the senses and the will through detachment and mortification activities. These processes, then, are the 'means' or the 'disciplines' of mysticism. They are understood as transformative activities, either in terms of an outward quest or journey – in which one's preponderant focus shifts from the material world of external reality to a latent spiritual world which is source and ground – or in terms of a process of inner change or transmutation of the self.

Concerning mystical experiences, Underhill's 'illuminative' and 'unitive' types can be generally characterised as those powerfully affective experiences where the subject claims to encounter a greeeater reality, or to participate in union with this reality, a reality which is thought of as source and ground of all existent being, and which affects the subject's whole being in significant ways. Later we will see that these two types need to be distinguished and that there are other more important kinds of experiences such as the experienced intimacy between a subject and God which is typical of the Awakening process and the more negative states of divine abandonment which are typical of the dark night of the soul. But perhaps this suffices as a general introductory outline of mysticism, and we can now turn to a more detailed examination, illustrating some of the ways in which its processes and experiences affect issues of the theodicy of mysticism.

EXPERIENCES AND PROCESSES OF MYSTICISM

Although Underhill does not always clearly distinguish between processes and experiences of mysticism, such a demarcation is implicit and very important to her thesis, and indeed crucial to mysticism. To draw out effectively Underhill's view we can begin with an outline that stresses these distinctive features. The following schema pictures mysticism in terms of phases that involve specific processes and corresponding experiences that arise out of these processes:

Phases	Processes		Experiences
Awakening	Crisis Mental Stress Restlessness	$\longrightarrow$	Conversion
Discipline	Recollection and Purification	$\longrightarrow$	Detachment Quiet
Enlightenment	Quiet and Active Contemplation	$\longrightarrow$	Illumination
Self-surrender	Self-surrender	$\longrightarrow$	Abandonment (Dark Night of the Soul)
Union	Infused Contemplation	$\longrightarrow$	Unitary Life

This schematic lists the diverse processes and experiences by which Underhill characterises mysticism. We will begin to fill in the picture in a moment, but first we must make a qualifying note about the diversity that the schematic naturally expresses. For these categories are not as distinctive as the outline would imply. The processes, for example, blend into each other. They are not that dissimilar; to some degree they are necessary for *all* the experiences, and involve in some cases experiences which are designated by the same terms, for example, 'detachment' and 'quiet'. Also, what Underhill considers higher level experiences are thought to be in some sense anticipated in those of the lower level. The whole schematic thus represents highly interconnected as opposed to distinct stages, even though Underhill insists there is a certain natural progressive order to these processes and experiences, and a correlation between the experiences and the processes.

Conversion and Discipline

Keeping these qualifications in mind, I begin with the conversion experience. Underhill refers to conversion as 'the awakening of the transcendental consciousness' (p. 176). It is an awareness that arises sometimes very gradually out of the practice of a pious religiousness, but more often it is a consequence of a profound internal turmoil and 'dis-ease' that is symptomatic of the individual's defensive egotistic reaction to the intrusion of the intuitive mystical consciousness. The experience that arises out of this 'unselfing' (p. 176) process, as E. T. Starbuck calls it, is considered to be a movement out of instinctive self-centredness, to a converted sense of self, and to the realisation of a greater reality present and active in existent things. Underhill describes the experience as an

> intense, and joyous perception of God immanent in the universe; of the divine beauty and unutterable power and splendour of that larger life in which the individual is immersed, and of a new life to be lived by the self in correspondence with the now dominant fact of existence. (p. 179)

Quite naturally, then, these experiences are accompanied by the emotions of awe, rapture and love, as well as a sense of inferiority and unsatisfactoriness in the face of this higher reality. Conversion is accompanied not only by positive affective emotions, but also by negative feelings of imperfection and sin. As a consequence of this converted sense of self, this imperfection, and the belief that this higher reality can be experienced more fully, the mystic undergoes transformative measures that Underhill characterises as the recollection and quiet of the introversion process. So the individual naturally moves in conversion from the phase of Awakening to that of Discipline.

The recollection process of introversion involves the purification disciplines of detachment and mortification that are intended to rid the subject of the distracting factors that inhibit mystical experience. The point is to eliminate those aspects of the self that hinder mystical realisations; to 'recollect' that which began to surface in the conversion experience, the underlying inner but latent self free of the individuating forces of the egoistic impulses. Since each individual has his or her own particular desires, prejudices and attachments to overcome, the type, manner and degree of purification depends upon the nature of the individual subject (p. 212).

But in each case the processes of mortification and detachment involve a very radical self-transformation. In *Practical Mysticism* Underhill clarifies this goal in reference to Plotinus. She describes the converted mystic as at the mid-point between a 'higher' and a 'lower' life, as incompatibly attracted to two diverse ideals.[7] The lower life is the world of natural order, the material realm within which the ego finds its home. She characterises this state of affairs as the enslavement to the verb 'to have', where the individual is subject to conflicting passions, interests and desires that arise out of the egoistic centre.[8] The point is to stop these self-dispositions, to move towards participation in the higher life of the source and underlying order. Yet against this apparent Plotinian dualism of higher and lower life, Underhill goes on to stress the potential compatibility of the higher and lower orders; through mortification and detachment one does not transcend the material-temporal realm, but rather one changes one's egoistic attitude toward that realm.

Underhill distinguishes between negative and positive purification processes. Detachment is the negative. It is 'the stripping or purging away of those superfluous, unreal, and harmful things which dissipate the precious energies of the self' (p. 204). This she describes within the general framework of poverty, in terms of the virtues of chastity and obedience. Chastity is poverty of the senses and obedience is the poverty of the will. The main goal, then, is an indifference to existent things, an expurgation of egoism, and the elimination of independent selfhood. This she considers preliminary to positive purification; detachment 'purifies' the soul and the positive processes of mortification raise 'to their highest term' these 'permanent elements of character' (p. 205). The goal of mortification is the resolution 'of the turbulent whirlpools and currents of [one's] own conflicting passions, interests, desires'.[9] One pursues 'freedom from the fetters of the senses, the "remora of desire", from the results of environment and worldly education, from pride and prejudice, preferences and distaste: from selfhood in every form' (p. 224).

Towards this end the mystic undergoes a deliberate mental and/or physical process of painful suffering, a process that might involve simply the neglect of personal appearance and hygiene, like that of the highly bred and refined St Ignatius Loyola, or crude and barbaric self-torture, as in the case of the ascetic Henry Suso (1295–1365).[10] The severity of measures depends upon the individual needs of the person, but in all cases the goal is an indifference to all aspects of life, the good and the bad, the beautiful and ugly, the positive and negative.

Mortification is very illuminating in terms of the issues of evil and suffering for mysticism. In certain cases, the stress on mortifying activities as necessary mystical means becomes very acute, leading to quite incredible heights of self-inflicted torture. One of the best examples of this is Henry Suso, who in his autobiography recounts a life of incredible suffering for the sake of mystical experience. In this account he brings himself close to death through self-inflicted torture, claiming that 'God showed him that this severity and all these austerities had been just a good beginning and a breaking down of the outer man'.[11] In fact, he interprets all the many unusual calamities he encounters as actively brought upon him by God.[12]

There are problems with this view. Surely it is not the case that *all* suffering is to be interpreted as mystical means. As we saw in Chapter 2, Dostoevsky effectively illustrates the fact that in certain cases suffering destroys the person. Mortification is not without dangerous side effects. Indeed, one has only to begin to read Henry Suso's autobiography to appreciate the very fine line that exists between mortification as a spiritual process and mortification as a perverse and crippling masochism. Such, however, is not to argue that all mortification processes reduce to masochism, or that they cannot be justified by a theodicy. But it does illustrate the negative aspects of mortification, that this kind of suffering can cripple rather than benefit the practitioner. And it raises the questions of how far suffering of all kinds is to be interpreted in terms of a spiritual learning process, and what the criterion for such determination might be.

When approached from another angle this view of purification raises other issues. In considering such severe purification processes as necessary to one's spiritual life, one raises questions about the omnipotence and benevolence of the Divine. Simply put, one wonders if there is not a less painful way by which human beings can progress spiritually. Almost all mystics consider mysticism to be a difficult and painful undertaking, though they do not generally go as far as Suso in this respect. Spiritual development requires a self-transformation that involves a great deal of mental, emotional and physical suffering. Indeed, in mysticism we have views of human nature and spiritual transformation that have a significantly different flavour from that which we saw earlier in Hick's soul-making theology. Hick emphasises the practice of moral virtue in human relationship in overcoming the self-centredness that inhibits epistemic closeness to God. But the goal of mystical experience requires a peculiar detachment, what might also be referred to as a kind of disinterested concentration, a freedom from all aspects of selfhood in so far as they inhibit mystical realisation. This goal is not thought to be achieved solely through positive moral practice. As Donald Evans points out, egoism that inhibits mystical self-transformation is 'not eliminated merely by involving oneself in the service of other human beings'.[13] Indeed, such service can be but a consequence of egoism.

Mysticism espouses goals that require a radical self-transformation which can involve much anguish and pain. Mysticism is difficult, and not something to be achieved simply by following moral rules and prescriptions. This magnifies the problem of theodicy for mysticism. Mortification is not an essential element of Hick's teleology and neither is the kind of self-transformation mysticism espouses; but in mystical theodicy we must ask why mortification should be necessary and why such a radical and difficult self-transformation is requisite. In Chapter 9 we will examine Jacob Boehme's response to these questions. He explains the necessity of these mystical processes in terms of the first principle of the Divine Essence, the *Ungrund*, the dark side of the Divine Essence and human nature which the human being must overcome in mystical teleology. He thus provides, as we will see, an effective theodical response to these issues of mysticism.

Underhill goes on to depict mortification and poverty of will and senses as conducive to a detachment which leads to the experience of quiet. This is a non-intellectual and non-sensual state accompanied by a silence and an emptiness, what Underhill calls a deprivation, where sense of personality vaguely remains in the context of a passivity. Left at that, this state issues forth in the quietism that I mentioned earlier in this chapter. One wants to remove the will from what one anonymous Christian mystic has called its 'enslaving passions, obsessions, and attachments'.[14] Indeed, the goal of purification is a detachment and a quiet that is quite unlike the processes and experiences Hick has in mind, and a very difficult goal to achieve. It is referred to paradoxically as a concentration without effort, what our anonymous mystic calls

> the profound silence of desires, of preoccupations, of the imagination, of the memory and of discursive thought. One may say that the entire being becomes like the surface of calm water, reflecting the immense presence of the starry sky and its indescribable harmony.[15]

So these processes of detachment and mortification issue forth in a profound quiet, a passivity that when regarded as an ideal Underhill considers 'utterly at variance with all we know of the laws of life and growth' (p. 325). For, sought as an end in itself, this state demands and involves an indifference to all internal and external realities. Referring historically to the more extreme quietists, Underhill says they 'taught that the turning of the soul towards Reality, the merging of the will in God, which is the very heart of the mystic life, was *One Act*, never to be repeated . . . Pure passivity and indifference were [their] ideal' (p. 325). However, Underhill distinguishes between a true 'active' quietism and a passive extreme type. She stresses that the indifference espoused is not a 'holy indifference'. She says the mystics 'are indifferent to all else save the supreme claims of love' (p. 326), pointing, as we shall see, to a key aspect of teleological mysticism for issues of theodicy. Quietism is properly a transitional state, a means to higher and purer experiences that involve an active component. This new activity she characterises as the process of contemplation. The experience of quietude allows one to move into the contemplative mode, which in turn allows for the illumination experiences of the Enlightenment phase.

Enlightenment

In the detachment of the purification processes the mystic moves to the contemplative process that Underhill considers an extension of the preceding quiet. Contemplation, that is, 'the extreme form of that withdrawal of attention from the external world', is most properly a process of the unitary state, but also an aspect of the phase of Enlightenment. The purification processes of the earlier phases continue, with an emphasis on concentrative meditation. Through these methods the mystic acquires one or another of the three experiences of illumination, that is, either a profound sense of the divine presence within aspects of the natural world, or an inner encounter with what is understood as the divine Reality, or a variety of experiences of a paranormal nature.[16] Perhaps the three experiences can be understood in terms of a kind of mystical continuum beginning with the paranormal and moving through the spiritual experiences of the divine presence and reality, and culminating in an inner experience of a divine Source or Transcendent.[17] Underhill does not propose this kind of continuum for the illumination stage, though she does regard the inner encounter with a divine Reality to be 'the most constant characteristic of Illumination' (p. 241).

The experience of the divine presence in the world has a pantheistic flavour. It has been referred to as 'cosmic consciousness' by R. M. Bucke, and termed 'extrovertive' mysticism by W. T. Stace. Underhill describes it as 'the discovery of the Perfect One self-revealed in the Many' (p. 254) where a peaceful harmony of vision sees the world in a joyous unified light. She says, 'A harmony is thus set up between the mystic and Life in all its forms. Undistracted by appearance, he sees, feels and knows it in one piercing act of loving comprehension' (p. 258). The anonymous mystic emphasises the intoxicating effect of this experience, and the apparent subject–object coalescence that occurs. He says it is aptly termed, in the words of Levy Bruhl, 'mystical participation', designating 'the state of consciousness where the separation between the conscious subject and the object become one'.[18] He also associates it with certain drug-induced experiences, and cites the Dionysian mystery religions of ancient Greece as illustrative of the 'sacred intoxication' that occurs in the union of the self with nature.[19] And though Underhill and the anonymous mystic at times speak as if this experience is only of the natural world, excluding the sense of the Divine, such need not be the case. As Stace emphasises, the experience involves a sense of the 'One', the 'Unity', or 'God', as *'shining' through* the natural world.[20]

This state, then, is one wherein the evils and suffering experienced in the processes of mortification are reconciled and harmonised with the divine presence in all things. As I stated above, the objective of mortification is an indifference to all features of life, a condition realised in this illuminative experience. Underhill puts the point bluntly: 'Real detachment means the death of preferences of all kinds; even of those which seem to other men the very proofs of virtues and fine taste' (p. 223). But she does not stop here; much to the discomfort of the morally sensitive mind she adds in *Practical Mysticism*: 'you find in every manifestation of life – even those which you have petulantly classified as cruel or obscene – the ardent self-expression of that Immanent Being whose spark burns deep in your own soul'.[21]

This experience, then, possesses tremendous consolatory power. So mysticism contains a much more pronounced and powerful positive/affirmative theodicy than we saw in Hick's soul-making theology. Mysticism stresses the possibility of experiencing a comforting presence and support in the encounter of an omnipresent divine reality. But what is the nature of this consolatory force? How does such an experience affect the reality and negative force of evil? As we saw in Chapter 1, mysticisms which claim the complete elimination or non-reality of suffering and evil in this experience possess serious theodical problems. Indeed, at first glance it seems rather odd that the negative means (the experience of these negative realities) in achieving the experience should be themselves positively transformed in the experience. Yet, as Underhill puts it, 'everything will be seen under the aspect of a cosmic and charitable beauty; exhibiting through the woof of corruption the web of eternal life' (p. 224). The suffering of mortification, indeed, all suffering of the world, is somehow redeemed. As Donald Evans characterises it, there is an appreciative awareness of the mystic 'that everything is okay as it is – indeed, not merely okay but wondrous and radiant and harmonious and good'.[22] This contemplative mode, along with emphasis upon *individual* transformation and spiritual awareness, is seen by Evans as standing in tension with 'social activist' spirituality. Indeed, the mystic's concern with *self*-transformation and spirituality and his or her appreciative awareness often lead to a neglect of social activity.

But do these contemplative modes possess active moral imperatives? If they do not, then they pose severe problems for theodicy. Do they naturally lead to an amoral or non-active stance on the part of the mystic? In terms of appreciative awareness, how is this experience to be reconciled with social obligations? Is not a deep sense of the injustice and imperfection of the world, perceptions which would seem to be transformed in illumination, necessary as impetus to social activity? Returning to the question of mortification, it is easy to understand how one can be moved out of one's self-centredness through a profound compassion aroused in the mortifying process of witnessing the torture of children. But surely this does not 'justify' such an outrage or render the incident illusory? How could it be illusory, if it had such a spiritually powerful effect upon the observer? And what about the victim in this case? Is he or she left behind, so to speak, in the mystic's illuminative experience? Is such brutality justified as the mortification process of the witness? And is such brutality to be understood as an 'aspect of charitable beauty'?

There is great danger that mysticisms that espouse an appreciative awareness as their *teleological end* will issue forth in a pronounced moral callousness. If evil in these kinds of mystical teleologies loses its negative reality and force then these mystical teleologies prove to be without theodical power. In the overcoming of evil, evil itself is denied as a religious problem. So this kind of teleological mysticism possesses very serious theodical problems. But even those mystical teleologies which espouse a moral imperative in the context of the movement to higher mystical experiences are pressed with difficult questions regarding the consolatory power of these experiences. What is the nature of such consolatory force, where is the source of a mystical moral imperative, and how can the tension between social activism and self-transformation be reconciled? As we shall see shortly, and develop more fully in Chapter 8, theistic mystical teleologies more effectively address these questions than other mystical teleologies.

If the first kind of Enlightenment involves both strengths and weaknesses in relation to theodicy, this is also true of the second kind, the inner encounter with divine Reality. This experience of the divine Source or Reality differs considerably from the experience of the divine presence in the natural world. This experience of the divine Source in the Enlightenment phase is not unlike the unitive state that Underhill locates as the appropriate telos of mysticism. In this realisation the mystic experiences a 'harmony with the Infinite' or a 'joyous consciousness of His Presence' (p. 242). It is described as 'a kind of radiance, a flooding of the personality with new light' (p. 249), and it issues forth in an equanimity that overcomes the distracting anxieties and worries that normally accompany day to day tasks.

The Reality which is experienced is described by mystics either cataphatically (in positive terms) or apophatically (in negative terms).[23] In the former case the Reality is described in relation to an experience of 'love' and 'God' in the heart. At its best, as it moves towards the phase of Union, it involves the kind of theodical evidence we briefly discussed in reference to Kant. Underhill refers to it as 'a positive contemplation of truth; an ecstatic apprehension of the secret "plan"' (p. 340). In *Practical Mysticism* she says,

> thanks to the development of the higher side of your conscious-
> ness, you are now lifted to a new poise; a direct participation in
> that simple, transcendent life 'broken, yet not divided,' which
> gives to this time-world all its meaning and validity.[24]

But further she comments:

> Certain rare mystics seem able to describe to us a Beatific Vision
> experienced here and now: a knowledge by contact of the flam-
> ing heart of Reality, which includes in one great whole the planes
> of Being and becoming, the Simultaneous and the Successive,
> the Eternal Father, and His manifestation in the 'energetic Word'.
> (p. 340)

This aspect of mysticism claims to offer evidence verifying the-odicy. In Chapter 8 we will examine this claim as it is espoused by Meister Eckhart in order to determine its significance and validity as theodical evidence or verification. The concern will be regarding the content and nature of such a realisation for the mystic, and its status for non-mystics. As we will see, this realisation can offer, both for the mystic and the non-mystic, a much more effective theodical position than is the case in non-mystical theodicy.

Meister Eckhart also has much to say about the apophatic inter-pretation of the experience that Underhill speaks about. The experi-ence is formulated in negative and impersonal words such as unity, other, infinite, absolute, qualityless, groundless, mystery and nothingness. As an example of these conceptions, Underhill mentions Johann Tauler who speaks of the unfathomable divine Abyss that stands apart from the Trinity (p. 339), but there is also Meister Eckhart who speaks of Godhead beyond the Creator God, and Jacob Boehme who is noted for his view of the *Ungrund*, the divine Nothing or first principle of the Divine Essence.

These three mystics tend to regard this experience as an encounter of the essence of God in an uncovering of the ground of one's soul that mirrors and shares in this essential Divinity. It is considered an experience of that which precedes the personal, active, and creative God and Trinity. As we shall see in Chapter 9, this claim is very important to mystical theodicy both in terms of the issues we raised regarding the self-transformative and mortification processes of mysticism, and in accounting for the origin of evil in human nature. Nicolas Berdyaev describes Boehme's *Ungrund* as the source of meonic freedom within which evil arises. Evil, for Berdyaev and for Boehme, is uncreated by God, and is impenetrable to God.[25] In Boehme we find a profound and highly unique Christian mystical theodicy that effectively distances God's responsibility of evil through a provocative account of its origin in the *Ungrund*. Thus, we will see, it reconciles evil with a personal benevolent Divine.

Self-Surrender and Union

As I said, these cataphatic and apophatic experiences of the illuminative stage are not unlike those of the unitive life. However, Underhill sets them apart in terms of the sense of distinctive individuality that remains at this lower stage, where, she says, the mystic experiences but 'a brief foretaste of the Unitive State' (p. 245). She also maintains that these experiences precede the experience of the abandonment by the higher Reality, the phase of Self-Surrender where the mystic experiences the 'dark night of the soul'. Underhill describes this dark and trying experience:

> psychic fatigue sets in; the state of illumination begins to break up, the complementary negative consciousness appears, and shows itself as an overwhelming sense of darkness and deprivation. This sense is so strong that it inhibits all consciousness of the Transcendent; and plunges the self into the state of negation and misery which is called the Dark Night. (p. 382)

Most of us are familiar with the kinds of negative experiences where the purpose and vitality are sapped from an individual or community following a tremendous output of creative energy and activity. The mystic understands the experience in a spiritual context; the fatigue involves a spiritual sense as well as its physical and mental aspects. Not only is there emotional lassitude, moral helplessness, a stagnation of will and intellect, but there is also the mystical experience that Underhill describes as a dark ecstasy, negative rapture and divine absence (pp. 394–5). Now this experience is not wholly unlike the apophatic illumination experience just mentioned. But according to Underhill, the mystic sees the experience either as the abandonment of divine companionship or as a deep sense of imperfection. These interpretations reveal the dark night as more than an experience, as also a necessary process of mysticism where the mystic completes the process of self-surrender. Underhill says 'the whole "value for life" of the Dark Night is revealed to us: as an education in selfless constancy, a "school of suffering love"' (p. 394). She goes on to refer to it as a 'state of passive suffering which is to complete the decentralization of your character, test the purity of your love, and perfect your education in humility'.[26]

This is a state where the mystical quest for experiences as consolations is voluntarily renounced in the effort of eliminating remaining self-centredness. The Divine is thought to withdraw from the mystic, even to 'send' various trials in order to facilitate the voluntary renunciation of the mystic's self-centredness. So the dark night is a mystical means, a form of divine mortification, if you will, where the Divine is thought to distance itself purposely from the mystic, and to set obstacles intended to induce the mystic's spiritual growth towards the unitive life. The dark night, then, as a form of mortification, raises a further issue in the theodicy of mysticism. It adds a slightly different dimension to the questions of mortification raised earlier in that at this stage of spirituality the Divine is thought to be taking an active role in the subject's suffering. Underhill cites Henry Suso as an exemplar of the trials and tribulations experienced in this phase of mysticism, as he interprets his unusual trials as divine tests intended for his spiritual development. Here we have God *actively* treating evil as means to a future end, a view that makes the questions of divine benevolence and omnipotence that much harder.

The dark night of the soul brings about the final phase of Underhill's mystical teleology, the state of final self-surrender, where the last remnants of distinctive individuality are eliminated. At this point the intense concentration upon the Divine which occurs in the contemplative processes leads to the unitary life. The movement to this last phase Underhill describes by the term 'infused' in contrast to the 'active' striving in the contemplative and purification processes of the previous phases. At this point one ceases 'all conscious, anxious striving and pushing'.[27] She says: 'An attitude of perfect generosity, complete submission, willing acquiescence in anything that may happen – even in failure and death – is here your only hope'.[28] The emphasis here is on reception rather than activity, a complete cessation of the senses, emotions, will and the intellect. She says, 'it will come to you through the darkness: a mysterious contact, a clear certitude of intercourse and possession'.[29] Though these experiences are properly ineffable Underhill speaks of an unsolicited energy beyond your control, infusing itself into the soul. She cites the general characteristics of these experiences as an 'absorption in the interests of the Infinite' involving 'a consciousness of sharing Its strength', hence 'a complete sense of freedom', serenity, a creative activity, and a 'spiritual vitality' as source of strength for others (p. 416). At this stage there is the experience of oneness with the Divine, the sense that one acts through and in this higher reality and that one's fundamental being is in complete harmony with this primary force.

As I pointed out, Underhill considers this experience to be singular,[30] but interpreted in either (or both) positive or negative terms. In apophatic and non-personal terms the 'Reality is apprehended as a state or place rather than a person', and it is described in the language of deification that involves a 'rebirth or transmutation' whereby the subject annihilates his or her self in a mergence with this higher reality (pp. 418–19). This is the impersonal interpretation that neglects, according to Underhill, the personal and emotional features of the experience. The cataphatic and personal interpretation, on the other hand, involves characterisation more of self-fulfilment than self-abandonment, in words of a *loving* union and spiritual marriage with a personal Divine.

Others have referred to the apophatic experience in different terms. R. C. Zaehner refers to it as monistic mysticism, claiming that the transcendent Reality that is experienced here is best characterised as the universal Self. He cites as examples *Advaita Vedānta*, where the teleological point is the experience of *Atman* (the eternal Self underlying the phenomenal self) and classical *Sāṅkhya* which espouses the separation of *Puruṣa* (spirit) from *Prakṛti* (nature) as the mystical goal.[31] Similarly, the anonymous mystic speaks of a realisation of the transcendental Self, the higher immortal Self in, behind, and above the phenomenal.[32] Both these thinkers, like

Underhill, consider this experience to be of a non-personal nature, excluding the notions of relationship and love.

But Zaehner characterises Underhill's personal unitive experience of the Divine as distinct from the experience of universal Self. He refers to it as theistic mysticism and considers it most typical of the Christian tradition, though also found in the Hindu traditions of *bhakti* (devotional) oriented emphases such as that of the *Bhagavad Gita*. In this regard the anonymous mystic cites the Hindus Rāmānuja, Madhva and Caitanya, who, like Christian mystics, stress the communal and relational aspect of the unification experience. He says: 'Their union with the Divine is not absorption of their being by Divine being, but rather the experience of the breath of Divine Love, the illumination by Divine Love, and the warmth of Divine Love'.[33] He is harshly critical of those mysticisms that emphasise experience of Self, that 'aspire to true being' rather than aspiring to love.[34] Citing John 10:8, he refers to them as 'thieves and robbers' since they teach a 'depersonalisation' in their mystical espousal, a robbing of the personality from the human being. He further says 'The characteristic of this mystical way is that *one loses the capacity to cry*'.[35] He claims that one becomes what one seeks, resulting in the loss and absence of love, compassion and personality in those who pursue the transcendental Self. On the other hand, in Christian theism the stress is on personal love and compassion. The anonymous mystic says, 'nothing is extinguished in the human personality but, on the contrary everything is set ablaze. This is the experience of "legitimate twofoldness" or the union of two separate *substances* in one *essence*'.[36]

Louis Dupré recognises this kind of teleology in theistic mysticism as well. Such a communion issues not in a staticity and passivity. This theistic goal involves a sharing, participation and living in God's dynamic creativity that is characteristic of His essence. Dupré says,

> in this blissful union the soul comes to share the dynamics of God's inner life, a life not only of rest and darkness, but also of creative activity and life. The contemplative admitted to this union is granted to see by the light in which God sees Himself and to follow the outflowing movement of the Godhead.[37]

In this picture one 'lives out' this experience of the Divine in a positive, personal and active compassion and concern. Eckhart is also very telling in regard to this experience, depicting his mystical teleology as culminating in the experience of divine compassion and justice, which, by its very nature involves its creative actualisation. As Dupré comments: 'The contemplative accompanies God's own move from hiddenness to manifestation within the identity of God's own life'.[38]

This point is very important to mystical theodicy. As we will see in Chapters 7 and 8, mystics that espouse this kind of end to self-transformation maintain an active and prominent role in the struggle against suffering and evil, a social–moral imperative that is grounded in the very nature of the Divine itself, a Divine that is described in active, positive, personal and passible terms. Non-personal mystical teleologies that are ordinated to individual transformation, on the other hand, offer no moral imperative in the context of their experience (though it might arise from other sources), and no sense of God actively striving against evil. But certain theistic mystical teleologies fundamentally *consist* in the actualisation of the creativity, love and compassion of the mystical experience. Thus Dupré says these teleologies restore 'a divine meaning to the finite that the mystic ignored in the early stages of the spiritual ascent and that negative theology permanently ignores'.[39] And, in so far as this union is thought to complete the cosmic process, God is considered passible, as affected by the experienced love in the teleological experience and as moved in the human experience of evil and suffering.

MYSTICISM DEFINED AND ISSUES OF MYSTICAL THEODICY

We are now in a position to define mysticism in a theodical context. Mysticism can be considered in terms of processes and experiences; the mystic purposely undergoes certain processes in order to achieve an encounter with or participation in a reality that is understood to be primary, the source of existent phenomena. The mystic life begins with a 'psychic push', an inner anxiety, turmoil, or 'dis-ease' that forces the person out of his or her natural self-centred bent, to a recognition of a greater pervasive reality in and around them. This involves a sense of closeness or intimacy with this greater reality, a reality that is interpreted as the Divine, as well as involving an accompanying sense of the divine presence as source of life and things. This is the conversion experience that Underhill speaks of. In the belief that a greater intimacy can be achieved with the Divine the mystic undergoes processes of purification which are thought to transform the subject's preoccupation with him- or herself and with all other realities that inhibit the mystical life. These processes involve negative methods intended to lessen and finally eliminate the debilitating influence of the senses and the will which hinders mystical realisation, as well as more positive painful moral, physical and spiritual mortification activities. Through these methods of detachment the mystic achieves a state of non-conscious and non-sensual passivity, states of quiet and contemplation, whereby she or he moves to the phase of Enlightenment and experiences the Divine (1) through cosmic consciousness, (2) as an inner loving radiance and/or (3) as the qualityless ground of the soul. Following this, the mystic might undergo further processes of mortification, involving the utter passivity characteristic of the dark night of the soul where this sense of intimacy or presence of the Divine disappears, and she or he undergoes further moral and physical disciplines intended to induce a more permanent and complete selflessness. The mystic experiencing this phase of Self-surrender then moves, through contemplative activities, towards the final phase of Union. This can result in more pronounced and continuous mystical experiences that take the form of either (1) non-personal, negative and passive realisation of a transcendent Self, or (2) more personal, positive, active and emotional union with the Divine, which by its very nature issues forth in moral concerns and activities that involve a highly charged sense of spiritual support and direction.

With this introduction to teleological mysticism in mind we can briefly outline mystical theodicy. A mystical theodicy is one that explains and justifies evil in terms of the mystical teleology it espouses. Like non-mystical theodicy, to be effective it must rely heavily on the free-will defense. Freedom is deemed necessary to progress in the mystical life, the final goal being one of the many experiences outlined by Underhill. But only mysticisms espousing a theistic teleology offer an effective response to the challenge of evil. In this regard we will be examining in Chapter 10 Śaṅkara's non-theistic theodicy. He proposes a retributive-rebirth hypothesis to explain evil, one that possesses serious moral difficulties. Indeed, that only a theistic mystical teleology can bring the various kinds of mystical experiences into a moral and sound theodical perspective will become more evident as we proceed through Chapters 7 to 10.

Also in Underhill's exposition of mystical teleology we saw that mystical experiences could provide evidence which supports the claims of a theodicy. In Chapter 7 we will examine the nature, content and significance of the theodical evidence arising in the various mystical experiences. In Eckhart's mystical teleology we find an effective response to the Kantian critique that we developed against non-mystical theodicy in Chapter 5, one that can have significant force even for non-mystics. And, closely related to this issue, we find in the structure of mystical teleology an emphasis upon the positive/affirmative aspect of theodicy, one that offers much more theodical consolation than does non-mystical theodicy. We will turn in Chapter 8 directly to the question of the nature of this consolatory power as it surfaces in various mystical experiences. In an examination of the mysticisms of Eckhart and Dostoevsky, I will argue that theistic mysticism's stress on the possibility of the Divine, on the affective power of mystical experiences, and on the moral imperatives inherent in certain experiences provide a morally acceptable and effective illustration of divine beneficence and participation in the world.

But in contrast to this positive aspect of mystical teleology there also arises the issue of the justification of the apparent pervasive self-centredness which requires such radical transformation and reorientation. An effective mystical theodicy will, while addressing this issue, distance the responsibility of the Divine from the moral evil this view implies. Boehme's account of the origin of evil in God and human nature will be particularly relevant here. In Boehme's *Ungrund* we find a pre-theistic or theogonic feature very important to the structure of coherent mystical theodicy, an aspect we will examine in Chapter 9.

The final facet of mystical theodicy is one that surfaced only indirectly in Underhill's account of mysticism. This is the notion of rebirth. Mystical teleology can only be adequately justified if persons are not unfairly ruled out of the spiritual process. Though dysteleological evils can be explained in a doctrine of probationary purgatory, rebirth provides a more satisfactory response to the problem. In Chapter 10 we will draw out the issues surrounding this aspect of mystical theodicy, showing that the hypothesis of rebirth as a process of soul-making provides a more effective treatment of the problems than does that of probationary purgatory.

So the basic structure of effective mystical theodicy consists of four features we discussed in this introduction to mysticism, elements by which we will respond to the four major problems we raised for Hick's soul-making theodicy. These are evidence verifying theodicy, positive/affirmative theodicy, the origin of evil in God and human nature, and the hypothesis of rebirth. Let us turn, then, to examine these issues in more detail.

7

Theodical Evidence in Meister Eckhart

Underhill considers Meister Eckhart (1260–1329) to be the founder of the fourteenth and fifteenth century Flemish and German schools of mysticism. She says 'all have passed under his hand, being either his immediate disciples, or the friends or pupils of his disciples'.[1] But his influence extended even further than this. Matthew Fox suggests that, among others, the English mystics Walter Hilton and Julian of Norwich, the Polish Angelus Silesius, and even Teresa of Avila and St John of the Cross of Spain are indebted to Eckhart. And his reputation goes beyond mysticism proper. More notable philosophical figures influenced by his thought include Schelling, Hegel and Heidegger.[2] Not only was Eckhart a mystic of the highest rank and influence, he was also a philosopher of some stature and an outstanding preacher. But Eckhart is perhaps most noted as a Roman Catholic heretic who, within ecclesiastical circles, is not highly regarded for his theology. However, recently there has been some renewed interest in his philosophy and his mysticism both inside and outside the church.[3]

Given his influence and the renewed interest in his thought, Eckhart seems a very appropriate figure to draw upon in this section on mysticism. This impression is reinforced in his development of a well-formulated mystical teleology that stresses a highly ethical and active component. His mysticism is clearly teleological and this-worldly oriented, possessing a strong imperative to moral consciousness. Furthermore, he addresses the problem of evil vigorously, though not always clearly, with the deep concern of a sensitive preacher. Thus his mystical theology illustrates very effectively certain features of coherent mystical theodicy. It will be a useful vehicle to examine the question of mystical theodical evidence and it will also be helpful when we turn to the issues surrounding the conciliatory power of mystical experience in Chapter 8.

But before we can develop Eckhart's thesis we must attempt to outline the epistemological assumptions behind the theodical evidence proposed by mystical teleologies. It is necessary to formulate the conditions by which theodical evidence might be said to arise in mystical experience and to begin to develop the nature of such evidence in order to determine and evaluate its significance. Only then can we effectively turn to the mystical theodical evidence that is proposed by Eckhart.

TELEOLOGY AND EVIDENCE

As we will see later in this chapter, in Eckhart's theodicy natural and moral evil are reconciled with the conception of an all-benevolent and omnipotent Divine much in the manner of John Hick's theodicy. Theodical justification occurs in the realisation of the teleological goal, wherein one realises the appropriateness of this world, including experienced evils and suffering, in actualising the final purpose of God. Kant calls such a vision an experience of artistic wisdom, an experience where one 'can see an indubitable light (and understand) the purposes of the Creator and his wise providence'.[4]

As we have seen, Leibniz, Hick and Kant point towards artistic wisdom as the future experience that will validate teleological theodicy. The problem occurs, as Kant points out so well, in the ineffectivenesss of empirical evidence to bear out divine artistic wisdom; such is well beyond its means. Thus traditional theodicies have generally looked to a future other-worldly eschaton as the hope of finally answering the problem of evil. Yet the empirical evidence against theodicy is very strong indeed, a fact that Dostoevsky so vividly portrays in Ivan's rebellion. This leads Dostoevsky to doubt the possibility of theodicy, gives some support to Schopenhauer's penal colony hypothesis, and pushes Kant to question the whole philosophical activity of theodicy.

Rather Kant pointed to a faith that arises from his moral argument, to the 'authentic' theodical stance as epitomised in the story of Job. This theodicy is an extension of Kant's postulative faith, a theodicy that arises in the postulation of the conditions for the possibility of moral existence. Now the anonymous mystic contrasts Kant's postulative faith with both faith from extrinsic authority and faith from first hand experience, suggesting that postulative faith is without any support external to itself. He describes it as a faith

> where one believes without any support, either from without or from within. It is the faith of the "voice of one crying in the wilderness" (Matthew iii, 3) – the voice itself of the soul who cries, i.e. postulates in complete solitude ("in the wilderness") the things without which it could not live. Kant's three postulates: God, freedom of will, and the immortality of the soul, are such a cry of the soul in the wilderness. For they are founded neither on extrinsic authority nor on mystical experience, but rather on semi-structural exigencies of the soul itself . . . "Freedom, immortality and God" – or the desperate night of nothingness – such is the cry from Kant's soul in the desert where he found himself.[5]

The anonymous mystic here raises some interesting questions. Is it not the case that Kant's search for a final moral purpose, his search for that which has an absolute worth, rests on the very possibility of an absolute worth, which in turn is grounded in the assumption of the existence of a soul? Yet this is not conclusive; is Kant really forced to promulgate the structure for soul actualisation in the face of unfaceable nothingness? Surely Kant himself considers his moral argument for God, freedom and immortality, an argument which is the foundation of his authentic theodical stance, to be much stronger than the anonymous mystic thinks. But on the other hand, Kant does not press his authentic theodicy in any absolute manner; indeed, he seems to remain doubtful of its 'authenticity', refers to it as a *mere* thing of faith, and stresses the tension existing between moral theodicy and certain empirical facts.

Yet Kant does establish the limits of speculative metaphysics in regard to theodicy. Theodical verification is not to be had in empirical observation. In retrospect, having surveyed speculative theodicies with Kant's position in mind, this truth seems rather obvious and unquestionable. But it took the intellectual power of Kant to establish the fact explicitly. The anonymous mystic takes this point further in proposing a rather intriguing historical observation, that Kant's postulative faith has pointed the way towards a faith of first-hand experience, that is, a faith that combines practical reason with the intuition arising in mysticism. He says:

Kant put an end to the speculative metaphysics of autonomous
intelligence and opened up the way to a mysticism which non-
autonomous intelligence or "practical reason" (*Praktische Vernunft*)
is capable of – Kant's "practical reason" being intelligence united
to the wisdom of moral nature.[6]

An example the anonymous mystic goes on to give in this regard
is the view of Paul Deussen, a neo-Kantian who considers that the
inability of intelligence to know the noumenon behind the phenomenon 'entails the task of resorting to the intuitive perception of the
essence of things'.[7] Now such an intuitive experience assumes that
one can override linguistic and conceptual categories and *directly*
encounter the phenomenon in question. Many neo-Kantians rule
out such an intuitive possibility.[8] However, as I pointed out in
Chapter 5, Kant himself seems to have left open such a possibility
in regard to the experience of theodical artistic wisdom. Now this
is not an experience of a particular phenomenon, but rather a
direct encounter of the source, harmony and purpose of such
phenomena – an experience of the final resolution of creation as
exemplified in Job's experience of artistic wisdom. But what would
such an experience be like? What conditions might exist in such
an experience? What kind of epistemological explanation could we
give for it?

Towards an answer to these questions let us begin with the
personal vision of artistic wisdom as described by the Canadian
mystic-psychiatrist, Dr R. M. Bucke:

> I became conscious in myself of eternal life. It was not a con-
> viction that I would have eternal life, but a consciousness that I
> possessed eternal life then; I saw that all men are immortal; that
> the cosmic order is such that without any peradventure all things
> work together for the good of each and all; that the foundation
> principle of the world, of all the world, is what we call love, and
> that the happiness of each and all is in the long run absolutely
> certain.[9]

Now Bucke goes on to say that this experience was very brief, only
a few seconds, but that it had such an affective force to it that he
remained convinced of its veracity, even during bouts of depres-
sion, for the remainder of his life. So the experience for Bucke
involved a change of consciousness that presumably revealed for

a moment the purposes of life in the context of a benevolent and wise Divine; a glimpse of eternity as it stands in relation to temporal creation. It was not a dialogue with a transcendent Thing, a kind of discussion with God about his plans and purposes, but a rather ineffable and highly affective consciousness and conviction of the fundamental goodness of creation, its grounding in 'what we call love' and of one's immediate participation in this source.

Bucke claims to participate, for the moment, in eternal life. He does not 'know', in the normal sense of the word, something or another that he is encountering. Rather he 'participates', he 'possesses' the reality he encounters. Louis Dupré comments upon this unitive aspect of the mystical experience:

> Where knower and known are substantially united, that union no longer allows any distance for subject–object oppositions such as determine ordinary epistemic processes. The mind functions here in the different mode of being-with reality, rather than of reflecting upon it.[10]

Now Dupré notes that this kind of experience of identity has been called an 'intellectual intuition' by Joseph Maréchal, a depiction which is strikingly similar to that which we saw proposed by the anonymous mystic who spoke of a certainty of intuition that arises in conjunction with intelligence, that is to say Kant's practical reason. But Dupré goes on in an attempt to outline a possible epistemological structure to account for the kind of transient experience that Bucke describes and, further, to depict it as it occurs in the more permanent union of the *unio mystica*. It does not involve the self-consciousness that we normally find in conscious epistemic experiences. Rather it is a turning away from self-consciousness to God-consciousness. This description is quite consistent with the detaching processes Underhill depicts as common to mysticism, and describes very well the letting-go and letting-be of the mystical process espoused in Eckhart's apophatic spirituality, as we will see in a moment. There is a need of a radical detachment on the part of the mystic, 'a slow and presumably painful process of self-emptying'.[11] For only in eliminating one's normal conscious self can one make room, so to speak, for God-consciousness.

Dupré refers to St Teresa and John of the Cross in his description of the experience of God-consciousness:

It commences with what she [Teresa] calls an intellectual vision, that is, an imageless intuition during which for a brief period all mental functions unite while receiving a comprehensive insight into the source and coherence of all reality. Though clearly not intellectual in any discursive, rational sense, such a "vision" possesses a distinctly cognitive quality to which John of the Cross refers as a "knowledge of naked truth," that is, a "comprehending and seeing with the understanding that truths of God, whether of things that are, that have been or that will be."[12]

So the mystic claims that in unitive experience with God one comes to envision, to comprehend, the artistic wisdom of creation. Now such an experience cannot be described – artistic wisdom cannot be spelled out – but this should come as no surprise. For if the experience is a 'participatory glimpse' of eternity, a state of 'being in' artistic wisdom, we should expect it to be ineffable in principle. It is not a normal epistemological knowing but a transformation of self *in* this encountered divinity. That is, the vision in this permanent union remains indelibly ingrained in the person's consciousness; it becomes a centring point out of which the mystic comes to see and act in the world. In this regard Dupré says that the 'final state of permanent union is characterised by an uninterrupted awareness of God's presence. That presence may not always be fully "sensed" but it remains the horizon against which all other phenomena appear'.[13] In so far as this presence is not *fully* sensed by the mystic, he or she maintains a sense of self, albeit transformed, and can actively participate in daily affairs. Dupré says the mystic's consciousness in this permanent union remains for the most part divided; there exists a deeper-surface level division of the mind that 'enables the mystic to combine a contemplative life with one of active service'.[14] For it is out of this deeper level of God-consciousness habitation that the mystic's active orientation and direction derives.

So a basic epistemological framework in the reception of mystical theodical evidence can be roughly given as follows. To attain artistic wisdom the mystic must, rather paradoxically, detach himself from himself. This perhaps explains the stress that we saw in Underhill on the inability of the mystics to achieve the unitary life on their own. The original centre of meaning and value, the self-consciousness of the person, must be eliminated. All processes of desiring and knowing must cease as the mystic seeks a state of consciousness-purity, a consciousness utterly empty and vacant of all concepts and images. Only then can the divine presence enter into the centre of the mind in a direct experience of God, and transform the self-consciousness of the mystic. Such a union can occur sporadically or take a more permanent form, but in either case there arises a vision of the very source, interconnection and purpose of all reality. Given the nature of the experience, however, such is not a discursive knowledge; artistic wisdom is not an intelligible concept, indeed, not properly a concept at all. Yet it exudes a cognitive quality about it and possesses tremendous affective power which establishes in the mystic an unyielding conviction of its veracity. More than this though, the mystic carries this experience of eternity into daily life. In this regard Dupré says the mystic 'takes the finite on its own terms and asserts the divine meaning of the finite as it remains in God's own Being'.[15] The mystic brings the experienced divine purposes to his transformed perspective of reality; she or he actualises this artistic wisdom.

ECKHART'S MYSTICAL TELEOLOGY

To illustrate the dynamic aspect of mystical theodical evidence, as well as to draw the nature of the evidence out a bit more, we can turn to Meister Eckhart who is very provocative in this regard. We can perhaps best begin with his view of the myth of the fall. Though Eckhart leans heavily upon the traditional Augustinian interpretation of the fall myth, his version shows some similarity to that of John Hick's Irenaean interpretation. It is typically Augustinian in its view of a fall from perfection, but it attempts, like the Irenaean strain, to shift the responsibility of this fall away from human beings and God, and to emphasise the progression to divinity. Human beings, though 'adorned with all virtues and knowledge'[16] fall in status to a state of mortality and suffering. However, Eckhart stresses the role of the Devil, the fallen angel, in instigating this fall. Satan, the 'father of evil',[17] fell from divine being in the attempt at perfection independent of God. In innocence, Adam and Eve are easy prey for the wicked angel, thus falling in their impropriety away from God and the divine life. The state of alienation they find themselves in is analogous to the damaged relationship between Satan and God; humanity stands distanced from the Divine. Eckhart emphasises the role of Christ as exemplar, as the teacher who shows the way for beings to realise their true latent divinity.

The fundamental telos is transfiguration to divinity; Eckhart says, 'Know that all creatures are driven and take action by their nature for one end: to be like God' (p. 63).[18] In typical scholastic terminology he emphasises that God as first cause of human beings is also their final cause. In this regard he speaks of return or reunion as the appropriate end of human existence:

> God in creating all creatures instructs and enjoins, advises and commands them, by the very fact that he creates them, to follow him and conform themselves to him, to turn and hasten back to him as the first cause of their entire being. (p. 62)

This realisation, this return to God, is the overriding feature of Eckhart's theology and towards this telos he proposes what might be distinguished as four interrelated paths that reach their culmination in this-worldly activity as a divine channel of the experienced Godhead. The progression begins in a transformation of consciousness whereby the human being comes to realise the divine presence in all of creation, and all of creation *in* God. This is Eckhart's panentheism, the mystical view that 'all is in God and God is in all' (p. 72). It involves a realisation that corresponds to Underhill's experience of divine presence in the phase of Enlightenment.

To illustrate this view Eckhart incorporates a number of powerful images drawn from scholastic philosophy and scripture. We can draw here on three of these to highlight panentheism effectively. The first image plays further on the scholastic depiction of God as first cause in describing God as the primary being from which all created being arises. Such a conception implies a peculiar perspective on how creatures are related to their Creator, a relation quite different from the way human artifacts are related to their human creators. Eckhart comments:

> God created all things, not that they might stand outside of himself or beyond himself, the way other artifacts (made by humans) do, but he calls them from nothing, that is from nonbeing, so that they may come into and receive and dwell in himself. For he is being. (p. 72)

Human beings thus are to be understood in intimate relationship to this primary being; they are made of nothing external to God. As will become even clearer later when we describe Eckhart's notion of emanation, there is no hard subject–object delineation between God and His creation; indeed, there cannot be in creation *ex nihilo*. Nevertheless, there is more than a subtle difference between Creator and creation. To illustrate this difference while at the same time upholding the intimate connection Eckhart cites the creative word, the spoken word which issues forth from the speaker yet remaining in the speaker's intellect and memory. Thus Eckhart draws upon the more familiar image of speech to illustrate path one. He says: 'the words that I am now speaking first spring up in me, then secondly I reflect on the idea and thirdly I express it and you receive it; yet it really remains in me. In the same way, I have remained in the Father' (p. 72).

So like the spoken word the Father retains an aspect of His creation in Himself in the issuing forth of creation from His very being. But creation is more than just in God. For God is omnipresent in His creation. He envelops humans and the world in a most inter-penetrative manner. He is in creation as it is in Him. Perhaps the most powerful image of path one is Eckhart's analogy of the fish in the ocean; though enveloped by the water, the fish finds the water also present in itself through its gills (p. 73). So God is present in all creation like the ocean in the fish, and creation is in God like the fish in the ocean. Such is Eckhart's vision of the omnipresence of God.

Now the point of path one is to become aware of this divine omnipresence, of the world in God and God in world. In this first stage one achieves a mystical awareness of God in the created world as the ground of existence and also as present in this existence. Naturally, this experience of divine presence includes a profound sense of harmony and unity; since 'opposition has no permanency in being' (p. 90) there will be no distinctions in this experience, no oppositions. Rather, the experience involves a realisation of inter-connection and oneness in the reception and alignment to a pervasive cosmic spirit.

In path two the emphasis moves to the divine presence in the human being. The shift is away from sensible reality to the human soul. Eckhart says God 'dwells in the innermost dimension of the soul . . . There where time never penetrates, where no image shines in, in the innermost and highest aspect of the soul God creates the entire cosmos' (p. 65). But path two moves deeper even than this active, creative aspect of the Divine, to that which precedes the personal God and the Trinity. This is the apophatic experience of illumination and the unitary life that we described in Chapter 6. The soul or intellect desires more than image, it seeks that essential unity that is beyond time and space, that oneness before all images, categorisation and characterisation, an indescribable experience of essential, primary God.

Referring to the final cause of the person, Eckhart asks what the soul desires. He replies: 'It does not know; it wants him as he is Father . . . It wants him as he is the marrow out of which goodness springs; it wants him as he is the root, the vein, from which goodness exuded. Only there is he the Father' (pp. 304-5). So Eckhart distinguishes God from underlying and essential Godhead of the Father. Indeed, he stresses their differences and distance:

> God and Godhead are as different as heaven and earth. I will go further still: The inner and the outer person are as different as heaven and earth. But God's distance from the Godhead is many thousand miles greater still. God becomes and ceases to become, God waxes and wanes. (p. 76)

Godhead is naked God. It is nameless, hidden, dark, mysterious and ineffable. It is the silent ground, the abyss, the divine waste-land. Nevertheless, this nothingness is the final goal of the human soul. Eckhart sees the human soul as so ennobled as to be able to penetrate the deepest recesses of the Divine. And it is rather surprising here that Eckhart speaks of this path two of the fourfold path as the culmination of the teleology. Yet he says, the Father

> remains within and is the goal of the Godhead and all creatures, the One in whom there is pure peace and rest for everything which ever received being. The beginning is for the sake of the final goal, for in that final end everything rests which ever received existence endowed with reason. The final goal of being is the darkness or the unknowability of the hidden divinity, which is that light that shines 'but the darkness has not comprehended it'. (p. 169)

This experienced Godhead is the appropriate end of human beings. It constitutes Eckhart's apophatic spirituality. It involves a very radical move away from sense perception and intellectual faculties as one withdraws in union with the Godhead beyond the Creator God. This is the *via negativa* where one experiences union with the formless, nameless, unknown Godhead in an other-worldly detachment from the sensible realm. It is the negative way to mystical experience of the negative God. To achieve this experience of Godhead the mystic must strip away the many layers of being that would prevent unity with non-being. The mystic must uncover the ground of the soul, the soul-point, the spark or apex of the soul or intellect[19] that mirrors this hidden Godhead and shares in its essential divinity. This requires a very radical detachment. Eckhart describes it as a 'letting-go' and 'letting-be', a letting-go of egoism and images, of names and forms, of everything that constitutes life in composite being, and a letting-be of things as they are in themselves. The mystic must become 'simple and one as God is' (p. 289). He says, 'Since it is God's nature that he is unlike anyone, we must of necessity reach the point that we are *nothing*, in that we can be removed into the same essence he himself is' (p. 328). Indeed, the mystic must let go of all positive attachments and connections, must let go even of the image of a positive and personal God: 'we pray God to rid us of "God" so that we may grasp and eternally enjoy the truth where the highest angel and the fly and the soul are equal' (p. 215).

Confirming this path as the appropriate teleological goal, Eckhart goes on to describe this experienced truth and transformation in very strong terms. He says:

> There every comparison must be driven out, so that I can be transported into God and can become one with him and *one* substance and *one* essence and *one* nature and in this way a child of God. And after this has happened, nothing more in God is hidden that will not be revealed or will not be mine. Then I shall be wise and powerful and all things, just as he is, and one and the same with him. Then Sion will be a true seer, a "true Israel", which means a "God-seeing man". For nothing in the Godhead is hidden from him. There a person will be guided to God. (p. 328)

Thus Eckhart depicts the mystical experience of Godhead in words which would no doubt raise the eyebrows of the ecclesiastical authorities of his time, as well as ours. One becomes divine,

becomes 'one substance, *one* essence, *one* nature' with God. One
realises that which is hidden in the Godhead, and becomes 'wise
and powerful' like God. But elsewhere Eckhart qualifies this picture.
He says 'When God draws the soul to himself, then the soul becomes
divine, but not that God becomes the soul. Then the soul loses
its name and its power but not its will and not its being' (pp.
319–20). But what is its will and its being? What becomes of the
being transformed in the likeness of God? Eckhart describes it as a
birth of the Son of God, the birth of Christ in man. One becomes as
Christ. Eckhart argues, 'It would mean little to me that the "Word
was made flesh" for man in Christ, granting that the latter is distinct
from me, unless he also was made flesh in me personally, so that
I too would become the Son of God' (p. 311). So Eckhart stresses
the role of Christ as the exemplar of human transfiguration. The
suffering and resurrection of Christ is not simply to be understood
as a cosmic undoing of original sin that has removed, quite distinct
from the person and once and for all, the distance of God from his
creatures. Rather Christ is the role model of human transformation;
people must suffer, die and be born again in God as Christ Himself
suffered, died and rose again.

It begins to become clear how Eckhart's mysticism can be characterised by four paths despite the realisation of telos in path two.
For the teleological goal is not a static and passive realisation. As
Fox says, the union with Godhead is 'a union of birthing and not
merely similarity' (p. 322). One does not unite in passive repose
in the realisation of God's essence. For God's essence is creative;
He gives birth in the union to the Son; He transforms the mystic
into divinity. But more than this, the Son becomes the Word as
the Father; He too is creative; He too gives birth. In the experience
of Godhead one is not united in static passivity. Rather, in 'the
supreme emptiness of detachment, man and God are united in
fertility; one sole determination joins them together: that of giving
birth' (p. 282). Indeed, God is *fundamentally* creative: 'The property
of the Father to give birth is nothing else than his being God, and
I have already said that he held nothing back. And I further say
that it is the very root of divinity which he fully speaks into his
Son' (p. 322).

Eckhart expands on this wonderful imagery of birthing by using
images of water overflowing. 'Life means a sort of overflow by
which a thing, welling up within itself, completely floods itself,
each part of it interpenetrating every other part, until at last it

pours itself out and boils over into something external' (p. 204). So the Son and the Spirit of the Trinity are the Father Himself, who has overflowed, melted or molted forth his essential goodness in a fundamental creative fertility. In the first path one has an experience, as an enlightened creature, of the world united in God. In path two one experiences God quite distinct from creation, realises the Divine *prior to* creation of even the active, personal God. In path three one has an experience, in unity with God, of God's creative activity. It is not, as in path one, a matter of 'seeing' this activity, but rather of participating in it. One lives out this fundamental birthing, one expresses oneself for creation's sake, one exudes one's essential divinity from within in a creative outpouring. This artistic expression is a consequence of divine transformation, arising out of the very experience of Godhead itself: 'Thus human beings should be communicative and emanative with all the gifts they have received from God . . . People who do not bestow on others spiritual things and whatever bliss is in them have never been spiritual' (p. 367). So Eckhart's teleology relates the cataphatic experience of the unitary life to the apophatic experience of Godhead. Out of Godhead gushes a spiritual overflow that springs the naked soul to life in the spirit; the mystic exudes out of this experience of nothingness the fundamental creative energy that naturally issues forth from it, and if he does not, he has not properly or fully experienced Godhead.

So Eckhart moves from the apophatic spirituality of path two to the more cataphatic explanation of union in paths three and four, drawing together the different experiences we outlined in our introduction to mysticism. The third path involves the expression of experienced Godhead through selfless activity; one expresses the divine through creative activity according to the experienced divine will. But in the fourth path Eckhart goes on to describe this selfless activity as divine compassion and justice, the latter being the natural extension of compassion. These features arise from the deepest essence of the experienced Godhead. Eckhart says, 'In the highest and purest acts that God works, God works compassion' (p. 442). Thus, to describe the process in a manner that neatly ties the final three paths together, one expresses the compassion and justice of the Divine as it arises out of the union with Godhead in an outpouring of creative activity. One plays out, so to speak, the justice and compassion of God that one experiences; one 'gives birth' to the Divine of the mystical experience, a Divine whose most essential nature is compassion. Eckhart says:

> compassion divinely adorns the soul, clothing it in the robe which is proper to God. Both the theologians and the Scriptures teach that in every work which God works in a creature, compassion goes with it and ahead of it, especially in the inwardness of the creature itself. (p. 420)

The experiences of this fourth path thus involve a unity and interconnection of a highly personal and dynamic nature. One moves from the realisation of the ultimate as detached and distinct from the world to that of a fundamental harmony of personal God participating in the world. The cohesive energy of the experience is a most fundamental compassion in a loss of otherness and a grounding in peace: 'When we are truly in God and in compassion we are grounded in peace and thrown into peace and end up in peace' (p. 448). Here there is a sharing of energies within the context of a profound sense of interdependent peace. As Fox puts it, the mystical side of the experience of compassion is 'that of our relation to all of the cosmos and its origins and goal in compassion', that all 'saints swim in an ocean of compassion and rejoice where it is shared and lived out' (pp. 436, 438).

This sharing and living out of compassion is Eckhart's justice. Eckhart says, 'compassion directs a person to relationships with his fellow human beings' (p. 421). It is a giving to one's neighbour that which is his, it is a rightness or fairness in ensuring one's neighbour receives his or her due. Eckhart comments:

> It follows that "and your justice will go before your face" applies to the neighbor. For this is the nature of justice. This is explicitly said insofar as compassion is just to the extent that it gives each one what is his. This is why Isidore of Seville says . . . that "it is a great crime to give the wages of the poor to the rich and from the livelihood of the poor to increase the luxuries of the powerful, taking water from the needy earth and pouring it into the rivers". (p. 422)

So compassion becomes justice as one expresses it in economic and political relationships with one's neighbour. One gives to others that which is properly due to them. Nevertheless, such a giving is not, in Eckhart's eyes, a calculated utilitarianism or contractualism utterly disconnected from mysticism. Indeed there is to be no motive for the just: 'The just person does not seek anything with his work, for every single person who seeks anything or even something with his or her works is working for a why and is a servant and a mercenary' (p. 464). Indeed, Eckhart goes on to say that works should not be done even for God's sake. There is no why arising in the compassion to which justice finds itself linked.

First of all there occurs a breakdown of dualistic thinking in the mystical realisation of the profound and fundamental interdependence of God's creatures. Experienced oneness and harmony is very important in the actualisation of compassion and justice. As Fox puts it, 'when we traffic in a consciousness of otherness, we destroy compassion and reduce it to philanthropy, pity, or moralizing' (p. 447). True compassion only arises in recognition of a fundamental interdependence and unity; one acts as if others are but an aspect of oneself. Thus in terms of justice one does not assume a social contractual responsibility for others but one recognises a responsibility for others in the awareness that they are not fundamentally independent others – that they are deeply interdependent and interconnected with one's essential being.

Second, at this stage one 'enters into all the properties of justice and truth' (p. 435). Eckhart says, a 'just person is one who is conformed and transformed into justice. The just person lives in God and God in him. Thus God will be born in this just person and the just person is born into God' (p. 464). He refers to the person born as the Son in the experience of path two as becoming equal to justice, because God is justice, and the Son and God are the same in nature (p. 433). So Eckhart speaks of justice as working without a why for the welfare of others, as actualising justice simply for the sake of actualising justice.

Thus Eckhart's eschatology is extremely this-worldly in its orientation. The egoistic impulses of lower human nature are transfigured through the grace of experienced God, and the person comes to live the divine compassion and justice that occurs at the core of God's creative act. One can become divinised in this life, one can in this temporal, mutable world participate in eternal, immutable life, and Eckhart urges people forward in this pursuit: 'we should never rest until we become what we have eternally been in him (Rom. 8:29ff.). For the Father runs and hurries in order that we be born in the Son and become what the Son is' (p. 466). Yet, when the eschaton is realised, once one becomes the Son, one is not involved in an eternal rest and peace of passive beatitude. Rather, in the manner of God one creates in compassion and justice, one does His singular work as it occurs in eternity:

> If a person is raised up beyond time into eternity, then the person works one work there with God. A person who is risen beyond time into eternity works with God what God worked a thousand years ago and will work a thousand years hence. This too is for wise people a matter of knowledge and for ignorant people a matter of belief. (p. 466)

So the enlightened person brings eternal activity to the temporal realm; he does the very work, compassion and justice, that God does before and beyond time. He sees and knows the point of creation, the reason to be; like Bucke's glimpse of eternal life mentioned earlier in this chapter, the mystic comes to a vision, in Kant's terms, of artistic wisdom. But more than this, more than the kind of transient realisation that Bucke had, he *participates directly* in the artistic teleology of creation, in the artistic wisdom of God. Indeed, vision and participation go hand in hand in Eckhart's mystical teleology, as he saw artistic wisdom to be only fully and properly realised *in* active compassion. He makes this point more clearly in answer to the following question: 'Now one might ask: Has the spirit no vision of God in eternal life? Yes and no. Insofar as it is born, it has no contemplation and no vision more of God. But in so far as it *is being* born, it has a vision of God' (p. 467). So one lives eternity only in the practical personal relationships of temporal life; until one comes to live out artistic wisdom in one's daily affairs, one has not fully realised its vision.

THE SIGNIFICANCE OF MYSTICAL THEODICAL EVIDENCE

Let us begin to evaluate the significance of Eckhart's mystical theodical evidence by setting it against that which is offered in John Hick's soul-making theodicy. Both propose a teleological view that involves a movement of human beings towards relationship with the Divine. The picture is one of human beings established in an environment free of divine coercion (for Hick, epistemic distance, for Eckhart, mystical distance) where they can, as autonomous personal and moral beings, develop their spiritual potential to capacity. Through the processes of moral and spiritual develop-ment the distance (epistemic/mystical) between the Divine and human being is reduced and ultimately eliminated.

In both teleologies evil is regarded as necessary. The emphasis for Eckhart is on the non-being of evil, its radical distinction from all that is divine. He says:

> It is evident first that evils, as nonbeing, are not from God nor is God in them, since there is no existence in them. They are evils in and of the fact that they are not in God and he is not in them. This is why they do not exist, are not creatures, and have not been created.[20]

In characterising moral evil as non-being Eckhart places the culpability on the evil-doer who in sinning freely distances himself from the Divine. For Eckhart, the sinner moves himself to the edges of the divine realm, to the outskirts of being. In sinful activity one moves towards a kind of non-participation in the teleological drama, distancing oneself from the divine source which is in fact one's appropriate end.[21]

Still, though Eckhart characterises evil as a mode of distance and distancing from the Divine, he does give it a positive place in his theology. He says, 'what is evil for one man is good for another or for the universe; and he who takes harm from it now and in the present instant will benefit from it later in other circumstances'.[22] Thus as Hick deems necessary some forms of evil in a soul-making teleology, so Eckhart regards it a necessary feature in his theology of mystical teleology. In both cases evil is ultimately justified in the future good of the teleological conception, no matter its severity or scope.

So, in Eckhart's theodicy we find natural and moral evil reconciled with the conception of an all-benevolent and omnipotent Divine, much in the manner of Hick's theodicy. Theodical justification occurs in the realisation of the teleological goal, wherein one realises the appropriateness of this world, including experienced evils and suffering, in actualising the final purpose of God. The major difference between the two theodicies is Eckhart's mystical emphasis, a stress which has significant implications for the nature and status of theodical justification. Like Hick, Eckhart justifies evil in terms of the greater good of the teleological end, but he goes well beyond Hick in maintaining that his theodicy can be verified in the present life. Whereas Hick's theodicy rests upon an envisionment of some future utopian spiritual state, Eckhart's hinges upon an experience of the here and now.

Indeed, Eckhart claims to have himself realised theodical justification and he passionately urges us on to pursue a similar realisation. He tells his readers that God is good and wise despite the hard reality of evil and suffering, that we ought to believe this on his authority and on that of others. Yet he presses us not to rest satisfied by the claims of the divinised mystic, but to investigate for ourselves, to validate his theodicy in personal experience, to replace ignorant belief by the wisdom of knowing (p. 466). In contrast with this, Kant's moral theodicy and the speculative or philosophical theodicies such as Hick's offer us no personal authority in this regard and they possess no experiential imperative.

Now the significance of this authority in mystical theodicy cannot be dismissed lightly. No doubt direct personal experience and conclusions established in reasonable thoughtfulness are much more valuable and reliable then rational faith in the word of another. But the importance of knowledge from authority should not be downplayed. For example, though evidence from authority is often belittled in scholarly circles of the day, any thoughtful student learns very quickly the importance, necessity and pervasiveness of authoritative dogma in the academic life. Indeed, the dependence upon knowledge from authority is a very common and accepted practice, extending to all facets of life. Why in Eckhart's case should its status be regarded negatively? Because it is not publicly verifiable?

Eckhart and other mystics implicitly challenge the assumption that public verification is necessary to establish the truth of all propositions. This view about the necessity of public verification in establishing the truth of a claim is very much in vogue today, a view that Donald Evans refers to as 'impersonalism'. Impersonalism is 'the dogmatic rejection of any truth-claim which requires personal transformation in order to be adequately understood and appraised; the only truth possible is truth which can be known impersonally'.[23] In Eckhart's case, impersonal verification of theodical evidence is impossible because theodical evidence *requires* personal transformation. The experiences involved are not *publicly* verifiable but only *personally*, in so far as one has undergone the appropriate personal transformation. The assumption for Eckhart is that one can only appraise or understand mystical theodical evidence through undergoing the mystical path and transforming self-consciousness. So one can only verify the claims by having the experiences. As Evans puts it, the 'meaning of spiritual and mystical assertions is linked with their method of verification'.[24]

It is important to note that such personal verification is not confined to the realm of mystical experience. One only has to consider the common human experiences of grief and love, whether they be regarded as spiritual experiences or not. The power and significance of these experiences are intertwined with personal transformation and can only really be known and appreciated in direct personal experience. Moreover, it also seems true that these experiences of grief and love, as well as compassion, can involve personal transformation of self-consciousness that in some instances is quite radical. These experiences can issue forth in a radical psychic upheaval that transforms a person's attitudes, beliefs and practices. Dostoevsky, as we will see in the following chapter, considers these experiences essential to the positive mystical theodicy he espouses

Regarding this issue of personal verification, Evans also cites as an example the truth-claims of depth-psychology, and refers to the necessity of a 'self-transforming exploration of the unconscious' for 'an adequate understanding and appraisal' of the Freudian unconscious.[25] Very much related to this, I would suggest that Jung's archetypes of the collective unconscious never become properly known or understood, except in a very minimal and superficial sense as rote memorisation of the terms and their use, until one experiences them to some degree directly in psychic experience. Until then Jung's theory can only appear as fantastic to the psychology student, who must accept the view and its significance on the authority of one who has directly experienced it.

So we can find in non-mystical knowledge cases that should lead us to question the impersonalist assumption. But more than this, we can also find other aspects of non-mystical experience that speak in favour of the significant status of theodical authority in Eckhart's view. For one thing, though the non-mystic has not personally verified the theodical evidence Eckhart proposes, it might be that she or he has had certain experiences, be they emotional or aesthetic, that are somewhat analogous to the various mystical experiences Eckhart espouses. Evelyn Underhill speaks of these experiences as 'Transcendental Feeling', describing them as preliminary to the mystical path:

> Few people pass through life without knowing what it is to be at least touched by this mystical feeling. He who falls in love with a woman and perceives – as the lover really does perceive – that the categorical term, "girl" veils a wondrous and unspeakable reality: he who, falling in love with nature, sees the landscape "touched with light divine," – a charming phrase to those who have not seen it, but a scientific statement to the rest – he who falls in love with the Holy, or as we say "undergoes conversion": all these have truly known something of the secret of the world.[26]

Certain aesthetic and emotional experiences, then, are analogous to the mystical; more than this Underhill suggests that they can be mystical, albeit lower level and transient glimpses of the transcendental world underlying reality. Indeed, she says the artist shows the way to the mystical path, evoking the mystical consciousness through their artistic endeavours. The artist 'perpetually demonstrates the many-graded character of human consciousness; the new worlds which await it'.[27] In the case of Eckhart, we find paths three and four characterised by concepts familiar to all moral beings. Mystical experiences of justice, compassion and creativity are described in terms that do not contradict their standard meanings, though Eckhart claims they surpass normal connotation and require and involve processes of radical self-transformation to be experienced.

Surely it is not the case that all aspects of the processes and experiences of the unitary life are utterly foreign to the experience of the non-mystic. This should lend *some* plausibility to the mystical teleology Eckhart espouses and the claim of the theodical evidence it evinces. This point is strengthened by the fact that Eckhart's moral teleology is typically raised up, both within and without religious traditions, as the highest and most virtuous goal, and the authority figures he has in mind are considered appropriate moral and spiritual exemplars. That is to say, the moral ideal he espouses and the apparent moral integrity of the authority figures he has in mind make it highly unlikely that there is any deliberate attempt at deception on Eckhart's part. But perhaps Eckhart himself is the one who is misled, deceived and deluded?

What evidence do we find to justify such a position? His ideal of actualising the compassion and justice experienced in the unitary life seems most noble, a goal that draws a moral imperative from the mystical experience itself. His delusion, then, would involve a bizarre kind of self-deceiving egoism, if that was from which it derived. And Eckhart was not an illiterate and superstitious peasant. He was a well-educated, practically minded Dominican, schooled in the classics of the scholasticism of his time, a *Magister in Theologia*, the Regent Master for Externs in Paris and directing the Dominican *stadium generale* in Cologne. Still, there will be some who suggest he was deluded in the very scholastic Christian theology of his day, unwittingly drawn into a power structure that determined his view, and mistaken in considering his fundamental philosophical and mystical framework to be veridical, to be more than superstition. But to these people we can only point out that there is no logical inconsistency implicit or explicit in his theodicy and there seems to be no inherent epistemological impossibility to the mysticism he espouses. Moreover, the self-transformative personal verification he deems necessary is also indispensable in the evaluation of certain non-mystical truth-claims, and he is not alone in his mystical teleological view.

If he were alone in this regard then the evidence he asserts on his authority would be highly questionable. Further, if the experiences he talks about were utterly private and unverifiable in principle then the evidence he proposes would be at best dubious. However, though the mystical experiences Eckhart describes are not verifiable by the non-mystic, they are, according to him and other mystics, verifiable by those who undergo the appropriate practices. With this in mind, I think the authoritative theodical evidence that Eckhart proposes offers the non-mystic, both in terms of consolatory power and reasonable response to the theodical sceptic, a great deal more than Hick's theodicy can; Eckhart's theodicy displays a cogency that Hick's cannot possess. Nevertheless, much more must be said about the nature of this consolatory force of mystical experience, and we have not yet begun to examine the issues arising from the *necessity* of evil and suffering in Eckhart's thesis, a necessity that cannot be merely assumed in mystical teleology. Let us turn now to the question of the status of evil in mystical teleological theodicy, a question which will naturally lead us into the issues of the necessity of evil and suffering in mystical teleological theodicy.

8

The Consolatory Power of Mystical Experience

As we have seen in our introduction to mysticism and in Eckhart's theology, mystics claim in certain experiences to encounter a powerful consolatory force which significantly reduces or eliminates the negative force of evil. In such experience evil is often referred to as a non-reality, non-being or nothingness which no longer has power or influence upon the enlightened mystic. As R. C. Zaehner has so provocatively pointed out in *Our Savage God*, this mystical perspective can in some cases have horrible consequences. To illustrate he refers to Charles Manson who apparently 'passed beyond good and evil' in the realisation of the harmonious unity of cosmic consciousness.[1] Likening Manson's experience to non-theistic mysticisms of the ancient Greeks and Zen Buddhism, Zaehner describes it as one where the 'discursive mind *disintegrates* and you *see* that right *is* wrong, and that good *is* evil':

> Once you have reached the stage of the eternal Now, all is One, as Parmenides taught in ancient Greece. "After all", Manson said, "we are all one". Killing someone therefore is just like breaking off a piece of cooky.[2]

From Manson's perspective the temporal world of human activity and moral categories is to be regarded as fictional – as insignificant in relation to the 'eternal Now' that he encountered in his mystical experience. In combination with his psychopathic yearnings this amoral perspective culminated in brutal atrocities. Manson and his 'enlightened' family turned to indiscriminate torture and killing, as they went out of their way to drive their amoral perspective home to those still clouded in moral pretension.

Zaehner vividly illustrates the dangers of non-theistic mysticisms. The realisation of harmonious unity underlying differentiated reality involves an affective experience of such power that the mystic

is led to deny the reality of evil. Evil becomes neither a problem nor a concern, and without a moral imperative arising outside of the experience there occurs an amoral indifference on
the part of the mystic. Indeed, for the Manson family such is
a profound understatement; they illustrate the perverse extreme
of the positive or assertive aspect of mysticism. The affective
consolation of mystical experience is characterised by a denial
of the reality and power of evil on the part of the illumined
gnostic elite. So Manson, who never espoused a moral perspective
prior to his mystical seeking, attempts to *justify* his immorality
through mystical realisation of the harmonious unity underlying differentiated reality. Hence it is not surprising to find an
extreme immoral perspective and no theodicy associated with his
mysticism.[3]

In this chapter we are interested in mystics who are concerned
with morality and theodicy before and after undertaking a mystical
way. This naturally directs us to mysticisms that go beyond an
individualistic quietism, to mysticisms which espouse a theistic
teleology. But even theistic mystics often severely downplay the
power and scope of evil. As we discussed in Chapter 6, Donald
Evans describes the redemptive power of mystical experience as
an 'appreciative awareness' that issues forth from it. In the experience of a pervasive benevolent and harmonious energy, everything
about the world comes to be regarded as good. As Underhill has
put it, 'everything will be seen under the aspect of a cosmic and
charitable beauty'.[4] In this regard, as I briefly mentioned in Chapter
7, Eckhart stresses the non-being of evil, its radical distinction from
all that is divine. He says:

> It is evident first that evils, as nonbeing, are not from God nor is
> God in them, since there is no existence in them. They are evils
> in and of the fact that they are not in God and he is not in them.
> This is why they do not exist, are not creatures, and have not
> been created.[5]

Though Eckhart does go on to stress the positive and more
substantial nature of evil, this quotation raises questions regarding
the status of evil in theistic mysticisms. Indeed, the fourth article of
the papal bull in condemnation of Eckhart's theology pertains to his
view of evil. Taken from his *Commentary on John*, the proposition in
question reads 'Also, in every work, even in an evil, I repeat, in one

evil both according to punishment and guilt, God's glory is revealed and shines forth in equal fashion'.[6]

No doubt this particular article should be properly read only in its context, and the reference to punishment and guilt is a qualification that significantly reduces its heretical flavour. Surely Eckhart here is thinking only of retributive evils, as they are appropriate in bringing about the teleological end. Nevertheless it is easy to see how someone like Manson, for example, who considered himself to be the 'divinely appointed agent of the wrath of God',[7] might have cited Eckhart in justification of his actions. Be that as it may, these quotations from Eckhart raise a number of issues regarding mysticism and evil. Does the enlightened mystic have no experience of evil? More importantly, perhaps, is it the case that evil is only real for the unenlightened non-mystic? Is evil only properly perceived as non-being – as in fact fictional and illusory? How, indeed, are we to understand Eckhart's description of evil as non-being?

In addressing these questions we will be returning to the views of Meister Eckhart who has much to say in this regard. For as we saw in Chapter 7, his mystical teleology goes beyond the consolatory experience of harmonious unity characteristic of mystical quietists and immoral activists such as Manson, to include the consolation and moral imperative of more theistic experiences. We will also look to Dostoevsky, to his positive theodical stance which was just barely mentioned in Chapter 2. Though Dostoevsky illustrates very effectively the problems of evil for theodicy he also moves to the other side of the coin, pointing the way towards accepting a theodicy within the framework of mystical theodical evidence and consolatory power. But we begin now with the question of evil as non-being, as it is developed in Plotinus, the Pseudo-Dionysius and Eckhart.

EVIL AS NON-BEING: PLOTINUS AND PSEUDO-DIONYSIUS

To answer these questions surrounding the consolatory force of mystical experience we can begin with a brief reference to Plotinus. The notion of evil as non-being goes back at least as far as Plotinus who locates the source of evil in a formless matter situated at the far end of a spectrum that begins, so to speak, with the unified One. Reality is perceived in terms of a Platonic form–matter conjunction that derives from the One. There exists a hierarchy of unified form and matter, with the matterless triad of hypostasis (One, Mind, All-Soul) as the source and goal of human beings. Now since matter as we know it is always associated with form, absolute evil can never really exist. As John Macquarrie puts it, for Plotinus 'matter [is] without form, [has] no qualities and [is] virtually indistinguishable from nothing'.[8] As such evil is without an ideal form. This is in contrast to the sensible world which, in typical Platonic fashion, has its reality in its likeness to an ideal form.[9] So Plotinus refers to evil as non-being, a non-being, however, which he is quick to qualify. He says:

> By this Non-Being, of course, we are not to understand something that simply does not exist, but only something of an utterly different order from Authentic-Being: there is no question here of movement and position with regard to Being; the Non-Being we are thinking of is, rather, an image of being or perhaps something still further removed than even an image.[10]

Plotinus is caught in the tension between denying the reality of evil (since if evil exists it must derive from the One which is the Good, which is a logical contradiction) and affirming it (if evil is utterly unreal then it has no power and reality, which is a contradiction of fact). To get around this dilemma he proposes a hypothetical absolute formlessness at the far end of the emanated spectrum, a formless non-being that has reality in so far as we can choose in favour of it and move towards it.[11] He says:

> There must, then, be some Undetermination-Absolute, some Absolute Formlessness; all qualities cited as characterizing the Nature of Evil must be summed under an Absolute Evil; and every evil thing outside of this must either contain this Absolute by saturation or have taken the character of evil and become a cause of evil by consecration to this Absolute.[12]

The teleological emphasis of the thought of Plotinus is quite pronounced here. Unlike all existent reality, which is good because it is an emanation of the Good, evil is not good. But as not good, it is also not being; it does not exist for it is not good, and there are no ideal forms which evil images. Nevertheless, it does exist, and not just in terms of the privation of good. But it exists only in terms of its teleological effect of drawing one away from their appropriate end. As Macquarrie puts it, 'Evil does not belong to matter as such, but the preferring of the lower to the higher'.[13] In choosing against the good, the soul actualises evil at the practical level; in activity non-conducive to the movement towards the ideal forms (All-Soul, Mind and One), one fails to actualise their appropriate telos and falls towards the formless realm of non-being. The soul becomes 'shut out from the Forming-Idea that orders and brings to measure'.[14]

But let us pick up this theme in an influential Christian theodical version, that of Pseudo-Dionysius, a version which is very likely influencing Eckhart in his account of evil.[15] In the latter part of Chapter 4 of *The Divine Names* Pseudo-Dionysius gives an account of evil very similar to the Plotinian view. Like Plotinus, Dionysius considers all spiritual and material being to be an emanation of a transcendent God that can only be properly described negatively. But against God as One and Unity he also emphasises God's personhood in the Trinity, and His goodness and beauty. Indeed, it is in God's over-abundance of goodness that there occurs the creative process. He says:

> And we may be so bold as to claim also that the cause of all things loves all things in the superabundance of his goodness, that because of his goodness he makes all things, brings all things to perfection, holds all things together, returns all things. The divine longing is Good seeking good for the sake of the Good.[16]

In this seeking good for the sake of Good there occurs an emanation of a series of the forms and ideas of the intelligible universe from God, and the sensible world which in turn emanates from these ideas. Now, like Plotinus, Dionysius considers creation's origin in the Good to entail its being solely good. He says, 'there is nothing in the world without a share of the Beautiful and the Good'.[17] Nevertheless, evil, which is present in the world, 'does not come from the Good'.[18] But, Dionysius asks, how can this be?: 'What in fact is evil? Where did it come from? And where is it found?'.[19]

He begins to answer these questions in the manner of the response of Plotinus:

> Evil is not a being; for if it were, it would not be totally evil. Nor is it a nonbeing; for nothing is completely a nonbeing, unless it is

said to be in the Good in the sense of beyond-being. For the Good is established far beyond and before simple being and nonbeing. Evil, by contrast, is not among the things that have being nor is it among what is not in being. It has a greater nonexistence and otherness from the Good than nonbeing has.[20]

Since all being derives from the Good, evil is not properly being. Yet, on the other hand, since Good is that which transcends and precedes both being and non-being, non-being depends upon the Good. So evil is not properly non-being, and Dionysius speaks of 'a greater nonexistence and otherness' of evil than that which is associated with non-being. But how can Dionysius move to propose evil in this manner without espousing a fundamental good–evil dualism? In his attempt to distinguish evil from good is he not led to promulgate a substantive reality over and against that which arises from the Good?

But evil is in a privative sense connected to the Good; evil in its positive sense is understood as a lesser good. Dionysius says, 'A lesser good is not the opposite of the greater good. What is less hot or cold is not opposite of what is more so. Therefore evil is a being. It is in things that have being. And it is in opposition to and contrary to the Good'.[21] Evil in this sense can be contrasted to the Good. As an aspect of being, evil is associated with the Good, is in fact a good, albeit a lesser good. Evil here is positive for it naturally occurs in the emanative processes of creation that issue forth in a series of hierarchical beings which participate in the Good only 'in proportion to the capacity to receive it'.[22] But evil as a lesser good is productive of greater goods, and Dionysius justifies it in its contribution to the fulfilment of the teleological end. He says: 'Hence evil contributes to the fulfillment of the world and by its very existence it saves it from imperfection'.[23]

This is evil in its positive sense, however. Evil also exists in a more negative mode, the mode where we conceive of it as utterly removed from the Good. Dionysius distinguishes between evil in the context of the Good and evil in and of itself. He says:

evil, *qua* evil, never produces being or birth. All it can do by itself is in a limited fashion to debase and destroy the substance of things. And if anyone should say that it is a begetter of things and that by the destruction of one thing it gives birth to something else, the correct reply is that it is not *qua* destructiveness that it brings this about. Inasmuch as it is destructiveness and evil it destroys and debases. Birth and being occur because of the Good. That is to say evil in itself is a destructive force but is a productive force through the activity of the Good. Insofar as it is evil it neither is nor confers being.[24]

Evil in itself, then, is nothing: 'that which is totally bereft of the Good never had, does not have, never shall have, never can have any kind of being at all'.[25] It 'cannot produce and cannot sustain anything, cannot make or preserve anything'.[26] Only in conjunction with the Good does evil have any life or force, and we can only properly conceive and speak of it in terms of its association with the Good. Thus there is no such thing as substantive evil, and evil is only properly characterised as deficiency and lack in terms of the teleological goal:

> Thus, evil is contrary to progress, purpose, nature, cause, source, goal, definition, will, and substance. It is defect, a deficiency, a weakness, a disproportion, a sin. It is purposeless, ugly, lifeless, mindless, unreasonable, imperfect, unfounded, uncaused, indeterminate, unborn, inert, powerless, disordered. It is errant, indefinite, dark, insubstantial, never in itself possessed of any existence.[27]

Evil, then, does not exist in itself and only comes to life in terms of the Good. Nevertheless it has a reality in so far as one moves oneself out of the teleological picture in choosing and moving away from the Good. But in this movement one does not approach another realm of being or participate in a domain of non-being that has any relation to the Good. Rather one moves to the edge of a dark and empty nothingness, to annihilation. Speaking of demons in this regard, Dionysius comments:

> They are called evil because of the deprivation, the abandonment, the rejection of the virtues which are appropriate to them. And they are evil to the extent that they are not, and insofar as they wish for evil, they wish for what is really not there.[28]

This perspective of evil as nothing in itself, as totally dependent upon the Good for its reality, is a view that Jacob Boehme adapts anchor####aaa.. .

and extends in his provocative attempt to distance evil from God through his account of the *Ungrund*. This is the subject of the next chapter. But in the account of Dionysius this dependence means that so long as one desires 'to exist, to live, and to think',[29] one participates in the Good. Even the most radically evil beings are good in the minimal sense that they exist. But their movement is away from their appropriate telos, towards an end that cannot really be actualised since it is a goal that can only be characterised as utter annihilation, darkness or emptiness. Teleologically speaking, then, evil is not exactly nothing and non-being; it is not fiction or illusion in respect to the Good, but rather very real in its potential of moving one to the outskirts of the realm of the Good. In contrast, one moves towards the Good in the positive movement of the teleology, one distances oneself from this nothingness and participates more and more in the Good purified of the disorder and error of evil, culminating in perfection in the Good.[30]

The enlightened mystic, then, located at the far end of the spectrum in the perfection of the Good, will not participate in evil. For him, evil is recognised as insubstantial and powerless, a non-being or nothingness. Nevertheless this does not mean that evil altogether loses its negative force for the mystic. For the universe is pictured as a dynamic hierarchy, a theme which Dionysius develops directly in *The Celestial Hierarchy* and *The Ecclesiastical Hierarchy*. It involves both a coming forth from the Good, a return to this source, *and a sharing of the Good*. As Macquarrie comments: 'Hierarchy is not the static stratification of reality, but something very dynamic, the reciprocal communication among the different grades of being'.[31] Dionysius himself describes this relationship to God and participation in the hierarchy:

> Hierarchy causes its members to be images of God in all respects, to be clear and spotless mirrors reflecting the glow of primordial light and indeed of God himself. It ensures that when its members have received this full and divine splendour they can then pass on this light generously and in accordance with God's will to beings further down the scale.[32]

So there occurs in the teleology of Dionysius a moral imperative very similar to that which we saw in Eckhart's treatment of path four compassion and justice. There is a fundamental interdependence and relationship amongst creation that issues forth in a

concern, sharing and helping in the return to the One. More than
this, however, Macquarrie suggests that Dionysius emphasises the
concept of synergism.[33] God as co-worker actively participates in
the hierarchy. Dionysius says: 'A hierarchy has God as its leader
of all understanding and action. It is forever looking directly at the
comeliness of God'.[34]

EVIL, CONSOLATION AND MEISTER ECKHART

Eckhart's view on evil is very similar to that of Plotinus and Pseudo-
Dionysius, though he emphasises even more than Dionysius the
suffering, consoling God, and, more than either, goes on to describe
explicitly the enlightened experience of evil in terms that radically
downplay its power and significance. For Eckhart the experience
of evil for the mystically astute is unproblematic, even joyful.
He says:

> I say again that if there were any person who looked with his
> or her reason according to truth into the bliss that is within this
> power, then everything that he or she could suffer or that God
> might wish to have this person suffer could be for him or her
> insignificant, or indeed, a nothing. I say even that it would be
> totally a joy and a pleasure.[35]

In the mystical experience all is made right and good; supposedly
one rises above the categories of good and evil, enveloped in the
ineffable bliss of the divine union. In the beatific vision one comes
to know the highest good, to experience the good inherent in God
and all of His creation, transforming the pain of suffering evil into
the ecstasy of a higher knowledge. Evil, then, loses its force in the
mystical experience, and Eckhart begins to sound very much like
an amoral mystic. In this regard he writes rather shockingly: 'If a
child were born in me, and if I were to see my father and all my
friends killed before my eyes, my heart would not be moved as
a result'.[36] Indeed, it would appear on this reading that Eckhart's
mysticism culminates in an amoral insensitivity that renders evil
meaningless, and one wonders about the nature and status of his
theodicy. But Eckhart often incorporates hyperbole to illustrate his
view and one must be careful not to read him out of context.

In his *Book of Consolation* Eckhart qualifies this perspective. He says 'For a good man everything that is alien to God and unlike Him, and that is not God Himself alone, should be pain, not comfort'. He also says 'that if anyone for the sake of God and of goodness forsakes father and mother, brother and sister, . . . [then] all people . . . will become incomparably dearer to him'. Later he says 'In order to be a son it is essential that one should suffer', and that one should encourage and comfort a friend who is in sorrow and pain. Further he says that God 'suffers with man, indeed He suffers in His way before and incomparably more than the man who suffers for His sake'. And, finally, he also argues 'If my suffering is in God and God sympathises with me, how can suffering be painful to me then, if suffering loses its pain, and my pain is in God and my pain is God?'.[37]

Evil, then, loses its destructive power for the enlightened mystic. However, Eckhart here does not suggest that evil is fictional, that it has no force and reality, but rather that it is shouldered by God, that it is not encountered alone. For Eckhart the ideal encounter of evil is one where the individual is firmly grounded in the Godhead, one where the passions are not overwhelmed by the evil action or event. Nevertheless, the evil should disturb and move one to respond because it is something contrary to one's nature and end as Divine, and because one's ultimate role is to express the compassion and justice of the experienced Godhead. But Eckhart is careful to emphasise that one should not be moved overly much, either to the degree that one is unable to act or to the point that one turns away from the Divine. Such responses to evil would merely add to it. In this regard he comments:

> Do you think that, so long as words can move you to joy and sorrow, you are imperfect? It is not so! This was not the case even for Christ . . . Christ was so grieved by words that even if all the woes of creation befell a single creature, it would not have been so bad as the woe Christ felt. This was because of the nobility of his nature and the holy union of the divine and human nature in him. Thus I say that there have never been saints whom sorrow did not grieve and love did not please, and there never will be such saints . . . Whatever may happen to such a person does not hinder his or her eternal happiness so long as the very peak of the spirit is not affected in the place where the spirit is united with God's most precious will.[38]

Eckhart says that even the mystically astute person experiences the effects of evil, and he suggests that the mystic is, while abiding in divine union, able to appreciate and react to evil and suffering. Here we are reminded of Louis Dupré's proposal of a division in mystical consciousness which enables the mystic to participate in the world while at the same time remaining grounded in God-consciousness.[39] He says:

> A divided consciousness enables the mystic to take care of ordinary duties, even to suffer and to be disturbed on one level while preserving tranquility on another. The 'center of the soul' remains untouched by what preoccupies the mind's surface. No pain or unrest enters that inner sanctuary.[40]

So the mystic experiences and encounters evil with a concern and an empathy that is nevertheless accompanied by a consolatory force that leads Eckhart to describe evil in terms that severely downplay its seriousness. Evil is not to be taken as literally non-being or a nothingness since it threatens the well-being of human beings in a very real manner. A divinised mystic, however, encounters evil with an equanimity that reduces the power of the effect of the evil. Ideally, at the highest stage, the mystic is firmly grounded in the eternal Divinity that supports and permeates all creation. In such a condition the encounter with evil can be distinguished from a non-mystical encounter according to two characteristics. First, in this enlightened condition egoistic concerns are eliminated. Love, compassion and justice flow naturally from the mystic in an indiscriminate manner; egoistic preferences are overcome. The mystic acts out of the eternal love for humanity rather than a temporal love of this or that individual or thing. He regards all people equally, and he acts according to the love, compassion and justice of the experienced Divine. This is a key point in Eckhart's mysticism; at the highest levels of spirituality one expresses the compassion and justice of the experienced Divine by acting against that which inhibits the teleological attainment of others.

The second distinguishing characteristic of the mystical encounter with evil is the notion of a suffering God. For Eckhart the evil is real, and the suffering from it painful even for the mystically astute. However, if one stands steadfastly within the divine source this suffering is easily managed. For in the Godhead it is not the ego that stands suffering alone but the soul that rests

within the eternal Divinity that it itself is. In the mystical experience one experiences a profound consolatory power as the pain
and suffering of evil is somehow shared or transferred to God.
Eckhart says:

> It is God who carries the burden . . . If there were a person who
> liked to suffer for God and purely for God alone, and if this
> person felt in a single blow all the suffering the entire world
> bears, it would not hurt him and would not weigh him down,
> for it is God who would carry the burden.[41]

In effect, then, God *is* the evil-suffering.[42] God carries the burden
of suffering; one suffers, but finds consolation in a profound and
essential camaraderie of the mystical experience.

Eckhart thus stresses the possibility of God. Consistent with his
mysticism of God's immanence, he suggests that God actually
participates in human affairs, and that the Divine is affected and
moved by His creation. In contrast, traditional Catholic and Protes-
tant theology typically stress God's transcendence and impassibil-
ity in this regard. In *In Search of Deity*, John Macquarrie recognises
the kind of dialectic at play in theologies such as Eckhart's. For there
is a sense in which for Eckhart God must be understood as both
passible and impassible. Solely impassible, God is not depicted in
a manner worthy of admiration and worship, as a truly caring
and loving Divine. On the other hand, if conceived as passible
in the sense of existing only in process then God becomes, as
Macquarrie puts it, 'a puny godling, not so much the source of
anything affirmative [but] as the hapless victim of a world that has
got completely out of control'.[43]

Eckhart of course would deny both conceptions; his view is one
of a possibility which includes the notion of God's transcendence,
that God cannot be destroyed, and that the world would not
exist without Him. Furthermore, Eckhart thinks that God cannot
be overwhelmed by suffering; like Macquarrie, Eckhart considers
God to possess 'an infinite capacity for absorbing suffering, and
even for transforming it'.[44] Thus God is understood to suffer with
human beings while at the same time maintaining the transcendent
features which distinguish Him from creation.

Ronald Goetz recognises the contemporary emphasis upon passibility, picturing the theopaschite heresy of God's suffering as
'the new orthodoxy'.[45] But he questions the effectiveness of such

a conception as a theodical tool. Referring to the suffering in the incarnation he says:

> there is a certain immediate psychological comfort in the notion that God does not require of us a suffering that he himself will not endure. However, if this comfort is to be any more than a psychological prop, it must show how God's suffering mitigates evil. This explanation has been, to date, curiously lacking in the theodicy of divine self-limitation.[46]

Traditional non-mystical theodicies, even those that might emphasise divine passibility, do not illustrate how divine suffering contributes as a theodical force. Indeed, as Goetz asks, what is the significance of a suffering God for the individual in the throes of great evil? How does divine suffering mitigate experienced evils? We have seen how in mystical theodicy Eckhart understands such mitigation. The mystically astute, that is, the saint, responds to those experiencing the effects of evil with an equanimity born of the experience of the Divine. Eckhart says: 'Your joy reaches to the greatest evenness; it never alters. Therefore Christ says: "No one can take your joy away from you"'.[47] Further, he comments: 'A person who has thus let go of all that is his would therefore be so completely enveloped in God that when one wanted to touch him one would first have to touch God'.[48]

The imagery is very striking here. In mystical experience one encounters a powerful consolatory force that goes well beyond our normal frame of reference. Nevertheless, we do know what consolation is like, and we can conceive how the mystic might remain responsive to the reality of evil in the midst of this powerful consolation. Though not seriously affected by the experience of evil themselves, the mystics act in the world, responding to the suffering of others. This is perhaps analogous to the kind of consolation that an adult, matured by life-experience, might give to the queries of a distraught adolescent. Though truly empathetic to the youth the adult can respond with the calm confidence born by the deeper understanding of the nature and outcome of the distressing experience.[49] Theodical evidence, then, will be very important in regard to mystical experience. The consolatory power will be accompanied by the assurance of the truth of divine wisdom; mystical consolation involves a confident assurance of the ultimate reconciliation of the experienced trial. The mystical experience is such that one will no longer doubt theodicy. Eckhart speaks of this certainty as arising in love-relationship with God. He says it happens 'when a man, through the love and intimacy that exist between his God and him, trusts in him so fully and is so certain of him that he cannot doubt. What makes him so certain is that he loves God in all his creatures without distinction'.[50]

So Eckhart's mysticism does not espouse an amoral perspective that inhibits active concern and response to the evils of the world. Rather it emphasises active love and compassion as the vehicle in actualising his mystical teleology. The consolation of mystical experience no more plays down the pain of suffering than in the imagined example of the adult responding to the youth. The fact that the saint does not experience the degree of pain of the evil-sufferer does not mean that the suffering of the victim is not real or that it is pointless. Thus Eckhart's theodicy is highly moral and, indeed, very comforting. Eckhart maintains that in his mystical teleology God comes to shoulder the burden of evil suffering. So Eckhart's theodicy offers a great deal more than traditional non-mystical theodicies, both in terms of practical consolation to the believer and a rational response to the sceptic. For God, in allowing evil, has not left his creatures 'high and dry'; he participates in evil-suffering in a very profound manner.

Now Eckhart's view of the mystical consolation is not unlike Dostoevsky's treatment of the subject. For Dostoevsky, this facet of theodicy is the basis of his positive theodical stance, in so far as it is connected to theodical evidence. Thus to conclude this chapter, and to draw together the relationship between conciliatory power and evidence in mystical theodicy, I turn to Dostoevsky's positive theodical stance.

DOSTOEVSKY'S POSITIVE THEODICY

If Ivan represents Dostoevsky's negative theodical perspective, as we saw in Chapter 2, it is in the characters of Zosima and Alyosha that we uncover his positive theodical view. Zosima provides the theoretical framework, but he is drawn into the plot through his relationship and influence on Alyosha. As a young man Zosima had been proud, reckless and wild – not unlike the character of Dmitri Karamazov. In the crisis surrounding a duel, however, he experiences a profound religious conversion. As his reputation as a holy man grows, he takes on the role of elder, and pilgrims journey great distances to confess to him and receive his blessings. Very much taken with the charismatic old man, Alyosha devotes himself to the elder.

Zosima is sensitive to the problems that Ivan raises for theodicy. He recognises not only the terrible suffering of the world, but also the logic of freedom that is expressed in 'The Grand Inquisitor'. He argues that there is no freedom apart from the religious perspective. He criticises the modern secular mind that puts faith only in science, and in this context he observes that the 'world has proclaimed the reign of freedom, especially of late, but what do we see in this freedom of theirs? Nothing but slavery and self-destruction!' (p. 292).[51] He argues that this pseudo-freedom does not unite the world, does not, in the manner that its proponents proclaim, tie humanity together in brotherhood, but rather inhibits this possibility, isolating the human being from the rest of humankind. So Dostoevsky speaks of the potential of choosing against the good for evil, evil that, as in Eckhart, is thought to dissolve finally into an annihilating destructive self-avowal. He sees the victim of this choice as subjugated by his pride, and likens him to 'a starving man in the desert sucking blood out of his own body' (p. 302).

But, confirming the logic of freedom that we saw evidenced in 'The Grand Inquisitor', Zosima does not propose rational evidence in support of his religious view.[52] As we saw, Dostoevsky thought such was not available, and that it would in any event contradict the nature of the ideal. Rather he points to a feature that Ivan earlier mentions; the thirst for life, and the natural love for the world, people and noble actions and events. Ivan says: 'I love the sticky leaves in spring, the blue sky – that's all it is. Its not a matter of intellect or logic, it's loving with one's inside, with one's guts. One loves the first strength of one's youth' (p. 212).

Like Eckhart, Alyosha and Zosima urge as their personal ideals the autonomous actualisation of love and compassion. Like Ivan, Zosima recognises the innocent and lovable qualities of children, and he emphasises them in regard to active love: 'Love Children especially, for they too are sinless like angels; they live to soften and purify our hearts and as it were to guide us' (p. 298). Zosima saw this personal love as a purifying force, that which draws and moves one towards the religious ideal. Sorrow and grief are closely connected to this process. To the mother, grieving over her dead child, he consoles:

and a long while yet will you keep that mother's grief. But it will turn in the end into quiet joy, and your bitter tears will only be tears of tender sorrow, that purifies the heart and delivers it from sin. (p. 42)

Active love and compassion are thus the vehicles of religious transformation. They are both the means and evidence in support of one's choice of the religious good. Like Eckhart's mysticism, Zosima perceives a spiritual link that ties the world together: 'all is like an ocean, all is flowing and blending' (p. 299). So he stresses the responsibility the individual has for all human beings: 'There is only one means of salvation, then take yourself and make yourself responsible for all men's sins, that is the truth, you know' (p. 299). This is what Zosima's brother Markel had recognised on his deathbed: 'in truth we are each responsible to all for all, it's only that men don't know this. If they knew it the world would be a paradise at once' (p. 277).

So Zosima points the way towards the religious ideal much in the manner of Eckhart. In recognising one's interdependent connectedness with all others, one comes to 'realise' heaven on earth. He says, 'we don't understand that life is heaven, for we have only to understand that and it will at once be fulfilled in all its beauty' (p. 279). Artistic wisdom is thus a dynamic concept, as we saw in Eckhart's path four justice. The point is to do that which Ivan in his religious scepticism deemed impossible, to love your neighbour him- or herself, to love everything to your utmost, to love to the point of mystical ecstasy. Zosima presses this point; he says we must love 'not only occasionally, for a moment, but for ever' (p. 298). For it is in and through this love that the religious process and ideal become evident, verified and finally actualised. In this regard Zosima makes the comment that,

Much on earth is hidden from us, but to make up for that we have been given a precious mystic sense of our living bond with the other world, with the higher heavenly world, and the roots of our thoughts are not here but in other worlds. (p. 299)

And he urges the pursuit of this mystic sense:

Kiss the earth and love it with unceasing, consuming love. Love all men, love everything. Seek that rapture and ecstasy. Water

the earth with the tears of your joy and love those tears. Don't be
ashamed of that ecstasy, prize it, for it is a gift of God and a great
one; it is not given to many but only the elect. (p. 301)

The consolation, then, that Dostoevsky expresses in Zosima, is
the mystical sense that 'all things are good and fair, because all is
truth' (p. 274), a profound mystical experience of harmony and
purpose present in the world that stands over and against the
apparent unpracticability of freedom for the many and the seeming
injustice of the innocent suffering and evil in the world. Yet in
stressing the mystical experience, Zosima nevertheless maintains
his perspective of personal love against the non-personalist ration-
alism of the Inquisitor who spoke of subjugating the many for their
benefit:

If you love everything, you will perceive the divine mystery in
things. Once you perceive it, you will begin to comprehend it
better every day. And you will come at last to love the whole
world with an all-embracing love. (p. 298)

Dostoevsky proposes a positive theodical view very much like
the mystical theodicy Eckhart propounds. Such theodical stances,
however, are not reasonable responses to the criticism of theodicy
that Dostoevsky raises. Such consolation is not *an answer* to the
problems of theodicy that Dostoevsky witnesses; it does not eliminate the human sense of the unrealisability and the injustices of the
religious process that are raised by the rational mind. The mystical
experience does not give an intelligible explanation to account for
the suffering of the innocent, does not give a rational defence of
the dark side of human nature, and it does not replace the hard
human freedom by miracle, mystery and authority. And indeed,
this non-rational consolation is available only to the 'elect'; it is
no solace to the many, whose suffering, it would appear, can
at the most only serve the strong. Still, Dostoevsky chooses the
hard path of the Christian ideal, insists that if you love, 'you are
of God' (p. 44), and urges his readers to love life 'regardless of
logic', that 'it's only then that you will understand the meaning
of it' (p. 212).

This accounts for the final chapter of the novel, 'Ilyushenka's
funeral. The speech at the stone'. Missing the power and significance of this touching chapter of the book, R. Peace describes

it as 'mawkish', as 'merely catering for the nineteenth-century taste for bizarre sentimentality'.[53] But here we have the theme of active love expressed with great force, affecting the non-rational sentiments of the reader who has sensitively followed the sub-plot of Ilyusha's tragic trial. In witnessing the brutal and wholly unjust beating of his father at the hands of Dmitri Karamazov, the wretched ordeal of the innocent boy begins. In his simple sense of justice and his love for his father he responds indignantly, withdrawing into himself and lashing out at others, aggravating the situation. The problem is compounded in the poverty of his family, in his mother's illness, the cruel barbarism of his schoolmates who unabashedly torment him, and it climaxes in his slow and lingering death. But Alyosha patiently brings the boys to empathise and support Ilyusha in his trial, and his noble example inspires them to passionate active love, showing the way towards drawing good out of such an evil state of affairs. In the end, at the boy's funeral, he urges Ilyusha's young friends to always remember the noble selfless love of Ilyusha, the dark tragedy of the boy's life, and their united sensitivity and love for him. And, consistent with his antithesis of theodicy, this tension between the rational doubts of theodicy and active love and mysticism, Dostoevsky closes this chapter, and the book, with Alyosha's testimonial of faith to them:

> "Certainly we shall rise again, certainly we shall see each other and shall tell each other with joy and gladness all that has happened!" Alyosha answered, *half laughing, half ecstatic.* (p. 735)[54]

INNOCENT SUFFERING AND REBIRTH

Two key elements in the structure of mystical theodicy have surfaced in these last two chapters. Both Eckhart and Dostoevsky propose mystical theistic teleologies that illustrate the beneficence of the Divine in emphasising God's immanence in His creation. Both thinkers claim that this beneficence can be effectively realised in mystical experience, issuing forth in a profound consolation and theodical evidence or the assurance thereof. Moreover, the consolatory power of mystical experience is stressed in both theodicies without thereby downplaying or eliminating the force and reality of evil.

Freedom is another essential element of mystical theodicy. Dostoevsky shows the importance of freedom for any personalist philosophy. To deny freedom, or inhibit it, is to devalue, to eliminate the possibility of dignity of the individual person. Without freedom, human beings could be given neither credit nor criticism, they could be neither hated nor loved *in themselves*. This is the negative moral argument that Dostoevsky raises against those who would deny or take away the freedom necessary to this theodicy. So Dostoevsky's defence against the critique of theodicy is not solely non-rational.

But the problem of theodicy does not rest exclusively in its conception of freedom. The problems arise in considering the evil consequences of freedom and human nature in combination with the teleological pictures mystical theodicies propose. Dostoevsky proposes that freedom and the darker side of human nature are necessary for a person's spiritual growth to the religious ideal. Presumably, Eckhart has the same idea but he does not explicitly delve into this question of theodicy. Dostoevsky is uncomfortable with the obvious moral elitism at play in such a view, the fact that most people seem unfit to participate fully, or even at all, in this religious process. Many are unjustifiably crushed under the heavy burden of freedom, innocent victims of the suffering that arises in moral freedom. In this theodicy these people can, at best, only be understood as vehicles of compassion for the religious elite, as a spiritual means for the strong. Such a conclusion runs against Dostoevsky's deep moral sensitivity, and his dissatisfaction with it poses an intriguing paradox: the spiritual vehicle in the logic of theodicy, that is, moral compassion and empathy arising in and from active love, is that which gives force to his critique of theodicy!

But the main moral problem for theodicy is clearly expressed in Ivan's example of the suffering innocent child who tragically dies. The child's participation in the teleological process is brought to an abrupt end in suffering that is unexpiated in terms of the child. Justifying such an event in terms of the child's role as instrument is morally unacceptable. But what else would count as expiation in this instance? How do you reasonably justify the suffering of the innocent? For Dostoevsky and Eckhart, it is in terms of the future spiritual harmony; moral evils arise in human freedom, which is a feature necessary to human development towards such harmony. But what can you say against the moral criticism that innocent blood goes unexpiated? These people are unfit for the process, and unjustifiably cease to participate in this human development that justifies freedom and evil.

Given the religious teleologies of these thinkers, I would suggest that though expiation of these experiences is impossible here the evil might nevertheless be morally justified. It would require that the suffering innocents not be ultimately removed from the religious teleology, but that they be given the chance in a reincarnation[55] to bear this black mark in a positive manner, a chance to refuse to succumb to religious doubt in their misery, and the chance to pursue in active personal love the hard path to religious truth. This view, which I will develop in detail in Chapter 10, does not entail that the innocent be regarded as deserving of their suffering, nor that in every case the suffering be considered necessary to their spiritual development; hence it does not expiate the suffering of the innocent. But it does give a morally sound account of evil. If the innocent be understood as given fair chance to participate in the religious process – the opportunity to overcome their terrible experience of the minus side of human nature and the negative effects of freedom – then their trials need not be understood as utterly meaningless. If such were guaranteed it would constitute a rational response to those who, perceiving freedom as in many cases unpracticable and certain suffering as unexpiated, criticise theodicy on moral grounds. The suffering of the innocent is not explained as deserved; but the fact that the suffering innocent do not experience a final death, that they have the opportunity to transform these experiences into something more positive, to continue the spiritual journey towards the religious ideal, removes the force of the criticisms raised against the innocent suffering that occurs through evil. This kind of explanation gives credibility to the mystical theodical evidence espoused by the mystic authority, for the theodicy can no longer be criticised on moral grounds.

Because Dostoevsky does not move towards this kind of explanation, however, his theodicy possesses a pronounced antithesis between theodicy acceptance and rejection. In his view the 'harmony', the 'secret', the 'hosannah' possesses a mysterious reconciliation of our moral sense with the higher spiritual light. In this view we cannot understand how freedom is justified in those instances where individuals are unable, through no fault of their own, to handle such responsibility, and where the innocent suffer needlessly and tragically. Still, he thinks one can gain a confidence and assurance of the truth and reality of religious teleology. The spiritual vision of the mystical experience holds the dark mystery of the justification of the incredible suffering and evils that arise from our darker side and our freedom. This reconciliation remains unintelligible in Dostoevsky's eyes. He thinks one ought to pursue the personal active love and compassion that is pictured in his religious ideal, that one might thereby be rewarded in his or her efforts with a profound mystical experience verifying theodicy; nevertheless without such a realisation experienced first-hand, one must, in light of the great horrors of the human predicament, reasonably wonder if the price of the ideal is not too high to pay.

This price is compounded in Dostoevsky's view of the Devil. For there is in his view a good–evil polarity fundamental to human nature that must be explained in theodicy. Eckhart in his theodicy does not answer the question of this darker side of human beings; though he speaks of human nature as fallen and sinful he does not explain how or why such might occur. In so far as he considers a fall from likeness as necessitating a kind of 'recovery' of likeness, his theodicy gives rise to the problematic questions of how and why God created perfect creatures that fall from perfection.

But perhaps the more important questions are: why are people so inclined and drawn towards that realm of nothingness beyond the appropriate good to which they should naturally be ordered?; why is the darker side necessary to the teleological goal?; and from where does this sinfulness, this inherent impulse to evil derive? Indeed, though this nothingness does not arise out of the good, the impetus towards it certainly does. Is not God then responsible for evil? Does not the evil impulse arise in God's fundamental creative act? The answers to these questions constitute our third feature in the structure of mystical theodicy. Indeed, these questions, along with issues surrounding natural evil, cause the most difficult and significant problems for theodicy; how to explain the source of the rebellious and turbulent moral nature of human beings without thereby attributing responsibility to God. For a most provocative and insightful response to these questions we turn now to Jacob Boehme.

9

The Origin of Evil in Human Nature: Jacob Boehme's *Ungrund*

And he said, That which cometh out of the man, that defileth the man. For from within, out of the heart of men, proceed evil thoughts, adulteries, fornications, murders, thefts, covetousness, wickedness, deceit, lasciviousness, an evil eye, blasphemy, pride, foolishness: all these evil things come from within and defile the man. (Mark 7:20–23)

As we saw in Chapter 2, Ivan Karamazov suggests that if the Devil is but a creation of human beings, he is actualised in their image and likeness. The reference above from the Gospel of Mark looks for the source of such actualisation in the very heart of human beings. In Mark we find the suggestion that evil arises from the essence of human nature, that there exists in human nature an impulse to evil quite distinct from the influence of the external environment.

This view implies a fundamental polarity at play in the moral essence of human nature. In autonomy human beings are situated in moral struggle where good and evil are equally potential. In terms of religious teleology, the growth or destruction of the moral and spiritual self is at stake; the human being can choose the path of the good, subordinating, in Kant's words, the incentives to physical and practical self-love to that of personality (see Chapter 5), or she or he can reverse the ordination and thereby actualise the evil principle of this essential moral realm and inhibit spiritual growth.

Now this kind of egoistic-personalistic moral framework is not uncommon among moral theorists, though the details and terms of reference vary.[1] In a religious context the theme of free-will is often incorporated within this framework in the explanation

143

and justification of moral evil. In the attempt to distance God's responsibility from the evil actions of human beings, moral evil is thought to arise in human freedom. But in the traditional free-will defence we do not usually find the issue of the impulse to evil in human nature addressed.

However this is a fundamental issue that an effective theodicy ought to address. We must ask not only for the rationale of freedom but also about the nature and reasons for the darker side of human nature, a negative aspect that can become very pronounced and dominant. Human beings possess what seems to be a very strong and dangerous impulse to evil, one that can take such radical and destructive forms that we must ask, with Ivan and the Grand Inquisitor, if freedom is really worth the price we must pay. How and why are freedom and the negative aspects of human nature necessary to the spiritual teleology? And, indeed, how are we to distance the darker side of human nature from God?

Certain mystics, as we saw briefly in Chapter 5, claim an apophatic experience of that which precedes the active, creative and personal Divine. This experience uncovers a feature that constitutes the third element in our structure of mystical theodicy, a chasm of darkness in the eternal theogonic process that explains and justifies the origin of evil in human nature while at the same time distancing evil from the personal Divine. Perhaps the most insightful and well-developed exposition of this theodical view is offered by Jacob Boehme (1575–1624).

Boehme, who is most noted as a mystic,[2] was very sensitive to the questions and problems associated with the theology of his German Lutheranism. Though a shoemaker by trade, he wrote a number of influential[3] philosophical and theological treatises where he gives a great deal of attention to the problems of theodicy. Still, he remains a rather enigmatic figure in the history of philosophy, and somewhat neglected in recent time. This neglect can perhaps be attributed in part to the esoteric nature of his writings. Boehme's thought is often hidden behind a fantastic symbolism of magic, astrology and alchemy.

In order to properly outline the nature and significance of this mystical account of the origin of evil, we must provide a rather detailed exposition of Boehme's abstruse theology. We must first examine closely Boehme's theogonic picture as he presents it in the recondite imagery of alchemy and the natural forces, before drawing the view into our structure of mystical theodicy later in the chapter.

The problem of evil is a major concern of Boehme; he returns to this issue again and again,[4] and it is the primary theme of his comprehensive theological treatise, *The Three Principles of the Divine Essence*.[5] Here he examines the nature of the Trinity, heaven, hell, creation, incarnation and humankind, in the context of the problem of evil. Indeed, it is in his conception of the three principles of the Divine Essence that his theodicy has its coherence. He himself refers to the book as one of his major works, as 'a key and alphabet for all those who desire to understand my writings'.[6] This alphabet, however, is sometimes obscured in the alchemist imagery of the text.[7] Still, his theodicy is well formulated in this work, and can be clarified in reference to *Six Theosophic Points*.[8] This latter text, composed after *The Three Principles*, gives more of a summary account of the origin and nature of the three principles, and is considered by Boehme as also very important in understanding his thought. He says, this book 'is the six points, treating . . . how the three principles do mutually beget, bring forth, and bear each other out . . . it is key to all'.[9]

Boehme most clearly formulates the problem of evil in Chapter 4 of *The Three Principles*. He says:

> Here open your noble mind, see and search further. Seeing God is only good, from whence comes the Evil? And seeing also that he alone is the Life, and the Light, and the holy Power, as it is undeniably true, from whence comes the Anger of God? From whence comes the Devil and his [evil] will? Also Hell-fire, from whence hath that its Original? Seeing there was nothing before the Time of this World, but only God, who was and is a Spirit, and continues so in Eternity: From whence then is the first *Materia*, or Matter of Evil? For Reason gives this Judgement, that there must needs have been in the Spirit of God a will to generate the Source or Fountain of Anger.
>
> But now the scripture saith, *The Devil was a holy Angel*. And further, it saith, *Thou art not a God that willeth evil*. And in *Ezekial*, *As sure as I live, I will not the Death of a Sinner*. (4.33–34)[10]

In this passage Boehme denies any spirit–matter dualism in his account of evil. There is no primordial matter by which God creates, but only spirit alone. God as spirit is the eternal singular source of all life. Moreover, Boehme regards God as solely good. So the problem becomes clear: from where does the evil of the world derive? Presumably it must originate in the will of God. But this, he says, does not explain the Devil's fall and it contradicts scripture. Nevertheless, as we will see, Boehme does in a qualified sense locate the source of evil in the will of God. This is the first principle of the Divine Essence, a principle that despite being essential to God is *not*, Boehme insists, to be properly understood as God, nor as standing over and against God. To unravel Boehme's answer to the problem of evil, then, we should begin in examination of this first principle of the Divine Essence.

THE FIRST PRINCIPLE: THE *UNGRUND*

Boehme incorporates a rather wide variety of images in reference to the first principle. It is 'the Original', 'the Mother', conceived as the origin of good and evil, and of love and anger (1.4). It is also 'the Father' himself (4.45), in contrast to the second principle ('Word') and the third principle ('Spirit'). This first principle is the source of the essence of God and of all things. The principle is the *Ungrund*, the unground, that which precedes the creative aspect of God, and which is perhaps best described simply as primary Will, though it is impossible to characterise fully or properly. Boehme speaks of a mystical knowledge of the *Ungrund*, the comprehension by the *Spiraculum Vitae* (Spirit of the Soul) of the Divine Essence, but such an insight 'cannot be wholly expressed by the Tongue' (2.1). And, indeed, the eternal Godhead is beginningless and thus not properly distinguished in terms of three essences. Nevertheless Boehme insists that these aspects of God can be distinguished for purposes of theodicy (1.4) and that the Essence can be made intelligible to some degree through natural imagery.

Boehme presents the three principles largely in terms of alchemy and the natural forces. Again, it is important to keep in mind that Boehme is attempting to convey a mysterious mystical experience through alchemist imagery. Like Eckhart he emphasises feminine images of motherhood and birthing. He says that 'a Principle is nothing else but a new Birth, a new Life' (5.6). The first principle is the source of this birthing. But Boehme explains it in terms of alchemy, as MERCURIUS, and the PHUR of SULPHUR. As PHUR, the first principle is the *prima materia*, or the 'Essence of the most inward Birth, out of which God generates or begets His Son from Eternity, and from thence the Holy Ghost proceeds' (2.7). It is essentially nothing, but must be understood as a power or virtue or potentiality to essentialness. It is that through which Spirit and the natural world is generated. He describes the process as follows:

> In the first Principle (as I have mentioned above) is Harshness, Bitterness, and Fire; and yet they are not three Things, but only one Thing, and they one generate another. Harshness is the first Father, which is strong, (fierce or tart) very sharp and attracting to itself; and that Attracting is the (Sting) or Prickle, or Bitterness, which the Harshness cannot endure, and it will not be captivated in Death, but rises and flies up like a strong fierce Substance, and yet cannot remove from off its Place: And there is a horrible Anguish, which finds no Rest: and the Birth is like a turning Wheel, pulling so very hard, and breaking or bruising, as it were furiously, which the Harshness cannot endure, but attracts continually more and more, harder and harder; as when Steel and Flint are struck one against another, from which the twinkling Flash of Fire proceeds. (1.49)

The process expressed in the alchemist imagery of PHUR and MERCURIUS in this passage is vivid. PHUR is the first matter, the harshness (astringency) that acts as prime mover. MERCURIUS includes this harshness, along with bitterness and fire. In harshness there occurs a contraction that generates desire, a craving for self-creation that Boehme describes as magical (1.11).[12] This desire is an attraction that, given the primary uncaused nature of harshness, works only upon itself; as a consequence it is characterised by a bitterness, a bitter sting or prickle wherein the harsh desire only encounters its cold, hard and sharp self. In *Six Theosophic Points* Boehme describes this harsh desire as

> a stern attracting, like an eternal elevation or motion. For it draws itself into itself, and makes itself pregnant, so that from this freedom where there is nothing a darkness is produced. For the desiring will becomes by the drawing-in thick and full, although there is nothing but darkness.[13]

This process constitutes the lower triad of Boehme's metaphysical picture. As Will, this harshness desires to create, thus it attempts

to move out of its dark self. But it encounters only itself. Its movement is pictured as a dark circular motion of anguish. Harshness
swings to bitterness as it attempts to move above itself, and it
rises in a circular motion like a wheeling: 'it cannot rise higher
than its Seat, but is thus continually generated from beneath,
therefore it falleth into a Turning or Wheeling' (2.8). Boehme thus
shifts his imagery of the first principle to that of a wheel of a
fire-clock that strikes the burning fire of anguish in its circular
motion, not like a burning fire, but likened to a fire in stone
(1.10). Will desires to give birth, to manifest itself, but does not
possess properties to do so (1.52). In its turning, Will creates the
non-substantial harshness, bitterness, fire and brimstone water
that stands as essence of *all* life – it is the essentialness of all
things. As Boehme says, 'These four Forms are in the Originality
of Nature, and from thence the Mobility exists, as also the Life in
the Seed, and in all the Creatures, has its Original from thence'
(1.13). In this regard Boehme likens it to a mirror, an object that
contains an image but cannot retain it. With respect to nature,
this fundamental Will 'hides' the image of all forms. In itself the
mirror is a clear brightness, a non-essential nothing, but it has the
potential to reflect all forms, all life. Yet, like a mirror, it is not the
image that it reflects; it is *not* that which it reflects, for it is without
essentiality.[14] Referring to this Will as the *Ungrund*, Boehme says:

> It is the unground, and yet sees all, all has been hidden in it from
> eternity, and therefrom it has its seeing. But it is not essential, as
> in the mirror the brightness is not essential, which yet embraces
> all that appears before it.[15]

Continuing with this imagery of sight and mirror, Boehme
describes his Will as a spirit that reveals itself in its sight. Boehme
thinks that it is in sight that a will is moulded, and that all seeing
requires a ground of sight, a source or object of sight. But given
the groundlessness of this Will of the *Ungrund* it finds no ground
nor limit to see. It needs a grounding that it can only find in itself:
'hence its mirror goeth into itself and makes a ground in itself,
that is a will'.[16] Boehme goes on to describe it as the finder that
encounters nothing, as that which 'goes forth again from the centre
of the ground, and seeks in the will'.[17] So this process of the first
principle is one that is characterised by a vitality, a dynamism of
movement wherein the Will, in itself, finds 'no ground where it

might rest',[18] nor stability. It is ever involved in a circular motion of self-seeing. It is an ever-seeking Will for a ground that, in itself, only encounters its groundless self.

It is thus an ever-frustrated volatile process of Will aptly characterised as the negative MERCURIUS. It is a necessary principle of life for without it there would be only a static nothingness. But on the other hand, Boehme refers to it as dark and malicious. He says: 'it is a poysonous or venemous, hostile or enimicitious Thing: And it must be so, or else there would be no Mobility, but all [would be as] nothing, and the Source of Wrath or Anger is the first Original of Nature' (1.13).

Thus MERCURIUS is the energy or driving force behind nature. It is the dynamism and vitality of the natural processes. Nevertheless, in itself MERCURIUS is but a nothingness. It has no quality, number or substance; it is without essence and is lifeless. Having 'no feeling, understanding nor substantiality',[19] Boehme likens it to a shadow. But in terms of God, Boehme refers to MERCURIUS as His wrathful, vengeful, angry and jealous aspects (1.8). It is thus the cause, though not a sufficient cause, of the dark and negative features of the natural world. It is the source of evil (1.8), and the domain of the anger of God (4.23). Yet it is not in itself God: 'God is not called God according to the first Principle' (1.8). Rather it is but a feature of God, the impetus behind the creative force of the Divine. Boehme refers to it as 'the driving of the essences'.[20] He says: 'The first Principle lies in the fire of the will, and is a cause of the two others (Principles), also of life and understanding: and is an upholding of Nature, as well as all the properties of the Father'.[21]

The first principle is the will-to-life of God. Without this principle there could be no God, spirit or natural world. It is the dynamism of the Divine Essence, and as such Boehme speaks of it as preceding and as the cause, though not sufficient, of the other two principles of the Divine Essence. For Boehme speaks of this principle as inseparable from 'the Word' and 'the Spirit'; Boehme defines God as the Father (Will), the Son (Word) and the Spirit (Love), and he stresses the nothingness of the *Ungrund* apart from the second two principles of the Divine Essence.[22] But in nature and human beings, however, this Will is distinguished and distinguishable from the soul and spirit. In moral terms Boehme describes this Will as a terrible evil: 'The dark world is called death and hell, the abyss, a sting of death, despair, self-enmity and sorrowfulness; a life of malice and falsehood, in which the truth and the light is not seen and is not known'.[23]

To better illustrate this origin of evil in human nature let us return to the fire imagery of MERCURIUS. As I pointed out earlier, Boehme depicts the harshness and bitterness of the first principle to lead to the fire of the fire-wheel, painfully turning itself in its unsatisfied desire. Boehme understands this point as the boundary mark between the amoral and the moral, the moment when the good–evil dialectic comes into play. Boehme says:

> there is the dividing-bound mark of spirit, there it is born. It is now free. It may by its imagination go back again into its mother the dark world, or, going forward, sink down in the anguish of fire into death, and bud forth in the light. That depends on its choice. Where it yields up itself, there it must be; for its fire must have substance, that it may have something to feed upon.[24]

Herein freedom surfaces in the process. Boehme considers the centre of the mind to be free. Spirit can remain within itself, in imagination, thereby swinging back into the dark abyss of harshness, bitterness and fire. Or, its imagination can die to the fire, and thereby move in transformation to the spiritual realm of the Word, the domain of real freedom. Either way, the fire needs fuel, and the fuel is that which determines the property of the fire. In the former case the darkness itself becomes the fuel. The Devil stands as exemplar in this move to evil. Boehme pictures him as self-willing against freedom in God, as substituting the strength of the fire for the light of the Word. Boehme says:

> for his [the Devil's] bitter Sting in the Birth climbs up thus eternally in the Source of the Fire, and affords him a proud Will to have all [at his Pleasure] but he attains nothing; his Food is the Source of Water, *viz.* the Brimstone Spirit, which is the most aking Mother. (4.71)

The Devil thus consists of a lightless fire; his source is the fearsome abyss where the fire 'burns in the dark, harsh, stern source, and sees in itself as a flash; it has the mirror of darkness, and sees in the darkness'.[25] The fire of the first principle, the *Ungrund*, is lightless. It is likened to the fire in a stone. It is the source of light, but only potentially so; it is a necessary but not a sufficient condition for light. For light, the fire requires a fuel external to itself, a fuel that Boehme expresses in the image of SUL of SULPHUR of the second principle.

THE SECOND AND THIRD PRINCIPLES: THE WORD AND LOVE

Up to this point I have concentrated upon the first principle of the Divine Essence in order to make clear the nature of the primary Will, the *Ungrund*, the abyss of nothingness that stands as source of evil. In dwelling upon this first principle I have only given one side of Boehme's explanation of evil. His theodicy only becomes coherent in the context of all three principles. Indeed, Boehme generally speaks of the first and second principles together. Though he distinguishes fairly clearly between the effects of these two principles, he does not always dissect the principles themselves in a clear and precise manner. But this is not surprising. For he understands God as eternal (beginningless and endless), and the essences of God (Father, Son and Spirit) as indistinguishable.[26] God does not undergo the movement from the first to the second principle and, as a consequence, to the third, but He *is* these principles eternally. Thus there is no substantial *Ungrund* standing over and against God, or preceding God, and it is important to keep in mind that Boehme's 'God' is neither the first nor the second principles in themselves, and is always positive, personal and active.

As we pointed out, the two principles, in themselves, are as nothing. Independently they constitute Boehme's apophatic theology, the negative, non-personal Divine. Thus Berdyaev perceives a similarity between Boehme's *Ungrund* and Eckhart's Godhead, the completely abstract absolute that 'escapes all worldly analogies, affinities, dynamism'.[27] It is also important to mention that Berdyaev recognises a theogonic process common to the mysticisms of Eckhart and Boehme. Both mystics maintain that the absolute, non-personal, passive Divine that lies behind and beyond the active personal God can be realised in mystical experience; indeed, Eckhart argues that such an experience is imperative to religious teleology. This suggests that there is an inner birthing of the Divine. As Berdyaev says, 'It appears, therefore, that there is in eternity a theogonic process, a Divine Genesis'.[28]

Boehme incorporates the image of SULPHUR to illustrate this divine genesis. As I have pointed out, PHUR symbolises the first principle. SUL stands as the second principle in Boehme's alchemist picture. It symbolises 'God the Son, or the Heart, the eternal Power and Virtue' (7.22). It is the spirit of substance, that which gives quality and property to the Will of the first principle. In terms of the brimstone fire of the first principle, it is the kindling (1.6nh) and the water brought to MERCURIUS. It is the fuel which gives light to the potentiality of the *Ungrund*, that which reacts with the brimstone in the yielding of the fire to the light of the Divine. Like the first principle of the Divine Essence, it is only properly encountered in mystical experience, and Boehme similarly incorporates the figurative illustration of alchemy in his attempt to describe it:

> For the Harshness is as hard as a Stone (or Flint) and the Bitterness rushes and rages like a breaking Wheel, which breaks the Harshness, and stirs up the Fire so that all comes to be a terrible Crack of Fire, and flies up; and the Harshness or Astringency breaks in Pieces, whereby the dark Tartness is terrified and sinks back, and becomes as it were feeble or weak, or as if it were killed and dead, and runs out, becomes thin, and yields itself to be overcome: But when the strong Flash of Fire shines back again upon or into the Tartness, and is mingled therein, and finds the Harshness so thin and overcome, then it is much more terrified; for it is as if Water were thrown upon the Fire, which makes a Crack: Yet when the Crack or Terror is thus made in the overcome Harshness, thereby it gets another Source (Condition or Property,) and a Crack, or Noise of great Joy, proceeds out of the wrathful Fierceness, and rises up in fierce Strength, as a kindled Light. (2.9)

The harshness of PHUR contracts in the diffusion of bitterness sending the primal source into a wild oscillation, agitating itself into a great crack of fire. In this flash, harshness splinters and sinks into the fire, weakened, thereby allowing the external light of the SUL to enter into the realm of darkness. The process here corresponds to that noted earlier regarding the dying/yielding of the spiritual Will to the light of the Divine, and this light is the Word, Virtue or Power of the second principle. We will turn more directly to this aspect of the Divine Essence in a moment. But here it is important to note that the crack of fire thus brings light to the brimstone spirit, as it enters into the first principle and transforms its propertyless features according to the divine nature. This incoming light to the fire expands, sweetens and softens the dark source of being, like the sun melting ice (4.49). The brimstone fire then transforms to a bright burning in the darkness, abandoning, in freedom, the primary Will for the power, joy and love of the divine life. This completes the process of the first two principles, wherein PHUR and SUL become SULPHUR, naturally springing forth in the Holy Spirit and eventually the natural world of substance. Boehme draws the picture together:

> So now a Spirit is nothing else but a Springing Will, and in the Will there is Anguish to the Birth, and in the Anguish the Fire generates itself, and in the Fire the Light, and from the Light the Will becomes friendly, pleasant, mild and sweet, and in the sweet Will the Kingdom and the Glory generates itself. (8.20)

So Boehme associates the Kingdom of God with the third principle. But this association begins with the notion of the Holy Spirit as Love. The third principle is that which properly depicts God as a personal and creative being – it is that which manifests the eternal Deity (5.6). Thus it explains the origin and telos of creatures and the natural world. In this regard love is the fundamental property of this third principle:

> The Propagation of the Love is most especially to be observed, for it is the loveliest, pleasantest, and sweetest Fountain of all. When the Love generates again a whole Birth, with all the Fountains of the original Essences out of itself, so that the Love in all the springing Veins in that new Birth is predominant and chief . . . (3.17)

This is the fundamental telos of Boehme's conception of the Divine Essence. Out of the first and second Principles is generated the Holy Spirit or Love. In the Son–Father conjunction the Will of the first principle is transformed from its negative mode into the positive and creative mode associated with the third principle. Love is generated in this transformation, a love that by its very nature entails a birthing, the process of creation of distinctive creatures for its realisation. The highest quality of the Divine Essence, the seventh form, requires for its fulfilment the birth of creatures who participate in the divine life:

> and in the whole Birth it is as a Growing or Multiplying in one Will; and the Birth attains here the seventh Form, *viz.* the Multiplication into an Essence of Love. And in this Form consists Paradise, or the Kingdom of God, or the numberless divine Birth, out of one only Essence, into all Essences. (4.53)

In the first and second principles we find the third, that principle which Boehme describes as issuing forth in the world and human life and which relates this creation to the Divine Essence. The Trinity requires for its realisation participants of relationship. Such is the nature of Love. God generates the third principle so 'that he might be manifested by the material world' (5.16). The third principle is associated by Boehme with 'the Beginning and Birth of this World' (5.8), but the substance and energy of the natural world derives from the first principle, and its power and direction originates from the second principle.

Boehme is heavily influenced by Paracelsus and Sebastien Frank in what is a very obscure account of material creation.[29] But it is important for us to note that the material world consists of the three fundamental qualities of the first principle: fire, bitterness and harshness, that out of which all things are generated (4.32), via the creative power of the Word, Light and Virtue of the second principle (8.17). Though the dynamic energy and differentiation occurring in the creative process is associated with the first principle, and the rationale for creation is found in the third principle, Boehme describes the second principle as the source of power and direction to creation through the creative Word. The material world is thus the similitude of the paradisiacal world and God is present therein. Moreover, human beings are created in similitude of the three principles of the Divine Essence.

But this is to jump ahead a bit in Boehme's cosmological picture. In the Divine Essence there is first born a spiritual paradise, a realm or realms of spiritual beings that emanate forth from the third principle. It is here, in paradise, that the problem of evil arises, for from this beatific state falls the Devil and his legions. Paradise was manifested in the third principle so that angels and spirits might participate in the love therein, so that they 'could thereby understand the eternal Birth in the third Principle' (5.16).

They are born out of the first and second principles and are thus the similitude of this Divine Essence. But their fall is explained through the first principle. In the autonomy that resides in primary Will the Devil and his legions choose against the second principle. Rather than submitting their will to the external light of SUL they choose the darkness of the self-generating fire: 'but they cast their Imagination back into themselves, and formed (or created) a Will (or Purpose) in the Matrix, to domineer in the Fire over the Light of God and Paradise' (5.25). So they distance themselves from the second and third principles. In self-willing they cannot experience the Word and Love. So they set themselves against the processes of the Divine Essence, and remain outside and apart from the divine life. Boehme pictures these beings as eternally cast out by God; for they stood in paradise, fully experienced the Word, yet rejected it. Thus they do not participate in the second and third principles but remain eternally immersed in the harsh anguish of the *Ungrund*.

But the fulfilment of the Divine Essence entails the realisation of the third principle. Despite the Devil's fall, 'the Purpose of God must stand' (8.4), and so we have the generation of the material world and human beings for the sake of the third principle. Now at this point in his theology Boehme attempts to synthesise the Christian fall myth with his views of the three principles of the Divine Essence. The result is a rather obscure theology that appears somewhat contradictory.[30] However, a coherent and simplified version of his fall myth might run as follows.

A realm of temptation is necessary to secure against the Devil's fall, a domain where creatures can be tried and assisted towards the Kingdom of God. Adam was created and placed in paradise to be tempted. In his fall he was removed to this temporal material world (the temporary 'matrix' or 'nature' in contrast to the eternal 'matrix') whereby the grace of God could actively guide him back to his original perfect image (11.26). Boehme explains:

And this was the Purpose of God, therefore to create but one Man, that the same might be tempted, [and tried] how he would stand, and that upon his fall he might the better be helped: And the Heart of God did before the Foundation of the World in his Love before intend [or predetermine] to come to help [him]; and when no other Remedy could do it, the Heart of God himself would become Man, and regenerate Man again. (11.25)

Humankind, then, is created in similitude of the three principles of the Divine Essence. Boehme associates the rational aspect of the soul with the darkness of the Will in so far as it desires light. That is, he associates the active processes of consciousness – consideration and perception – with the Father. The light within by which one orders one's life and knows the virtue is like the Word or Son of God, and that which arises from this inner light and directs the body, as well as that which gives vitality and substance to the body, is like the Holy Spirit (7.22–3).[31] So human beings are of material, temporal and distinctive natures, and they possess a dark and negative will that has the active potentiality in freedom and grace to transform itself, through the light of the Word, into the love and joy of the divine relationship of the Kingdom of God. But there is also the potentiality in this freedom of the dark will to prop self-will up as the centre and foundation, to abandon the meekness and humility necessary to this spiritual teleology. So Boehme stresses the importance of the fall myth as it applies to *all* persons of this natural world: 'in thyself thou shall find the Tree of the Temptation, and also the Will to have it, which made it spring up; yea, the Source (Lust or Quality) whence it sprung up, stands in thee, and not in God . . . (10.29)'.

BOEHME'S THEODICY

Boehme's theodicy has a strong teleological emphasis. Like Eckhart's view, Boehme's theodicy is much like John Hick's soul-making conception of the Irenaean formulation, where the fall is viewed as a mythic portrayal of humankind's condition on the hard road to soul-making perfection. Nevertheless, Boehme's theodicy possesses important differences, variations that hinge upon his view of the Divine Essence.

As we saw in Chapter 5, Hick understands the world as a stage for soul-making, a realm where human beings have been established in a state of relative self-centredness so that they might not be coerced to growth in likeness to God. To this end, they have been created free beings. Evils of the natural world are understood as impetus to such development, and moral evils arise in the autonomy of human beings. The possibility of moral evil is in this view necessary; Hick believes that if human beings were restricted from moral transgression they could never participate in an 'authentic' relationship with God. He says that freedom makes one 'good in a richer and more valuable sense than would be one created *ab initio* in a state either of innocence or of virtue'.[32]

In Hick's version, then, 'fall' is rather a misnomer. Human beings are not understood as falling from a relationship with God in paradise but as established in immaturity in this natural world.[33] The emphasis is on the freedom of human beings in a state of moral immaturity. Boehme's analysis goes a bit deeper, uncovering a fundamental impulse to evil that is intertwined with the very notion of the Divine Essence. Like Hick, Boehme stresses the teleological theme arising from the fall myth, but in contrast he sees human beings as falling in paradise to temptation. Adam is understood as in very great risk in his paradisiacal state, as very much *inclined* towards rejecting the relationship with God. In Hick's version the emphasis is on the freedom of human beings in a state of moral immaturity.

In maintaining a premise of moral immaturity, however, Hick distances evil from God; for God does not create moral evil, human beings do. Boehme, in establishing a fundamental impulse to evil in human nature, raises the question of God's connection to evil. Indeed, God has created human beings. Is he thus not the source of this dark impulse inherent in human nature? In establishing the first principle, the *Ungrund*, as the source of evil in human nature, does not Boehme thereby place the ground of evil in God?

Yet Boehme considers God to be solely good, good in such a strict sense that He could not do evil even as a necessary means to a good end. Rather, Boehme places the source of evil in the *Ungrund*, the primary Will, the dynamic source of desire, motion and substance. This first principle of the Divine Essence is a potential power to substantial being; it is that out of which arises the forces of the natural world and human will, the sources of evil in this temporal realm.[34] Moral evil arises in the process of self-willing, the propping up of the individual will which places the human being outside of and against the ontological order of their divine teleology. But, Boehme argues, this first principle in itself is not God. For outside of the second principle of the Divine Essence it is nothing, and inside the Divine Essence it is wholly transfigured. In God this primary Will is transformed by the second principle into the power, joy and love of the divine life. Its harsh and bitter forces are transformed into positive activities in the divine light, thus extinguishing any potential to evil. In God, the first principle is not a source of evil but a source of love and life. Therefore, Boehme argues, God is solely good, possessing not a trace of evil. In God Boehme does not find a good–evil dualism; there is no moral bipolar nature in God.

It is in the fulfilment of the Divine Essence that we uncover evil, however. When we consider the role of human beings in the Divine Essence we find a moral bipolarity, for there is in God that which, if separated out by a creature, is evil. God, as the transformed first principle in the second, issues forth in the third – the power, joy and love of the divine life. However, the second principle is such that it requires the first principle as source of the creative processes of the third principle. The second principle is in itself a static unity, a non-generative light, and a passive oneness. It cannot in itself give rise to the plurality and activity of relation that is inherent to the third principle. In this regard Boehme comments:

> Now the Question is, May not the Mind stand in one only Will, (*viz.* in mere love) like God himself? Here sticks the Mark, the Ground, and the Knowledge: Behold, if the Will were in one only Essence, then the mind would also have but one Quality that could give the Will to be so, and it should be an immovable Thing, which should always lie still, and should do no more but that one Thing always: In it there would be no Joy, no Knowledge, also no Art or Skill of any Thing at all, and there would be no Wisdom in it also if the quality were not *in infinitum*, it would be altogether a Nothing, and there would be no Mind nor Will to any Thing at all (10.35).

The fulfilment of the third principle requires the existence of conscious, active and independent beings, beings who possess an individual will, desire and freedom. So there occurs an 'Out-Birth [generated] out of the Darknesse by the Virtue of the Light' (7.21). And in this out-birth is born the human being in similitude of the three principles of the Divine Essence, possessing the will and desire of the first principle, and the potential in freedom to transform this dark source of will by the light of the second principle, into the power, joy and love of the divine life.

So, although evil does not exist in God, it does arise in God's creative processes. But this is not to say that it arises out of a primordial good–evil dualism. Boehme says: 'God created all Things out of Nothing, but only out of Himself; and yet the Out-Birth is not from his Essence, [or Substance,] but it has its Original from the Darkness' (7.21). Though evil is to be found in an aspect of the Divine Essence, God's essence is not evil; the first principle is utterly transformed in God. Nevertheless, human beings are not God. Rather, they are to become like God; the human telos involves the autonomous transformation of this first principle.

Thus Boehme recognises God's indirect responsibility for evil. Although evil does not derive from God, Boehme maintains that it is God who creates human beings, and He is omniscient. But without the first and third principles the creative power of God is severely limited. The second principle of the Divine Essence is not, in itself, a generative power. Boehme refers to the first and third principles as the generative powers of God (10.36), the forces that emanate the dynamism of the plurality of being, where in the actualisation of love the creative spirit might spring forth in joyful, active, relational activity of a positive nature. So in separating evil from God Boehme places limitations on the omnipotence of the Divine. The fulfilment of the third principle requires that God allow the human being, in freedom, to play out the dark aspects of the primary Will that is essential to the dynamic creativity of human life. But this negative Will finds its actualisation in the creative forces of nature as well as in human nature. Indeed, God could not create a natural world that is potentially less evil or more good. Although natural evils can be construed as features conducive to the actualisation of Boehme's mystical telos, Boehme maintains that God is limited in material creation in terms of the creative power of the first principle, leading to a kind of blind creative dynamism at work in the forces of nature, as if the natural world is involved in the seeking for the divine light like that which is depicted of human nature. There is in Boehme's thought, then, the sense that though God could intervene in the forces of nature for the better, he could not create a material world without the blind creative dynamism that is associated with the first principle of the Divine Essence. Our world is the *only* world God could create as a soul-making environment. This places limitations on divine omnipotence by supposing an external constraint upon divine providence.[35]

This issue will reappear later, but for now it is important to note that for Boehme, God could not improve on either the creative dynamism within nature nor the fundamental moral chemistry of

human nature. God could not eliminate evil without also eliminating this dynamic world and human beings. So God allows the
evils of the natural world and human beings in order that human
beings can, in the experience of this negative foil, submit their
dark will to the higher light of the second principle, and thereby
participate in the divine life of God. Boehme says that God

> brings himself out of himself into a divisibility, into *centra*, in
> order that a contrariety may arise in the emanation, *viz.* in that
> which has emanated, that the good may in the evil become
> perceptible, effectual, and capable of will; namely to will to
> separate itself from the evil, and to re-will to enter into the one
> will of God.[36]

In the Divine genesis the eternal One, the light or virtue of
the Word, together with the *Ungrund* emanates forth the Holy
Spirit, which in its fulfilment involves an emanation of a plurality of independent participatory beings. To actively love, these
distinctive individuals require will and desire, potential sources
of evil, features that have their origin apart and distinct from
the positive features of God. These negative aspects of human
nature must be worked out in autonomy so that we can fully
and eternally participate in the divine life. Thus the transformative light is hidden in the natural processes of will and reason.

Boehme's mysticism completes the emanative circle. It is not
reason that justifies his theodicy, but the higher mystical realisation of God wherein one comes to know the three principles
of the Divine Essence. The mystical goal of Boehme's teleological
perspective is the experience of the power, joy and love of the
divine life as human beings fulfil the third principle of the Divine
Essence. This is the goal of Boehme's teleological perspective, the
experience that justifies the evils of the natural world and human
nature. Yet in this experience of the eternal One the subject is
neither dissolved not passively static. The emanative circle does
not return to its centre, but ever expands in the active love of unity
of will with others and with God. As Boehme says, the divine life
eliminates the separateness of human kind and God but not that
of the individuality.[37] And in the experience, the taking of the
will is transformed into a giving, as 'the will of love gives itself,
as light from fire, which gives itself to all things, and produces in
all something that is good'.[38]

EVIL AS NOTHING, AND DOSTOEVSKY'S DEVIL

The theodicy of Boehme is in many ways profound; it maintains a peculiar view of evil as the privation of good while at the same time giving evil an active and positive place in the world. Evil in his system is real yet it has its reality only in reference to the teleological goal. Thus it does not have ontological reality; as James McLachlan observes, for Boehme evil is 'the reverse of the ontological order'.[39] Its power rests in its ability to move one towards a fiction of self-destructive, disharmonious independence, a realm of nothingness quite apart from the appropriate teleology of the divine life centred in God.

Yet in this view of the dynamic character and reality of evil, Boehme is consistent with Christian monotheism. His view does not reduce to a good–evil dualism in the manner of Zoroastrianism or Gnosticism. Though evil is in his system an independent and active force in human nature, it is not thought to arise from an evil deity set in opposition to the contrasting good. For the *Ungrund*, the source of evil in nature and human beings, is not a God, has not consciousness nor substantiality, and has no force and life on its own. Rather, it is a kind of primeval potentiality to will and desire, the hidden principle to dynamism that requires for its actuality as evil the choice of human beings in its favour.

Human beings receive this negative potentiality in the context of God's creative act, however, so although God is not the source of evil in human nature, He brings it to life and permits it. The justification of this authorisation of evil rests on the fulfilment of the third principle. The third principle is the completion of the Divine Essence, and human beings are conceived as potential participants in the divine life. They are born in the conjunction of the first two principles of the Divine Essence. In the first principle we find the vehicle to activity and differentiation. Primary Will is the source of multiplicity in essence, the ground of the dynamism of individuality and activity that is necessary to fulfil the third principle. It possesses, however, the terrible side-effects of natural and moral evils that arise in nature and in individual wills that are separated, in their autonomy, from God. Multiplicity of being is necessary for the realisation of the power, joy and love of the divine life. But it begins in a separateness of will and a freedom that stands over and against this goal, a distance which can lead to hell if it is not worked out and overcome. Hell in Boehme's theology is not created by God and it does not involve any active involvement on His part. Rather, it is understood as the domain of non-being, as the state quite apart and distinct from the Divine Essence, where the spirit can witness but not participate in the divine life, remaining ever immersed in the isolation of the self-will of the first principle, over and against the positive light and virtue of the second.

Here Boehme brings depth and scope to the view of evil as a 'nothingness' that we saw developed in Plotinus, Dionysius and Eckhart in Chapter 8. In itself evil is nothing; it has no sub-stantive existence apart from the good, and it does not exist if the will is transformed in God. It is a dark and empty nothing-ness that nevertheless has a reality in its potential of moving one away from her or his appropriate teleological ordination. Thus it is best understood as a deficiency or lack in terms of one's mystical teleology.

So the mystical teleologies we have described in reference to Eckhart and Dostoevsky are given some expansion in this account of primary Will, and the structure of mystical theodicy is given further clarification. Freedom and the impulse to evil in human nature are explained and justified in the account of a primeval chasm of darkness, a primary Will which originates in the very essence of God. This primary Will is necessary and fundamental to human beings, but it is the principle of egoism that stands in the way of personal and spiritual transformation. In human will we find an unconscious desire, a will-to-be, a self-willing that finds itself in tension with mystical teleology. Human will seeks a pur-pose, a direction for its dynamic creative impulses, one which it can find in 'it-self' or in terms of mystical teleology – that is, moral, personal and spiritual growth to divine life. In the former move the will remains in egoistic isolation, in the latter it is gradu-ally transformed to divinity. But this spiritual transformation is a long and difficult process involving much anguish and pain. Autonomous growth to the mystical life requires the transforma-tion of a fundamental and pervasive egoism, what Donald Evans (see Chapter 6) has referred to as a defensive self-contraction. This self-contraction resists the many positive realities of mystical life, aspects such as those of theodical evidence and consolation that were developed in Chapters 7 and 8. Hence the necessity of the arduous processes of mystical transformation, as described in Chapter 6.

Primary negative Will powerfully inhibits personal and spiritual growth. Dostoevsky characterised it in terms of his Devil. It is the negative principle of human nature that finds itself actualised in the kind of atrocities Ivan observed so vividly in his rebellion, and issues forth in the internal agony of conscience that Ivan himself experiences in his nightmare. And for what reason does this fundamental moral polarity exist in human nature? Dostoevsky suggests that without this darker side of human nature everything on earth would be extinguished at once; without the Devil in us 'no events could have occurred'.[40] Boehme provides the thearchical background to this provocative view. The *Ungrund*, though in itself nothing, is essential to God's creative activity. Indeed, God does not become a personal active God without the *Ungrund*. Understood as distinct from the first principle, God is but a static unity – a nothingness, really, in the context of human encounter. Personal God–human encounter requires a dynamic focus and environment that the light of the Word cannot in itself create. Only the energy of the primary Will, the magical *Ungrund*, brings the dynamic power that is necessary to divine relationship.

Thus Boehme's theodicy brings interpretive scope to Dostoevsky's view of the Devil. Like Boehme's first principle of the Divine Essence, Dostoevsky's Devil is necessary for the events of human history. In the words of Boehme's thearchy, the teleological goal of human history is understood in terms of the third principle of the Divine Essence. Spirit or Love requires the personal and moral growth of individual personalities in likeness to God. But to secure the third principle requires the participation and transformation of the first principle, the *Ungrund*. This necessitates a realm of natural and moral evils wherein the human being can freely play out and overcome the negative aspects of the first principle, to transform it in the second, and thereby participate in active personal love of the divine life.

But though this theogony provides a context in which to interpret Dostoevsky's Devil, Dostoevsky considered this theodicy morally reprehensible. He ironically displays this criticism in his portrayal of the Devil's own discomfort and distaste for his role. And the reasons behind Dostoevsky's objections to this theodical theme become clear in the question the Devil raises regarding Job: 'How many souls have had to be ruined and how many honourable reputations destroyed for the sake of that one righteous man,

Job, over whom they made such a fool of me in the old days'.[41] Dostoevsky agonised over the justification of the suffering inno- cent. How, in this mystical theodicy, can dysteleological suffering and death that arises in natural and moral evil be explained? Thus we turn to our final issue in mystical theodicy, the question of dysteleological evil.

10

Dysteleological
Evil and Rebirth

THE PROBLEM

Dostoevsky was tormented by the many instances of apparently unexpiated suffering to which he bore witness in *The Brothers Karamazov*. He expresses his anguish through Ivan Karamazov, who concentrates upon moral evil in his rebellion against God and critique of theodicy. Ivan confines his illustration to that of suffering children. How, he laments, can we explain and justify the atrocities committed upon children? 'The innocent must not suffer for another's sins, and especially such innocents!'[1] He goes on to describe in simple but vivid detail certain macabre events of his time, such as the little girl's suffering at the hands of her parents and the case of the serf-boy who is put to death for inadvertently stoning the General's favourite hound. Both of these horrors I mentioned in Chapter 2. Another example is the treatment of the Bulgarians by the Turkish soldiers, how they 'took a pleasure in torturing children . . . cutting the unborn child from the mother's womb, and tossing babies up in the air and catching them on the points of their bayonets before their mother's eyes'.[2]

Paradoxical as it may seem, Dostoevsky considered tragic events such as these not to be always without their positive religious effects. As was discussed in Chapter 8, Dostoevsky saw this suffering as a possible vehicle of love and compassion, and he recognised the significance of grief as a force in spiritual transformation. He never denies the view that human freedom and the darker side of human nature are necessary for spiritual growth to his religious ideal – in fact he presses the point home in sections such as 'The Grand Inquisitor' and Ilyusha's tragic trials. However, the theodical problem he recognised here arises in consideration of those who turn away from the religious ideal in

165

witnessing these evils, and especially in reflection upon the victim; though some might grow spiritually in their witness of such cruelty, there are some who will not, and there is the victim who often cannot. Indeed, Ivan stresses in his rebellion those children who apparently suffer and die without realising any spiritual benefits at all. Unjustifiably removed from participation in their spiritual teleology, they can in these instances be regarded merely as instruments in the spiritual teleology of others. So Ivan questioned the providence of God and rejected theodicy on moral grounds.

These evils, then, are dysteleological; they are not adequately explained in terms of Dostoevsky's religious teleology. If the *point* of human life is autonomous moral and spiritual growth to the religious ideal, how are we to account for those who, through no apparent fault of their own, experience incredible suffering and are unable to participate in this process?

Dostoevsky stresses moral evils and their consequences in this regard. Moral evils arise in human freedom and the dark side of human nature which Dostoevsky deems necessary to his religious teleology. John Hick delves into the related question of natural evils. Countless numbers experience suffering and death in natural disasters such as famines and earthquakes, and there are a great variety of mental and physical diseases that plague humanity. Hick asks, with David Hume, about the scope and severity of such natural evils and the equity of their distribution. But the more important question for teleological theodicy resides in their dysteleological character; if evil is justified in terms of the religious telos, how can we account for it in cases where people, because of moral and natural evils, are unable to participate in the teleological narrative?

Hick suggests 'further scenes of "soul-making"'[3] as a possible answer to this query, implying a kind of future purgatory beyond this particular realm of soul-making. In *Death and Eternal Life* he speaks of a future 'series of lives, each bounded by something analogous to birth and death, lived in other worlds in spaces other than that in which we now are'.[4] This type of answerr seems to me to be the only saving response for teleological theodicy, to propose a continued participation in the teleological narrative following the experience of tragic suffering and death. This is the final feature in our structure of effective mystical theodicy. In this chapter I will develop this answer as it is expressed in two different ways: probationary purgatory and rebirth. I will argue that rebirth is more plausible than purgatory and more effective for theodicy. However, I will move to dissociate this notion somewhat from its typical connection to retribution. The traditional Indian notions of *karma* and *saṃsāra* are effective theodical concepts and more plausible than the concept of probationary purgatory, but only when significantly qualified in regard to retribution.

PROBATIONARY PURGATORY

Though purgatory had been present in Roman Catholic thought since the second century, it did not become a clarified and sanctioned dogma of the Church until the Council of Florence (1434 CE). At that Council it was formulated along Augustinian lines, described as a temporal state of punishment for the expiation of venial sins that is reserved exclusively for Roman Catholics. E. H. Plumptre describes Cardinal Julian's interpretation at that time:

> The souls of the saints ascend straight to heaven and enjoy eternal rest. Others who have sinned and have not completed on earth the full measure of their penance, nor brought forth good works as its fruits, are cleansed by the purgatorial fire, and are freed from it, some more quickly, others more slowly, according to the measure of their guilt, and then join the company of the blessed. For those who die unbaptised or in deadly sin there was simply the punishment of hell.[5]

From the official Vatican standpoint, then, purgatory is understood as a realm of physical or mental punishment, more in negative terms of painful retribution than in positive conceptions of spiritual learning and growth. Indeed, though the latter function is not ruled out in the traditional formulation, there is the sense that one can 'burn off', as it were, the actions and effects of past moral improprieties, simply through passive suffering. However, such a stress on purgatory as primarily a realm of punishment offers no theodical power in relation to the question of dysteleological evil; for the main issue here is the question of those individuals who are unjustifiably exempted from the teleological progression, not that of the just dealing of the wicked.

Thus it is important to recognise the historical line of thinking that tended to regard purgatory primarily as a probationary and learning period and only secondarily as a realm of punishment, in contrast to the interpretation of purgatory as fundamentally a punishing realm for previous moral indiscretions. For example, thinkers such as Clement of Alexandria, Origen and Gregory of Nyssa emphasised purgatory as an opportunity for further spiritual education. Origen propounded this view in terms of a universal restoration, speaking of 'different stages in the education of the great school of souls, and their upward and onward progress'.[6] Plumptre describes the basic thrust of this view of purgatory as the teaching

> that a redeeming and purifying work might be carried on in the intermediate state, giving fresh opportunities, and therefore a fresh probation to some, if not to all, who, at the time of their death, were not qualified by their faith or works for the peace and rest of God.[7]

This conception of a purification period of growth and development after death is also held by the Eastern Orthodox and the Anglican Churches, though apparently neither refer to it as purgatory.[8] Of the latter, Joseph Butler (1692–1752) is cited as influential in his speculation of a future realm of probation. Indeed, Butler is extremely teleological in his philosophy, and in this regard he understands this world and human life as essentially a realm and period of moral probation. The point is the acquisition of virtue – the development of moral consciousness – but such progression requires the autonomous learning activity of the human being. As Terence Penelhum comments:

> The suggestion is that the difficulties virtue encounters are necessary for its real possession: that to fit ourselves for the next world, we have to confirm our possession of virtue by *exercising* it. Hence this life is a period of probation, or testing.[9]

The teleological perspective here is reminiscent of Hick's soul-making version, as we illustrated in Chapter 5, and it is open to similar criticisms. Butler himself recognises the kind of moral difficulties Dostoevsky observes in his critique of teleological theodicy and he moves to account for dysteleological evils in terms of a future probationary period after this life. Virtue, he says, is militant here, and various untoward accidents contribute to its being often overborne: but it may combat with greater advantage hereafter and prevail completely, and enjoy its consequent rewards in some future states. Neglected as it is, perhaps unknown, perhaps despised and oppressed here, there may be scenes in eternity lasting enough, and in every way adapted to afford it a sufficient sphere of action . . .[10]

Purgatory, then, if we can understand it in terms of Butler's future probationary period, is a necessary supposition of teleological theodicy. If the tortured child is removed from the teleological scheme without the chance to realise the telos that justifies moral and natural evils of the world, then that theodicy fails. To suggest that the child simply passes away is to deny divine goodness. To suppose that the child is granted eternal life is to render divine providence arbitrary or elitist. And, in any case, both proposals imply that evil cannot be fully explained in terms of the teleology.

Thus the necessity of a kind of probationary purgatory to any coherent teleological theodicy. Though in reference to Butler's cosmic scheme, Penelhum states this general theodical case:

the fact that some people choose to act viciously rather than virtuously in the face of their temptations and opportunities may create a situation in which others are confronted with adversities which are overwhelming and not merely probationary. For them, forced to live out the evil consequences of the freedom of others, a future state of regeneration and opportunity might be required. Such speculations are of course no more than possibilities. What is not speculative is that certain understandings of what God's general purposes might include, would render intelligible some of the evils which human beings have to undergo; but that they could not do so without its being held that God's providence extends into another life.[11]

The speculative possibility, then, of a realm and period of probationary purgatory is necessary to coherent teleological theodicy, necessary to account for the kind of dysteleological evils over which Dostoevsky agonised. But is probationary purgatory the most plausible possibility – is it the best account of dysteleological evil? To answer this question we begin by examining some of the issues surrounding probationary purgatory.

In the examples given by Ivan Karamazov, infants are born into the most deplorable conditions to suffer a very brief period of torment and anguish. In certain cases these children can at best serve, from a religious standpoint, the role of instrument in the religious progression of others; they function briefly as spiritual means for the benefit of their fellow human beings, only to vanish from earthly existence. This tends callously to depersonalise the children in question. Is their earthly life only significant as a means to the ends of others? Does their life have value only in so far as it serves their more fortunate companions? The hypothesis of probationary purgatory supposes another realm and period of existence for these unfortunate beings. So the intrinsic value of souls tragically lost to dysteleological evil is guaranteed in their future progression, removing the force of the moral criticisms Ivan raises against God. Though the child's tragic experiences are not *justified* by the hypothesis in the sense that they are thought to be deserved, they are *explained* in the possibility of future spiritual progression where the child might overcome the tragedy, perhaps even drawing the terrible experience into the transformative process. The child, then, is not to be understood simply as a vehicle in the religious transformation of others, but a future participant in this progression. So the intrinsic value of the child is guaranteed in the conception of probationary purgatory.

Nevertheless, the child's significance in this life is in these cases confined to that of spiritual means of others. His or her life on earth does not involve the kind of teleological movement of their more fortunate companions. Why should this be the case? How are we to explain this discrepancy? Why should certain individuals be excluded from the teleological processes of this life? This is an issue left unresolved in probationary purgatory, an issue that is further complicated by the question of the relationship between this earthly life and future probation. It is assumed in the hypothesis that one's future probationary period is dependent upon one's past life on earth. But the relationship and connection between these diverse orders of existence are obscured by these instances of dysteleological evil. Presumably an infant consumed by the ill effects of moral freedom and the darker side of human nature must make that spiritual progression in a future probationary purgatory which more fortunate human beings undergo, more or less, in this life. What, then, is the relationship of these tragic experiences to the child's future existence, and what, if anything, are the criteria of exclusion from participation in this-world teleology?

This brings the whole theodical assumption of the necessity of life on earth into question. In this case the child's life on earth is not necessary to his or her spiritual teleology. But teleological theodicies suppose this world to be the best of all possible worlds in terms of divine providence. Probationary purgatory suggests there to be another realm that can achieve these aims *regardless and in spite of this world* – that God indeed does much better. So to suppose another realm of soul-making distinct from this natural world brings into question the significance of life in this realm of existence. Theodicies attempt to justify God's creation of *this* world, but if *another* realm is more appropriate to divine purposes then we must ask about the significance of this world. This problem becomes even more acute in the mystical theodicies of Eckhart and Boehme because of their emphasis upon a participatory teleology in this world.

Within the Christian tradition there is a stress on the historical religious development of a communal people. In the mystical theologies espoused by Eckhart and Boehme there is the understanding that this world is undergoing a cosmic process to divinity, that human beings are ever-evolving to the communal ideal of mystical participation in divinity. Indeed, it is in the context of this eschatological theme that Eckhart emphasises the way in which mystical participation in divine creativity is followed by mystical experience of compassion and justice towards people in this earthly life. One *expresses* that which is experienced in Godhead, one actualises in practical daily affairs the creative love, compassion and justice experienced in mystical vision. Similarly, Boehme characterises the natural world as a realm in process towards the Divine Essence. For Boehme the teleological goal of human history is explained through the third principle of the Divine Essence. Spirit or Love requires the spiritual growth of individual personalities in likeness to God, and the natural world is the appropriate realm for such realisation. The point is to subordinate and subsume the will in the love of the creative Word, issuing forth in an active sharing and giving as the communal ideal.

Now to adapt the notion of probationary purgatory to the teleologies of these mystics is difficult because of their stress on an historical progression towards a communal goal. Both mystics must presume a future realm of spiritual growth in order to account for the dysteleological evils described above. To cohere, their theodicies require this kind of a supposition. However, to suggest a future realm of probationary purgatory is to severely downplay the historical significance of this life. One must suppose a similar progressive movement occurring at a different realm and period of existence which is better in that it overcomes the destructive power of dysteleological evils of this life. This, however, raises theodical problems regarding the appropriateness and necessity of this realm of existence, a vital point to their theodical stance. For both mystics maintain that the communal ideal of the historical process is one of a moral and spiritual progression to Divinity that can and should be significantly realised and played out *in this world*. Clearly, significant qualifications must be made regarding the place and function of this natural world within a cosmic scheme which supposes a more effective future realm in realising the spiritual telos. Moreover, such elucidation must expand somewhat upon the characteristics of probationary purgatory; to be an effective theodical response this future realm of soul development must be made intelligible to some degree.

In so far as the future realm of probationary purgatory is described in terms of human nature and this world, it will be a conception very much like rebirth.[12] Rebirth, in fact, offers an explanation of future soul development that is much more cogent than that of probationary purgatory. When pictured within a mystical teleological framework the notion of rebirth accounts for dysteleological evils without raising these difficulties which are associated with the concept of probationary purgatory. We turn now to draw this concept out in terms of mystical teleological theodicy.

THE RETRIBUTIVE-REBIRTH HYPOTHESIS

The doctrine of rebirth is usually associated with Indian religious systems such as Jainism, Buddhism and Hinduism, but it was a belief present in ancient Greece and not unknown to certain Christian sects. Within Christian traditions, however, it has generally been regarded as an heretical belief. Thus it is not surprising that the notion is not usually incorporated in Christian mystical theodicies. But as we will see, when adapted to Christian mystical teleologies this doctrine provides an effective theodical explanation of dysteleological evils.

In Sanskrit the term for rebirth is *saṃsāra* – the succession of births or the course of worldly life. This concept is closely associated with *karma* – action or deed and its product or result. Though uniformly defined in the different Indian traditions, the religious import of these two concepts varies according to related anthropological and soteriological concepts. For our purposes it is sufficient to concentrate on the notions as they are developed in the *Advaita* (non-dualism) *Vedānta* school of Hinduism.

Śaṅkara (788–820) is considered to be the most profound and influential exponent of *Advaita Vedānta*. His religious view might be briefly described as follows. The mystical goal for Śaṅkara is *mokṣa*, which means release from the inhibiting bondage of *karma* and *saṃsāra* through the intuitive realisation of one's true identity with *Brahman* (Absolute or Supreme Being). The problem is *māyā*, the illusory superimposition of qualities upon *Atman* (eternal Self) which leads one to perceive the finite differentiated realm, including an individual self (*jīva*), as distinct and apart from *Brahman*. Śaṅkara proposes a particular mystical teleology that involves an illuminating knowledge of the identity of *Atman* and *Brahman*. The goal is liberation from *karma* and *saṃsāra*, freedom from the effects of actions which entail continued participation in the cycle of rebirth. The belief is that the *jīva* (embodied soul) is reborn according to subtle impressions that previous actions have left upon the sheaths of knowledge, will and activity that envelope the *jīva*.[13] These sheaths constitute the transmigrating subtle body, the condition of which determines the agent's nature and circumstances in a future life. As Nikhilananda puts it:

> Karma, literally meaning action, denotes both action in general and the fruit-producing subtle impressions which remain with the doer even after an action is outwardly accomplished. It is in the latter sense that an action plays an important part in moulding a man's future, not only here on earth, but after death as well. The law of karma is the application of the law of cause and effect both on the body and on the mind.[14]

Karma and *saṃsāra*, then, form the basis of theodicy in Śaṅkara's *Vedānta*, a theodicy that stresses the retributive theme. According to Nikhilananda, these notions 'explained for the Hindus the inequality between man and man at the time of birth and gave them reasons to believe in a moral foundation of the universe, in which virtue is, in the long run, rewarded and iniquity punished'.[15] All actions affect the person's future; a virtuous person will find him or herself in more fortunate circumstances in the next life and a wicked person will pay the price for impropriety.

In *Evil, Karma and Reincarnation*, G. C. Nayak argues that the retributive hypothesis as it arises in the Hindu notions of *saṃsāra* and *karma* provides the most adequate theodicy. In this view, he says, 'Our misery and happiness are in exact proportion to our wickedness and virtue, and God's justice consists in the fact that nobody suffers or prospers undeservedly'.[16] So this retributive-rebirth theme removes the responsibility of evil from the Divine. As Śaṅkara argues in his commentary on *The Vedānta Sutras*, the many inequalities in the world are not to be attributed to *Brahman*, but are rather to be understood in terms of *karma*. He says:

> If the Lord on his own account, without any extraneous regards, produced this unequal creation, he would expose himself to blame; but the fact is, that in creating he is bound by certain regards, i.e. he has to look to merit and demerit. Hence the circumstances of the creation being unequal is due to the merit and demerit of the living creatures created, and it is not a fault for which the Lord is to blame . . . the Lord, being bound by regards, cannot be reproached with inequality of dispensation and cruelty.[17]

Within the retributive-rebirth framework the evils that Dosto-evsky perceived as dysteleological are to be understood as a consequence of a person's improprieties committed in a previous life, and hence deserved. Circumstances of creation are determined by one's past existence, justifying present evils. But a question arises regarding first circumstances, an issue that Nayak neglects in his hypothesis. Śaṅkara himself recognises the problem, formulating it as follows: 'The Lord may be considered as acting with regard to religious merit after distinction had once arisen; but as before that the cause of inequality, viz. merit, did not exist, it follows that the first creation must have been free from inequalities'.[18] In the beginning creatures would be born meritless, having never before acted and thereby accrued any subtle impressions of *karma*. The inequalities of this first instance, then, would have to be attributed to the Divine. But to this criticism Śaṅkara responds by denying a first creation: 'The objection would be valid if the world had a beginning; but as it is without beginning, merit and inequality are, like seed and sprout, caused as well as causes, and there is therefore no logical objection to their operation'.[19]

This response is very intriguing, especially in light of Śaṅkara's belief in cosmic creation and destruction. The world, though without beginning, nevertheless undergoes cycles of involution and dissolution. In Hindu thinking there are four ages or stages (*yugas*) of world evolution that are generally characterised by a decline in virtue. At the end of the fourth *yuga* the world dissolves into a state of cosmic non-differentiation, only to creatively involve after a certain period into the first *yuga*. This schema is complicated further by the notion of *kalpa* (aeon), a major dissolution that occurs after 1000 cycles of *yugas*.[20] But the important points here are that although the cosmos is beginningless there is a sense of its dissolution and creation, and *karma* is carried forward throughout this cyclical regression and progression. The human being continues to work out the effects of his action despite the destruction of a particular cosmic period, and such has *always* been the case.[21]

This belief in the beginninglessness of the *jiva* and the natural world is consistent with Śaṅkara's identification of these apparent pluralities with *Brahman*, but it poses certain theodical problems. However, before turning to these problems we should note that Śaṅkara does indeed speak of a responsible Creator, and he must if his retributive-rebirth hypothesis is to have some foundation. This is *Saguna Brahman*, the personal, moral and active Divine in contrast to *Nirguna Brahman*, the impersonal, eternal and qualityless Divine. *Saguna Brahman* is Īśvara, the Lord, the Divine being that arises and creates through the *śakti* (power or will) of *māyā*. As Nikhilananda describes it: 'Brahman, through association with maya, . . . appears to be endowed with such activities as creation, preservation, and dissolution, and with such attributes as omniscience, omnipresence, and lordship, and becomes known as the Saguna Brahman'.[22] This creative power of *māyā* is further described by George Thibaut:

Māyā thus constitutes the upādanā, the material cause of the world; or – if we wish to call attention to the circumstance that Māyā belongs to Brahman as a śakti – we may say that the material cause of the world is Brahman in so far as it is associated with Māyā. In this latter quality Brahman is more properly called Īśvara, the Lord.[23]

Through Nikhilananda's and Thibaut's descriptions of Śaṅkara's theogonic speculation we begin to see its similarity with that of Jacob Boehme's. *Māyā* here functions very much like Boehme's *Ungrund; Brahman* only becomes an active personal and creative God through the power of *māyā*, which, nevertheless, has no reality or existence apart from *Brahman*. Similarly, as we saw in Chapter 9, the *Ungrund* has no power or existence distinct from the second principle of the Divine Essence, and yet without the *Ungrund* the second principle remains impersonal and inactive and cannot issue forth in the third principle and the natural world. The differences between the two theogonies, however, begin to show the theodical difficulties associated with Śaṅkara's view.

In Boehme's cosmology human beings fulfil the Divine Essence. The telos of Boehme's theology is a personal relationship between human beings and God, a dynamic communal ideal which requires for its fulfilment the autonomous moral and spiritual development which justifies the encounter and experience of moral and natural evils of this world. The goal of Śaṅkara's *Vedānta* is the realisation of one's true nature as impersonal, inactive and eternal *Brahman*. But this mystical goal does not justify the experience of evil in Śaṅkara's view. Rather evil is explained in terms of the notion of retributive rebirth; it is not necessary to Śaṅkara's mystical ideal but simply a consequence of human misdeeds. And, while Śaṅkara perceives *Nirguna Brahman*, that is *Brahman* minus the limiting adjuncts of *māyā*, as the appropriate ideal, Boehme depicts the personal and dynamic God – the *Ungrund* as it has been transformed in the second principle of the Divine Essence 'word' – as that to which human beings are ordered. So while Boehme's cosmology is theistic, Śaṅkara's is not fundamentally so.

The significance of this point for theodicy becomes clear when we recognise that because the telos is not theistic there is no divine teleology in Śaṅkara's system, no divine providence to creation. An all-encompassing purpose requires that the cosmos has a beginning and that there be a being who is ultimately *responsible* for creation. Though Śaṅkara supposes *Brahman* to be the force behind the cyclical involution and dissolution of the cosmos (in the form of *Saguna Brahman*) and so the upholder of a moral system, this is not to say that this force is Creator of the substance of the movement. The fact of the matter is there is no beginning to creation, hence no overall purpose. Śaṅkara himself explicitly denies divine providence, suggesting the creative activity of *Saguna Brahman* to be but *līlā* (cosmic play).[24] Evils, then, cannot be justified in any final sense. Since they have always existed, there can be no overall purpose which they might serve. Nevertheless, Śaṅkara insists that there is an overriding moral law within which evil can be understood as retributive. Though evils serve no final purpose, they are in each and every case deserved.

To return to our examples of dysteleological evils raised by Dostoevsky we see a rather different explanatory approach in the view of retributive rebirth from that which we examined earlier in terms of probationary purgatory. The fact that evils appear to be dysteleological is irrelevant for Śaṅkara because he denies cosmic teleology. Rather, they are explained and understood as recompense for moral improprieties of a previous existence. So the babes' suffering at the hands of the Turks, the boy's torture and execution by the General, the mothers' witnessing of these tragic events – all of these great horrors are but a consequence of misdeeds of these victims in a past incarnation. Within this vicious cosmic circle of beginningless impropriety and recompense, all are getting what they deserve according to the law of *karma*. Indeed, what atrocities they themselves must have committed to warrant such punishment!

But surely such a conception forces one to question the benevolence of Īśvara. For it is a strange system of retributive justice that punishes those who are unaware of their misdeeds; yet this is a common practice in this retributive rebirth hypothesis. Nayak himself recognises this difficulty for the theory. He says:

The person who is punished without the knowledge that he is being punished, and without the knowledge of the sin for which he is punished, does not learn anything from it, in which case the very aim of the retributive justice is defeated. A new-born babe does not know that his suffering is a punishment, nor does he know for which particular crime of the past he is being punished; what, in that case, could be the point in inflicting punishment upon him? Is such retribution any better than revenge?[25]

Surprisingly, Nayak goes on to argue that this objection is unfounded. Memory, he argues, is not always a good thing, and memory of details of past lives would not only lead to confusion but also perhaps to 'past habits and associations in stead of progressing through fresh experiences and ordeals'.[26] Furthermore, memory of past life experiences may be lost yet still contribute to present personality, analogous to the process as it occurs in a single lifetime. He goes on to develop this point in more detail:

> People are born with different innate tendencies, aptitudes, capacities, and inclinations, which may be explained as being due to their varied experiences in past lives; our initial variation in ability and aptitude not only points to a past life in which we might have acquired these specific qualities, but also shows that our experiences and ordeals of the past, though not remembered, have not gone in vain in so far as they have left sure and certain marks on the character with which we are born into this life.[27]

So, Nayak suggests, past-life experiences might have an effect on human character and personality though they go unremembered. In this regard he stresses rebirth as a positive process of progress and growth, rather than a negative one of punishment. 'Divine retribution', he says, 'is to be understood as being conducive to the highest good by making it possible for the person in question to have moral education as he proceeds'.[28] Thus Nayak edges towards a teleological explanation of the retributive rebirth theme, where certain evils are explained as necessary to cosmic teleology. The problem, however, is in the fact that Śaṅkara rules out cosmic teleology. Evil is justified as recompense for previous misdeeds, not as a consequence of certain necessities of the cosmic telos. Evil is explained through *karma*, not in terms of a cosmic teleology. So a retributive theme cannot be subordinated to a teleological within Śaṅkara's system.

This poses serious problems for the retributive-rebirth theme. For how are suffering children to be understood as making amends for their misdeeds if they do not understand the circumstances surrounding their tragic predicament? Nayak is quite correct in suggesting that certain experiences can have a profound effect on character and personality even though the individual retains no memory of them. But retributive punishment, if it is to be just, is the kind of thing that *requires* a recognition of the details surrounding one's punishment. If it is to have any positive effect, either upon the evil-doer or the cosmic moral imbalance, retribution demands a conscious knowledge of events which require the 'payment' of pain for wrong-doing. Surely it is the case that unless the suffering person *recognises* what they are being punished for, the punishment is but a crude form of retaliation, a kind of outlash of vengeance.

Even for retributionists who insist that guilty persons need not be presented with the details surrounding their punishment in order for retribution to be justified, there arises the problem of personal identity associations between lives. Since the bodily criterion of identity cannot obtain in rebirth, memory must be the sufficient condition of identity. But there is either an absence of past-life memories or an element of uncertainty in this regard; only very few people experience past-life memories, and even when they do they cannot, in the absence of the bodily criterion, be certain of the veracity of the memories. Hence, the retributivist requirement that a person be punished proportionately only for *his* or *her* particular crime is undermined, even in cases where past-life memories occur. Indeed, some criterion must be substituted for memory and bodily continuity in order to secure the identity connection between lives, and thereby justify retributive rebirth. But it is important to point out that even if an appropriate substitute is found for the bodily criterion we are still left with the serious moral issues surrounding the suffering of human beings, including infants and children, for past misdeeds which are not presented to them. For though such a criterion might assure the notion of continuous identity over lifetimes, it will not show to the sufferers the particular evidence which justifies their suffering to them.[29]

So, as it is expressed by Śaṅkara and Nayak, the notion of retributive rebirth possesses serious theodical problems. Though it does explain, in a fashion, Dostoevsky's dysteleological evils, it does so at the expense of our moral sensibilities, and it possesses problems of personal identity and raises questions regarding the benevolence of the Divine. It also has dangerous social ramifications; it justifies inequality and inaction, and it blurs the line between compassion and moral condemnation. For the poor and downtrodden are to be viewed in this hypothesis as justifiably paying the price for past misdeeds. And how, in this view, are the mothers in Ivan's examples to react to their children's 'punishments'? Are they to look lightly upon these horrors; indeed, could they ever accept such brutality as fair recompense for past misdeeds? Clearly, in light of these difficulties retributive rebirth cannot be regarded as an effective theodicy.

REBIRTH AS A PROCESS OF SOUL-MAKING

Like the conception of probationary purgatory, however, the notion
of rebirth need not be subordinated to a retributive hypothesis.
Nayak himself points towards a view which depicts rebirth primarily
as a vehicle of moral education rather than that of a mechanical punishing device. Sri Aurobindo, a contemporary Hindu (1872–1950),
suggests that the retributive theme must be subordinated to the
teleological if the notion of rebirth is to be morally acceptable.
He asks:

> And what of suffering and happiness, misfortune and prosper-
> ity? These are experiences of the soul in its training, helps, props,
> means, disciplines, tests, ordeals, – and prosperity often a worse
> ordeal than suffering. Indeed, adversity, suffering may often be
> regarded rather as a reward to virtue than as a punishment for
> sin, since it turns out to be the greatest help and purifier of the
> soul struggling to unfold itself. To regard it merely as the stern
> award of a Judge, the anger of an irritated Ruler or even the
> mechanical recoil of result of evil upon cause of evil is to take
> the most superficial view possible of God's dealings with the
> soul and the law of evolution.[30]

Aurobindo argues that the retributive rebirth hypothesis itself is
much too simplistic in its account of evil and that it must be
viewed in terms of the greater cosmological picture within which
it occurs. He criticises the *Vedānta* of Śaṅkara, referring to it as an
illusionist doctrine that mistakenly denies the reality and importance of the cosmic movement to the divine life in its misunder-
standing of the significance of rebirth. He says, in this conception
rebirth 'is reduced in its significance to a constant mechanism
of self-deception, and the will not to live is shown us as the
last acquisition, the highest good and the one desirable result
of living'.[31] The goal of Śaṅkara's view is the escape from the
cycle of 'an ignorant mechanical cosmic recurrence'. But this is an
other-worldly orientation that denies 'any divine meaning in life'.[32]
So rebirth is regarded here more as a burden and entrapment,
a cyclical process of punishment rather than a vehicle in one's
on-going spiritual realisation.

Aurobindo suggests the latter view, supposing rebirth to be a
blessing rather than an inexplicable bane to be overcome. In this

conception *karma* is conceived simply as the 'link between the lives that preceded and the lives that follow and that the past of the soul has an effect on its future'.[33] Rebirth, then, occurs in a general accordance of an individual spiritual evolution:

> What is behind us is the past terms of the spiritual evolution, the upward gradations of the spirit already climbed, by which through constant rebirth we have developed what we are, and are still developing this present and middle and human term of the ascension.[34]

Aurobindo sees a gradual spiritual evolution occurring in the historical processes of this world. This world is a realm of soul development, an environment that offers a great variety of opportunities and experiences through which the autonomous psychic being can unfold itself spiritually. As in Nikhilananda's view of the transmigrating *jīva*, Aurobindo considers only the essential elements of the person to be reborn, not the outer personality of human consciousness. In Aurobindo's view the soul or mental-vital consciousness develops by the 'figures of experience' it encounters through the character and personality it incarnates in a particular lifetime.[35] This psychic being, then, carries with it the essential moral and divine elements it acquires through life-experience – elements which find themselves expressed in the various activities of the personal character – in a gradual evolutionary movement towards the divine life.[36]

Thus in this reading of rebirth, punishment is not ruled out, but it hinges upon the teleological development of the soul. Like the doctrine of probationary purgatory developed earlier, punishment is here subordinated to the moral and spiritual development of the psychic being. Punishment, then, can be understood as suffering experiences for wrong-doing *which contribute* to the moral and spiritual progression of the psychic being. Here it is not a painful 'payment' for misdeeds that mysteriously sets right the imbalance of some kind of overriding moral law. Rather it is a personal learning experience that past improprieties would indicate are necessary to one's moral and spiritual growth. So, lack of memory of past wrong-doing does not in this view cause the serious problems that arise with it in the retributive hypothesis of rebirth. Though memories of past improprieties are important in just retribution (as evidence indicating that one's suffering in the present is to 'make up' for doing wrong in the past), such memories are not always necessary for spiritual growth. For one can learn and grow through present painful experiences regardless of the knowledge of past mistakes which might have hindered the progression of others and oneself.

Moreover, this idea of rebirth overrides the problems of personal identity that are associated with retributive rebirth. For one does not need to secure conclusive personal identity over lifetimes in order morally and rationally to justify the view. One's past lives are presumed to have affected the moral and spiritual status of one's present life, but one does not, in this view, have to have conclusive identification of past lives. Although punishment as it is understood in retributive rebirth requires that conclusive identification over lifetimes be established (so that people are punished proportionately for *their* misdeeds), spiritual development can occur without such conclusive identification over lifetimes, indeed, it can occur without any past-life identification at all.[37]

But this need not mean that all suffering be construed as beneficial to psychic progression. Ivan's examples of the tortured children need not be understood as teleological in order for the rebirth hypothesis to have theodical force. Indeed, a very brief but painful life can be explained as a tragic event arising in the conditions of human freedom and the natural world which are necessary to the soul's development to divinity, though they contribute not at all to such development. Though certain evils may be considered purposeless, as never being justified, they are explained as the brute facts of the soul-making environment. But with this conception of rebirth the person is thought not to experience a final and therefore meaningless death by them. The possibility of redemption of these experiences exists in so far as the person is able to incorporate or overcome this suffering in spiritual transformation.

This supposition, like that of probationary purgatory, maintains the dysteleological character of certain evils. This is very important to theodicy in that it confirms the negative force of evil, its tragic character; it explains evil without transforming it into good. For, as we showed in Chapter 1, if all evil is conducive to soul development, if all evil has its positive role as impetus to soul-making, then evil becomes but an aspect of the good. It loses its negative force. Indeed, as John Hick puts it, evil must 'threaten us with ultimate destruction'.[38] But if explained in every instance as teleological, evil becomes but a non-threatening form of the good.

The negative force and reality of evil is denied in the claim that all evil is teleological.

Thus the interpretation of rebirth functions theodically in a manner very similar to that of probationary purgatory. Nevertheless, it overcomes the problems that arise for mystical theodicies in association with probationary purgatory. These theodicies picture the human being in process of moral and spiritual growth to active mystical participation in the divine life. For example, Eckhart proposes four stages of mystical realisation, levels which culminate in the direct participation in the artistic wisdom of God. *Active* compassion and justice is the goal which justifies the experience of evil in the world; the telos is an active and communal ideal wherein the human being lives out those moral and spiritual virtues acquired in the mystical progression. This soul-making environment, then, is very important to his theodicy, in that it provides the suitable dynamic atmosphere to realise one's spiritual potentialities. Boehme similarly subscribes to an active-communal ideal, and stresses this natural world as the environment conducive to the fulfilment of the third principle of the Divine Essence.

The problem for their theodicies can begin to be illustrated in their apparent elitism. The mystical ideal they espouse is realised by very few people indeed, a telos that they nevertheless put forward as justification of evil. The experience of evil is deemed necessary to the spiritual growth to the communal mystical ideal. But the problem is further compounded in the fact that many people are unfairly ruled out of the spiritual progression; hence they cannot be blamed for the failure. So the theodicies can be criticised on moral grounds. Evil cannot be justified in terms of the telos because of the apparent unrealisability of the mystical goal for the vast majority. To cohere, then, their theodicies require a doctrine that ensures an equity in the cosmological picture. Probationary purgatory supposes another realm of soul-making for those who fail in this realm.

As we saw earlier in this chapter, this supposition brings into question the efficacy of this world as a soul-making realm, a very important premise in the theodicies of Eckhart and Boehme. This raises the issues of the relationship between two diverse orders of existence, the exclusion from this-worldly progression, and the practical actualisation of the telos in this realm of existence. The notion of rebirth overrides these difficult questions. When incorporated into the mystical theodicies of Boehme and Eckhart, it secures the significance of this world as *the* appropriate soul-making environment. So it eliminates the need to relate two diverse orders of soul development, denies the exclusion from this soul-making realm and points to a future actualisation of the communal goal *in this* world.

Now Eckhart and Boehme apparently did not espouse beliefs in rebirth. Though the doctrine was not unknown to Christianity, it was rejected by the Church and never gained popularity in the various Christian traditions. However, one significant Roman Catholic thinker who upholds a belief in rebirth as a process of soul-making is the anonymous mystic who I referred to in earlier chapters. He draws the notion into his particular Christian teleology, describing it as neither a dogma nor a heresy:

> For reincarnation is neither a dogma, i.e. a truth necessary for salvation, nor a heresy, i.e. contrary to a truth necessary for salvation. It is simply a fact of experience, just as sleep and heredity are. As such it is neutral. Everything depends upon its interpretation.[39]

The anonymous mystic considers it an acceptable interpretation of rebirth to understand it as evidence of God's infinite forgiveness, as renewed opportunities in one's spiritual progression. It is heresy when it is construed as the foundation of a deterministic law of cause and effect that rules out divine grace. But in itself it is either a matter of first-hand experience or it is not; it 'is either known through experience or ignored'.[40] Hence he thinks one should not be surprised that it is not generally held in Christian circles. From his mystical teleological perspective the anonymous mystic argues that such memories will arise if it is necessary 'to establish continuity of endeavour – of the quest of aspiration of the soul from life to life – so that particular lives are not merely isolated episodes but constitute the stages of a single *path* towards one sole end'.[41]

Here then we see the importance of past-life mystical experiences to mystical theodicies, as we briefly mentioned in Chapter 6 (see n.16). These paranormal experiences are thought to arise depending upon the particular spiritual ordination of the individual person, and to give some evidence in support of the truth of rebirth. The anonymous mystic considers these first-hand memories to support indisputably the hypothesis for those who experience them, but like Nayak he emphasises that memories of past lives might interfere with one's present stage of soul development. He says that one's present vocation often 'demands a maximum of concentration *in the present*' and requires no awareness of past-life experiences.[42]

Also important for the anonymous mystic are the possible practical abuses that might arise if rebirth became a popularised belief. He claims there to be grave dangers associated with orientating thoughts and desires to future incarnations. Citing G. J. Gurdjieff and P. D. Ouspensky as examples, the anonymous mystic speaks of a non-spiritual teleological orientation. This is an egoistic preoccupation with achieving one's own individual immortality, instead of being committed to the theistic-mystical telos of purification, illumination and celestial union. The anonymous mystic considers this to be a very real and dangerous possibility, one that was recognised by the Church. Since past-life experiences are not necessary, as is clear from the lives of Christian saints, and since popular belief in reincarnation can lead people astray, he argues that the belief should not be encouraged.[43]

The anonymous mystic does not, however, consider the positive force which a belief in reincarnation can have in theodicy. And he indicates how such a belief can be understood in ways which make it compatible with mystical Christian theism, even though the belief has been, and still is, viewed antagonistically by the Church. The doctrine is compatible even with a belief in purgatory. For with this conception of rebirth there remains the possibility of other realms and periods of existence where the soul might undergo moral-spiritual education that cannot occur in this world. Indeed, within the Hindu tradition we find speculation concerning various non-terrestrial realms of existence, and Aurobindo himself speaks of the soul's movement to vital and psychic planes of existence after death.[44] But the important point here in terms of theodicy is that the spiritual learning or healing occurring in a purgatory state be different from that which takes place in incarnate existence. For otherwise one must question the necessity of this realm of experience; why this world when God can do better, and indeed does better, in another realm? If the spiritual learning or healing can more effectively occur in another realm, then one must explain the significance of this world, and its relationship to other different and more effective realms of soul-making.

So the doctrine of rebirth seems not incompatible with the Christian theology of the mystical theodices we have examined and it overcomes the theodical problems surrounding the notion of probationary purgatory. It draws the structure of mystical theodicy together, as it were. As we have seen in the comparison of the teleologies of Eckhart and Boehme with that of John Hick's (Chapters 7 and 9), the structure of mystical theodicy is not wholly unlike that of Professor Hick's soul-making theodicy. The world is understood to be an appropriate soul-making environment, a world that is conducive to a person's growth to the mystical life of an active and communal nature. Freedom is necessary to personal, moral and spiritual growth to divine life. But in mystical theodicy we find in association with the apophatic experience of the Divine Essence an account of the impulse to evil in human nature. Human beings have in their freedom the very difficult task of transforming a fundamental egoistic stance, a self-contraction that arises from the very source of dynamic and creative life. Though having its source in the essence of God, this primary Will is nevertheless distanced from a personal benevolent Divine, a Divine whose beneficence is emphasised in the affective power of consolatory mystical experiences. In this context we also uncover ineffable experiences which verify this teleological perspective, and which confirm the providence of a personal, active and benevolent God. But in the face of dysteleological evils this providence only receives a clearly developed moral justification through the conception of rebirth as a process of soul-making, an hypothesis that also finds its support in certain mystical experiences.

Still there remains an issue regarding dysteleological natural evils, as I briefly mentioned at the beginning of this chapter. Though these evils are explained through rebirth in the same manner as moral evils, their scope and severity can be questioned. Like freedom and the darker side of human nature, they are understood to be necessary obstacles in autonomous soul development. In certain instances these evils are dysteleological, but they do not remove people from their spiritual progression in any final sense. Nevertheless, it seems very reasonable to ask if certain natural evils are necessary to soul development, or need be so severe. As Hick phrases the question:

> need there be volcanic irruptions burying whole cities, and earthquakes killing thousands of people in a single night? Man must (let us suppose) face harsh bodily consequences of over-indulgence; but need there be such fearful diseases as typhoid,

polio, cancer, angina? These reach far beyond any constructive function of character training.[45]

The hypothesis of rebirth does not help in the theodical justification of this issue surrounding natural evils. Indeed, mystical teleological theodicy has many strengths in regard to its explanation of moral evils, but is suspect in its account of natural evils. This is perhaps the most serious of the issues left unresolved in mystical theodicy. We have briefly raised it in the context of Boehme's qualifications of the omnipotence of God (Chapter 9), but it should be developed in more detail. Let us turn, then, to our final chapter, to draw out this problem and other unresolved issues, as well as the many positive aspects of mystical theodicy.

Conclusion

We have seen how certain mystical thinkers respond to various features of the challenge of evil. By drawing these mystical responses together in reference to the four major issues raised against traditional non-mystical theodicy, we have uncovered the basic structure of a unified mystical theodicy. As we have seen, this theodicy goes well beyond the response to the challenge of evil of traditional theodicies, overcoming, in many respects, the problems associated with these four issues in non-mystical theodicies.

Coherent mystical theodicy proposes a teleological scheme very much like the soul-making teleology John Hick espouses. The world is understood as a realm conducive to personal growth to spiritual life. The primary purpose of life is spiritual progression, a transformation which includes autonomous intellectual, emotional and moral development. Mystical teleology, however, stresses the potential divinity of the human being, his or her possible participation in mystical union with an active and personal Divine. In this regard mystical theodicy claims that theodicy is confirmed in certain mystical experiences which issue forth in evidence verifying mystical teleology. Mystical theodicy does not merely point to a future spiritual eschaton that justifies teleology, but emphasises, on the authority of enlightened mystics, experiences of God's purposes in the context of the very transformative processes which are associated with the teleology.

Very closely related to this feature of mystical theodicy is the stress upon the realisation of divine beneficence in mystical experiences of consolation. Traditional theodicies often neglect or only ambiguously treat the positive/affirmative aspect of theodicy. But in mystical theodicy we find in the response to the challenge of evil a very powerful pastoral thrust, one which nevertheless involves an active moral concern for others. Certain mystics emphasise the possibility of God and the consolation inherent to mystical experiences, while at the same time insisting upon a moral dynamic that issues from and in the experiences. So in its treatment of the problem of evil, mystical theodicy offers a much more effective practical response than that which we find in non-mystical theodicy.

Also, more than non-mystical theodicy, we find in mystical theodicy an adequate explanation of the teleological necessity for the incentives to evil, and an effective account of the depth and scope of evil. Boehme's mysticism involves a depiction of a theogonic process which explains the origin of evil and the darker side of human nature to be a consequence of the separation of the first principle of the Divine Essence from God. This principle is a necessary aspect of the transformative processes, one which is crucial to a dynamic creative world and a personal benevolent God. In God this principle is positively transformed. In human nature, however, this principle is separated from God, and finds its actualisation in egoistic incentives to evil. It must be overcome and transformed in mystical teleology, a teleology that arises out of the very nature of the Divine Essence.

So mystical theodicy offers a cogent response to the problem of moral evil. Indeed, mystical theodicy adequately accounts even for moral evils of a dysteleological nature. The fourth aspect of our structure of mystical theodicy includes an hypothesis of rebirth within which dysteleological evils might be understood as never utterly destructive. Though these evils have no teleological import for the suffering person, they cannot finally remove the individual from the realm of soul-making. The hypothesis of rebirth, when pictured in conjunction with the necessity of autonomous growth and transformation to the divine life, draws these evils into theodical explanation. This world, with all its terrible adversities, is justified as an appropriate realm of personal and spiritual progression to the divine life, a transformation that requires the overcoming of the negative primary will of human nature, and that involves very powerful consolatory experiences as well as verification of the truth of the mystical theodicy. This is the basic structure of mystical theodicy.

The Divine in this theodicy is theistic. The divine life is described in terms of the moral and personal anologues of creativity, love, empathy, compassion and justice. These are essential features of a personal, benevolent and highly passible God and they are realised in the highest mystical experiences. Their actualisation is what constitutes participation in the divine life, a life which requires human beings for its fulfilment. We are to become very much *like* God; great stress is placed on the potential divinity of human beings, their significance to God – their fulfilment of God's personal and active being. Thus the importance of autonomy and the long and arduous process of transformation. Indeed, in this mystical teleology becoming divine is considered no easy task and by no means guaranteed; it involves many lifetimes and much suffering, and there is the danger of finally succumbing to the negative aspects of primary will and removing oneself from the teleological process.

One must overcome one's darker side in an environment deeply affected by the negative will of one's fellow human beings, both present and past. Human beings have and continue to create abominable evils, not only the specific atrocities which Ivan Kara- mazov cites, but also social and religious structures that contribute, quite independently of individual human impetus, to a tragic human predicament. Indeed, for many people the world does not seem presently conducive to mystical soul development. In fact, such a spiritual teleology is alien to the dominant worldviews of the day, and it is often in these views regarded as preposterous. Nevertheless, in our structure of mystical theodicy we find a plausible explanation for the pervasiveness of evil; in the necessity of autonomy and primary will to the cosmic processes, evil is a significant feature of our world. Evil is an essential by-product of divine and human creativity.

So this mystical theodicy cannot be criticised for proposing a naïvely idyllic worldview. Rather, it looks the reality of evil in the eye, recognises its pervasiveness and power, and responds to the challenge by urging human beings to overcome evil in themselves and in the world. But there remain some unresolved issues sur- rounding their response. Perhaps the most serious involves those associated with the problem of natural evils. As we pointed out at the close of last chapter, we must wonder if certain natural evils are necessary to soul development, or need be so severe. As David Hume so provocatively argues, the principles and processes of physical nature possess a tendency to extreme and excess, and human nature suffers from severe physical and mental limitations (see Chapter 1). Is the degree of these natural evils necessary to soul development, especially in light of the seriousness of moral evils? Is this really the best of all possible worlds in regard to physical evils?

In our mystical theodicy, Boehme implies that this is the *only* soul-making world God could create, that He is limited in His creative act to this physical realm by the first and third principles of the Divine Essence (Chapter 9). Though it would seem that other realms of existence are possible for Boehme, these would not involve the dynamics necessary to soul development. But the creative dynamism of the natural world, its tendency to extreme and excess, and human limitations, arise from the very primeval Will that gives rise to moral evil. God is limited, then, by the first principle in the creation of this soul-making realm. Moreover, divinised human beings fulfil the Divine Essence; in some sense they would seem to perfect an active and personal God. So, not only could God not create a material world containing less physical evil, but there would seem also to be a significant *dependence* of God upon creation for His perfection.

The implications of this 'slight' upon divine omnipotence are significant. Following the tradition of Leibniz, non-mystical theodicies typically suppose that God, in His omnipotence, can create an infinity of possible worlds, realms which are unnecessary to a perfect Creator and which cannot affect His transcendent stature. Mystical theodicies, on the other hand, generally propose an emanative view of creation that pictures this world as a consequence of the overflowing or issuing forth of divine Goodness or Unity. This world, then, though an appropriate soul-making environment as an emanation of God, is the only possible world that God could create; omnipotence is limited by the emanative process. Moreover, within this emanative view there is the stress of divine omnipresence in creation – a view consistent with the nature of mystical experiences – as well as the implication that God's relationship with human beings positively enriches and enhances a personal and benevolent Deity.

Thus in mystical theodicy we find a stress on divine immanence that would seem on the surface to accentuate the problem of physical evils. Boehme, however, explains this reality in reference to the emanation of the three principles of the Divine Essence. Creation includes the negative aspects of the first principle. But in this theogonic speculation we find a view of divine omnipotence that is rather unorthodox; it implies a view of omnipotence that differs considerably from the traditional theistic standpoint. Though the view does not entail that God could not act in and upon the natural processes, even to extinguish them, it does suggest that

dysteleological physical evils are beyond any final divine determination. There is the sense that the physical soul-making environment is in important respects beyond the providence of God,
and that God's personal fulfilment is dependent upon the rather
hazardous soul-making journey. Divine providence is influenced
by, dependent upon, and even sometimes hindered by a force that,
though fundamental to an active and personal God, is, as the source
of the creative processes of the physical world and the darker side
of human nature, external and distinct from God. This dependence
of God upon external constraints also raises issues about divine
omniscience; the question arises as to how far the potentialities of
this creative primeval will are known by God.

Nevertheless, it must be noted that this theogonic view does
not mean that God cannot act upon creation; in fact it stresses
divine immanence. And it should be pointed out that this aspect of
mystical theodicy overcomes certain difficulties associated with the
supposition of this world as the best of an infinity of possibilities.
Indeed, perhaps this aspect of mystical theodicy best explains the
tragic character of human nature and the world. To regard this
world as the *only* possible realm of personal soul-making would
seem a more cogent account of the present and historical state of
affairs than if we regard it as the best of an infinity of possibilities.
For in light of the many dysteleological evils, that is, the severity
and excesses of physical evils, and the limitations of human nature,
its 'bestness' is open to considerable doubt.

The theodical sceptic, however, might consider these severities,
excesses and limitations to be evidence not only against the position
that this world is the best of an infinity of possibilities, but also
against the hypothesis of mystical theodicy. Indeed, why does God
not act more prominently against the severity of dysteleological
physical evils? A plausible case can be made that God presumed
a bit much in creating this world as an autonomous soul-making
realm, that he misjudged the effects of natural evils and this
darker side of human nature – that in any case the price, as
Ivan Karamazov puts it, is just too high to pay. But such a stance
should not perturb a mystic overly much, not if what he says about
mystical experiences of consolation and verifying evidence are true.
Moreover, a theodicy is the *religious* response to the problem of the
challenge of evil and not intended as a conversion tool. Though
this plausible account of evil might draw some sympathy towards
a mystical worldview, it is likely that mystical theodicy will have

little meaning for the religious sceptic. It involves a great many assumptions regarding spirituality and moral teleology that are not accepted by the sceptic – indeed, many that are unacceptable to more traditional theistic-minded believers.

For the non-mystic religious believer this mystical theodicy *might* possess a great deal of cogency and provide a comforting perspective in the face of the challenge of evil. This depends, of course, on how sympathetic the believer is to a mystical teleology of a theistic nature. In this regard there are many philosophical and theological issues associated with this theodicy, issues which I have in some cases developed only minimally. For example, mystics emphasise the significance of personal transformation in theodical and teleological verification as well as the importance of authority figures, features which many thinkers regard disapprovingly. Moreover, the theodicy involves many assumptions about the nature, teleology and veracity of mystical experience, issues that I have not attempted to fully resolve in this exposition of mystical theodicy. There are issues surrounding the epistemological status of mystical experience and the relationship of interpretation to mystical experience. There are also psychological and sociological explanations of the experience that bring into question its objectivity and veracity, and there is the evaluative assumption that theistic mysticism is the appropriate end-goal of healthy mysticism. Though our development of mystical theodicy has shown theistic mysticism to provide the most effective response to the challenge of evil, I have not attempted to justify the truth of this theistic eschatology.

There are other important issues. Mystical theodicy assumes a moral and spiritual teleology which has not been formally justified, and it proposes a particular belief in rebirth that many believers doubt. Moreover, there are questions about the relationship between the spiritual growth of personality and the reappearing spiritual entity, and the notion of rebirth could and ought to be drawn more explicitly into theories of heredity and evolution.

No doubt there are further issues that I have passed over in drawing out the structure of mystical theodicy. Nevertheless, though the many issues associated with mystical theodicy have not been fully resolved in this development of mystical theodicy, the structure of this response to the challenge of evil is intelligible and consistent, and, I think, plausible and cogent. It offers a coherent response to the challenge, one which is more effective in many respects than its traditional non-mystical counterparts. Given the unresolved issues mentioned above, the degree of its effectiveness is open to debate. But, clearly, the mystical response to the challenge of evil moves in a provocative fashion away from the difficulties associated with the traditional responses, into realms of experience and theology which demand further exploration.

Notes

Introduction

1. Paul Ricoeur, 'Evil, A Challenge to Philosophy and Theology', David Pellauer (tr.), *Journal of the American Academy of Religion*, vol. LIII (December 1985) no.4, p. 635.

1 Defining Theodicy

1. John Hick, 'The Problem of Evil' in Paul Edwards (ed.), *The Encyclopedia of Philosophy*, Vol. 3 (New York: Macmillan, 1967) p. 136.
2. Alvin Plantinga, *God, Freedom and Evil* (New York: Harper & Row, 1974) pp. 28–9.
3. J. B. Sykes (ed.), *The Concise Oxford Dictionary*, 7th edn (Oxford: Clarendon Press, 1982) p. 1109.
4. Ibid., p. 829.
5. R. Z. Friedman, 'Evil and moral agency', *Philosophy of Religion*, vol. XXIV (1988) p. 7.
6. Ibid., p. 8.
7. Ibid.
8. The most specific systematisation of theodical themes that I have come across is that by Arthur L. Herman, in *The Problem of Evil in Indian Thought* (Delhi: Motilal Banarsidass, 1976), especially pp. 79–80. Herman distinguishes between twenty-one proposed solutions to the problem of evil! However, such an analysis is severely inhibited by the close interrelationship of many of the themes. Moreover, I think his many solutions can be read in the context of my general typology except for six of them; three (Illusion, Metaphor, and Mystery solutions) are not in fact theodical themes proper and three (Not All-Powerful, Impersonal Substance, and Creator Limitations solutions) place radical limitations on divine omnipotence.
9. In Chapter 2 we will examine Dostoevsky's criticisms of this aspect of retributive theodicy. He illustrates the difficulties of understanding the sufferings of children as retributive.
10. In Chapter 5 we will examine Kant's criticisms of theodicies which are founded on a conception of divine justice. He argues that there is a disproportion between moral evil and punishment, that appropriate retribution often does not occur in this world, and that

suggesting a future realm of judgement is an unwarranted proposal which does not bring satisfaction to present injustices.

11.   H. L. A. Hart, *Punishment and Responsibility* (Oxford: Clarendon Press, 1968) p. 8.

12.   A very important version of the retributive theme that differs somewhat from that found in the Judeo-Christian traditions is the retributive-rebirth hypothesis that is espoused in many Indian traditions. In Chapter 10 I will examine Śaṅkara's version of it. The major difference between his view and the Judeo-Christian versions is in the denial of original sin. In the conception of rebirth human misdeeds are understood as 'beginningless'. Thus there can be no cosmic teleology, and punishment in this view involves the moral difficulties of punishing those who are not cognisant of their misproprieties; it is but a painful retaliation to past misdeeds that, for the most part, go unremembered. So Śaṅkara's 'backward looking' retributive view fails (see Chapter 10).

13.   In Chapter 2 I will be expanding upon how the free-will defence implies and requires a teleological context, in discussion of Dostoevsky's 'The Grand Inquisitor'. Indeed, the Grand Inquisitor questions the moral implications and feasibility of freedom, arguing that humanity is better without it.

14.   An exception to this is A. Plantinga, who suggests that natural evil might be thought to arise from the misuse of freedom of non-human spirits (see Plantinga, *God, Freedom and Evil*, pp. 57–9).

15.   In Chapters 6, 7 and 8 we will examine some of these mystical eschatological perspectives, especially that of Meister Eckhart and Dostoevsky. Eckhart's mysticism culminates in the expansive creativity, compassion and justice of divine union. Dostoevsky also perceives artistic wisdom as a dynamic concept, involving an active personal love through which the religious process and ideal are evidenced and actualised.

16.   David Hume, *Dialogues Concerning Natural Religion*, Henry D. Aiken (ed.) (New York: Hafner, 1948) pp. 77–8.

17.   Ibid., pp. 75–6.

18.   Ibid., p. 74.

19.   John Hick, *Evil and the God of Love* (London: Macmillan, 1966) p. 343.

20.   St Thomas Aquinas, *Summa Theologica*, Fathers of the English Dominican Province (tr.) (New York: Benziger Brothers, 1947) pt. I, Q. xxii, art. 2.

21.   Hume, *Dialogues*, p. 78.

22.   St Thomas, *Summa Theologica*, pt. I, Q. xxv, art. 6.

23.   It should be noted that not all theodicists depict these better possible worlds in terms of the processes of our present physical environment. In Chapter 9 and the conclusion we will examine Jacob Boehme's view, one which supposes that God could not create a better world that involves the creative dynamism of our natural world. For Boehme, a world containing less particular evil would be one radically different from this world. Although this book does

not delve deeply into the question of the suffering of non-humans, we will see that natural evil poses one of the most serious problems for mystical theodicy, raising issues regarding divine omnipotence and omniscience.

2   Dostoevsky's Critique of Theodicy

1.   For example, V. V. Zenkovsky points out that the fundamental question for Dostoevsky is 'Can human evil, the evil in history, universal suffering, be religiously justified and accepted?' See Zenkovsky, 'Dostoevsky's Religious and Philosophical Views', in René Wellek (ed.), *Dostoevsky* (Englewood Cliffs, N.J.: Prentice-Hall, 1962) p. 131. Also, Nicolas Berdyaev observes that 'no one has felt human suffering more acutely than Dostoievsky and his heart is ever bleeding'. Berdyaev, *Dostoievsky*, Donald Attwater (tr.) (London: Sheed & Ward, 1934) p. 107.

2.   In this regard scholars sharply disagree on the success or failure of Dostoevsky's theodicy. Robert Belknap provides a good survey of this issue in *The Structure of the Brothers Karamazov* (Paris: Mouton, The Hague, 1967) pp. 9–16. For a brief survey of scholars who consider Dostoevsky's critique of theodicy to be unassailable see Robert V. Wharton, 'Evil in an Earthly Paradise: Dostoevsky's Theodicy', *The Thomist*, vol. XXXXI (1977) pp. 567–84, esp. pp. 567–9. Wharton himself considers Dostoevsky's theodicy to be an effective response to Ivan's attack against God, a view which we will show to be mistaken in Chapter 8 (see especially n52).

      Also, Victor Terras refers to this theodical antithesis as a theodicy-'diabolodicy' contrast, one which he illustrates in his summary of the role of evil in Dostoevsky's metaphysical anthropology. See Victor Terras, *A Karamazov Companion* (Madison, Wisconsin: The University of Wisconsin Press, 1981) pp. 47–59. Terras also notes the disagreement among scholars regarding the status of Dostoevsky's theodicy (p. 48, n34) and he suggests that the 'success or failure of Dostoevsky's theodicy depends on the reader's accceptance of Dostoevsky's metaphysical anthropology' (p. 48). However, as we draw out the particular theodical themes of *The Brothers Karamazov* it will become clear that though Dostoevsky himself espouses a religious ideal which points the way towards theodical resolution, he nevertheless doubts theodicy on moral–rational grounds. This theodical tension is never fully resolved in *The Brothers Karamazov*.

3.   Henry Troyat, *Firebrand*, Norbert Guterman (tr.) (New York: Roy, 1946) p. 398.

4.   Zenkovsky, 'Dostoevsky's Religious and Philosophical Views', p. 130.

5.   Troyat, *Firebrand*, p. 404.

6.   D. H. Lawrence, 'Preface to Dostoevsky's *The Grand Inquisitor*', in Wellek (ed.), *Dostoevsky*, p. 90.

7.   Richard Peace, *Dostoyevsky* (Cambridge University Press, 1971) p. 226.

8. Fyodor Dostoevsky, *The Brothers Karamazov: The Constance Garnett Translation revised by Ralph E. Matlaw – backgrounds and sources, essays in criticism*, Ralph E. Matlaw (ed.) (New York: Norton, 1976). In this chapter all quotations from this edition are cited in the text.
9. Troyat, *Firebrand*, pp. 407–8.
10. Lawrence, 'Preface to Dostoevsky's *The Grand Inquisitor*', p. 94.
11. Ibid.
12. Peace, *Dostoyevsky*, p. 279.
13. Troyat, *Firebrand*, p. 413.
14. Ibid., p. 412.
15. Zenkovsky, 'Dostoevsky's Religious and Philosophical Views', p. 133.
16. Berdyaev, *Dostoievsky*, p. 58.
17. Ibid.
18. Zenkovsky, 'Dostoevsky's Religious and Philosophical Views', p. 134.
19. Berdyaev, *Dostoievsky*, p. 78.
20. Zenkovsky, 'Dostoevsky's Religious and Philsophical Views', p. 138.
21. Berdyaev, *Dostoievsky*, p. 75.
22. Ibid., p. 92.

3 Leibniz's Teleological Theodicy

1. C. T. Onion (ed.), *The Oxford Dictionary of English Etymology* (Oxford: Clarendon Press, 1979) p. 915.
2. G. W. Leibniz, *Theodicy*, E. M. Huggard (tr.) (London: Routledge & Kegan Paul, 1951). In *The Oxford Dictionary of English Etymology* the definition of the term refers to this text.
3. In this chapter references to Leibniz's *Theodicy* are cited in the text by page (for Huggard's translation) and essay paragraph number.
4. Austin Farrer, 'Introduction' to Leibniz, *Theodicy*, p. 35.
5. Richard H. Popkin, 'Fideism', in Edwards (ed.), *Encyclopedia of Philosophy*, Vol. 3 (New York: Macmillan, 1972) p. 201. Also see Popkin's 'Pierre Bayle' in Edwards (ed.), *Encyclopedia of Philosophy*, Vol. 1.
6. The teleological structure of Leibniz's theodicy only became fully clear to me in discussion with Michael Latzer. His insightful reading of the *Theodicy* helped me to clarify the antecedent–consequent will distinction and its relationship to the teleological goal.
7. According to Thomas this distinction between the antecedent and consequent will of God is introduced by John Damascene. Thomas quotes from *De fide Orthodoxa*: '"Antecedent will is God's acceptance of something on His own account"', whereas "consequent will is a concession on our own account"'. Though not in a direct theodical context, Thomas briefly discusses this distinction in *Truth*, vol. III, Robert W. Schmidt, S. J. (tr.) (Chicago: Henry Regnery, 1954) Q. 23, especially article 2, pp. 98–102.
8. Terence Penelhum provides an argument proving the logical impos-

sibility of foreknowledge of the free actions of human beings. His argument is easily adapted to show the failure of Leibniz's position: God knows at time T_1 that Leibniz will write X at time T_2 in *this* world. Now, if Leibniz *freely* writes X at time T_2 in this world, then he is capable of writing Y at T_2 in this world. But if he does the latter then he falsifies God's knowledge – a contradiction. See Penelhum, *Religion and Rationality* (New York: Random House, 1971) pp. 294–301.

Now perhaps one might defend Leibniz's view by doubting the premise of God's knowing *in time*. One might suggest that there is no past–present–future distinction in God's eternal knowledge, and foreknowledge is like our knowledge in memory. Just as our knowledge of the past does not impinge upon anyone's freedom, so God's knowledge of the future does not. However, this analogy breaks down in the fact that memory is *based* on past actual happenings while foreknowledge, by definition, has no such basis. To suggest that God *remembers* our future actions is one thing, and involves the nonsensical claim that God remembers events yet to happen. To suggest that God *knows* our future actions is quite another, and returns us to the question about freedom and foreknowledge with which we began: how can we freely do that which is known prior to our doing?

9. In the following critique of Leibniz's teleological theodicy I will be ignoring the moral problems of original sin and eternal punishment. Leibniz apparently holds both these views but he does not discuss them much. I think these notions are irreconcilable with the goodness of God, but I will postpone justification of this position until the next chapter, where I will clarify it in terms of John Hick's treatment.
10. Leibniz, *Theodicy* (paras 12–19) pp. 130–35.
11. Voltaire, *Candide*, in Edmund Fuller (ed.), *Voltaire* (New York: Dell, 1959) p. 10.
12. Ibid., p. 17.
13. Ibid., p. 20.
14. Ibid., pp. 14–15.
15. Hick, *Evil and the God of Love*, p. 172.
16. Ibid., p. 171.
17. Hume, *Dialogues*, p. 68.

4 John Hick's 'Soul-Making' Theodicy

1. In his most recent book, Professor Hick reaffirms the theodicy developed in his earlier works, in the context of the justification of religious belief from his religious pluralist perspective. See John Hick, *An Interpretation of Religion: Human Responses to the Transcendent* (New Haven, Conn,.: Yale University Press, 1989) especially pp. 118–122 for a brief summary of his theodicy.
2. Hick, *Evil and the God of Love*. References to this work will appear in this chapter as page numbers in the text.

3.   See W. Doniger O'Flaherty, *The Origins of Evil in Hindu Mythology* (Berkeley: University of California Press, 1976) pp. 4, 6–8.

4.   In Chapter 9 we will examine Jacob Boehme's interpretation of the fall. Though he does interpret the fall myth in terms of an original flaw in human nature, he nevertheless effectively distances this weakness from God.

5.   In an unpublished paper, 'On Rivalry in Theodicy: Irenaeus, Augustine, and John Hick', P. W. Gooch shows Augustine's version of the teleological theme to be very much like Hick's interpretation of Irenaeus. I think Gooch's argument is strengthened by the fact that at times Irenaeus does speak of a human fall from closeness to God. See Irenaeus, *Adversus Haereses*, W. W. Harvey (ed. and tr.) (Cambridge: 1857) pp. 100–101; and Irenaeus, *Apostolic Preaching*, in H. Bettenson (ed. and tr.), *The Early Christian Fathers* (New York: Oxford University Press, 1969) pp. 93–4. Perhaps the Augustinian and Irenaean versions are not as different as Hick thinks: both possess the views of a fall from paradise on the one hand, and that of spiritual growth on the other. However, for the sake of clarity I leave Hick's distinction because his version is necessary to coherent theodicy, and because the emphasis in Irenaeus is clearly the image-likeness progression that I will outline in a moment.

6.   This kind of interpretation of hell is not inconsistent with the views of the nature of evil of Meister Eckhart, Pseudo-Dionysius, and Jacob Boehme. See below especially Chapters 7, 8 and 9.

5   Problems and Issues in Traditional Theodicy

1.   Kant's 'On the Failure of all Attempted Philosophical Theodicies' in M. Despland (tr.), *Kant on History and Religion* (Montreal: McGill–Queen's University Press, 1973) pp. 283–97.

2.   Ann Loades, 'Kant and Job's Comforters' in Stephen Sykes and Derek Holmes (eds), *New Studies in Theology*, Vol. 1 (London: Gerald Duckworth, 1980) p. 129.

3.   In 'Kant and Job's Comforters', Anne Loades gives a very interesting historical account of Kant's changing views on the scope and limitations of theodicy, in the context of the ideas of Bayle, Pope, Leibniz, Hume and others. See ibid., pp. 119–38.

4.   This is the appendix of the second edition of the *Critique of Judgement*. In this paper I rely primarily on J. H. Bernard's translation (New York: Hefner, 1951) and quote from it, though I also turn to J. C. Meredith's translation (Oxford: Clarendon Press, 1951) for clarification.

5.   Kant, 'On the Failure', p. 283.

6.   Ibid., p. 290.

7.   Ibid.

8.   Ibid., p. 286.

9.   Ibid., p. 267.

10.   Ibid., p. 289.

11. Ibid.
12. Ibid., p. 290.
13. Kant, *Critique of Judgement*, J. H. Bernard (tr.), pp. 286–7.
14. Ibid., p. 288.
15. Ibid., p. 292. It is interesting to note Kant's changing view in this regard. In the *Critique of Practical Reason* he thinks that empirical data can give a much more powerful picture of the Author of nature, evidencing a good, wise and powerful Creator. He says there: 'Since we know only a small part of this world and even less can compare it with all possible worlds, we can very well infer from its order, design, and magnitude to a wise, beneficent, and powerful Author of it, but not that he is all-knowing, all-good, and all-powerful' (Kant, *Critique of Practical Reason*, Lewis White Beck (tr.) [Indianapolis: Bobbs-Merrill, 1956] p. 144). This is quite different from what he later proposes in the *Critique of Judgement*, as I have quoted above, where even limited wisdom and goodness are open to doubt.
16. Kant, *Critiques of Judgement*, J. H. Bernard (tr.), p. 292.
17. Ibid., p. 293.
18. Ibid.
19 Kant, *Critique of Practical Reason*, p. 145.
20. Kant, *Critique of Judgement*, J. H. Bernard (tr.), p. 295.
21. Ibid., p. 321.
22. Ibid.
23. Ibid., p. 307.
24. Ibid., p. 308.
25. Ibid., p. 322.
26. Ibid.
27. Kant, 'On the Failure', p. 291.
28. Ibid.
29. Ibid., p. 290.
30. Kant, *Critique of Judgement*, J. H. Bernard (tr.), p. 290.
31. Kant, 'On the Failure', p. 292.
32. Arthur Schopenhauer, 'On the Suffering of the World', in *Essays and Aphorisms*, R. J. Hollingdale (tr.) (Markham, Ontario: Penguin, 1981) pp. 49–50.
33. Kant, 'On the Failure', p. 293.
34. Ibid., p. 292.
35. Hick, *Evil and the God of Love*, p. 299.
36. Ibid., p. 322.
37. Ibid., p. 318.
38. Ibid., p. 395.
39. Ibid., p. 318.
40. On this point Hick does refer to the redemptive power of Jesus Christ (hence the great compassion of God), but he describes the crucifixion as Jesus' 'voluntary endurance of pain and suffering as God's *servant* and *agent*' (my emphasis). Ibid., p. 392.
41. Ibid., p. 299.
42. For these criticisms I raise regarding personal culpability I am

indebted to Paul Gooch who raises similar problems for Hick in 'On Rivalry in Theodicy'.

43.   Hick, *Evil and the God of Love*, p. 322.

44.   Immanuel Kant, *Religion Within the Limits of Reason Alone*, T. M. Greene and H. H. Hudson (trs) (Chicago: Open Court, 1934) pp. 15–49.

45.   Ibid., p. 17.

46.   Ibid., p. 23.

47.   Ibid., p. 22.

48.   Ibid., p. 21.

49.   Ibid., p. 22–3.

50.   Ibid., p. 23.

51.   Ibid., p. 31–2.

52.   Ibid., p. 32. Kant draws this conclusion from his observation of general human activity. He thinks this propensity 'need not be formally proved in view of the multitude of crying examples which experience *of the actions* of men puts before our eyes' (p. 28).

53.   Kant says 'The law, rather, forces itself upon [man] irresistibly by virtue of his moral disposition; . . . But by virtue of an equally innocent natural predisposition he depends upon the incentives of his sensuous nature' (ibid., p. 31).

54.   Hick, *Evil and the God of Love*, p. 376.

55.   Ibid., p. 377.

56.   Ibid., p. 365–6.

6 Defining Teleological Mysticism

1.   This is especially the case in regard to typologies of mystical experience. Perhaps the most notable of recent time are R. C. Zaehner's panenhenic, monistic and theistic ranking in Zaehner, *Mysticism Sacred and Profane* (Oxford University Press, 1957); W. T. Stace's introvertive–extrovertive distinction in Stace, *Mysticism and Philosophy* (Philadelphia: Lippincott, 1960); and Ninian Smart's numinous-mystical logical strand model, in Smart, *Reasons and Faiths* (London: Routledge & Kegan Paul, 1958). I will be referring to various aspects of these typologies throughout this chapter.

2.   Amoral and immoral mysticisms have, I think, aroused a great deal of the current philosophical interest in mysticism. Recent interesting and insightful developments of these ethical questions of religious mysticism can be found in James Horne, *The Moral Mystic* (Waterloo: Wilfrid Laurier University Press, 1983), and in R. C. Zaehner's highly provocative but meandering treatment of the topic which he developed around the demonic figure of Charles Manson in Zaehner, *Our Savage God* (New York: Sheed & Ward, 1974).

3.   For an excellent account of this historical religious diversity see Ninian Smart, 'History of Mysticism' in Edwards (ed.), *Encyclopedia of Philosophy*, Vol. 5, pp. 419–29.

4.   I am indebted to Donald Evans for these serious/casual and authentic/dilettante expressions.

5. Evelyn Underhill, *Mysticism* (New York: New American Library, 1974). In this chapter all references to Underhill's *Mysticism* will appear in the text.

6. Underhill does not always clearly distingush mystical processes from mystical experiences, but such a distinction is implicit in her account and helpful in understanding it. Concerning another important distinction, that between mystical experiences and mystical *interpretations* she is quite explicit. She says 'we have a mystical philosophy or theology – the comment of the intellect on the proceedings of spiritual intuition – running side by side with true or empirical mysticism: classifying its data, criticising it, explaining it, and translating its vision of the supersensible into symbols which are amenable to dialectic' (Underhill, *Mysticism*, p. 95).

   Recently some scholars have come to criticise this distinction; Steven Katz argues that the experience and interpretation are indistinguishable. He thinks the inherited beliefs, concepts, and values of mystics enter into the mystical experience itself – that the experience is over-determined by the mystic's socio-religious history. See 'The Conservative Character of Mysticism, in Steven Katz (ed.), *Mysticism and Religious Traditions* (Oxford University Press, 1983); and 'Language, Epistemology, and Mysticism', in Steven Katz (ed.), *Mysticism and Philosophical Analysis* (London: Sheldon Press, 1978). Though Katz has gained some support in this view, including John Hick (*An Interpretation of Religion*, especially pp. 170–71, 240–49, 292–6) I think it is mistaken in its extremism, and cannot account for mystical heresy. Ninian Smart effectively shows the separability of interpretation from experience in his distinction between 'lesser descriptions' and 'doctrinally specific'. See Smart, 'Understanding Religious Experience', in Steven Katz (ed.), *Mysticism and Philosophical Analysis*. Also, Donald Evans questions the epistemological assumptions Katz brings to his thesis in 'Can Philosophers Limit What Mystics Can Do?', *Religious Studies*, vol. XXV (1989) no. 3, pp. 53–60. It is my view that a mystical framework is to some extent *based* upon experience, and I will be drawing upon theistic frameworks, as we will see, because they provide the most effective theodicy.

7. Underhill, *Practical Mysticism* (New York: Dutton, 1943) pp. 60–61.

8. Ibid., pp. 67–8.

9. Ibid., p. 67.

10. Suso, a German Dominican mystic and disciple of Meister Eckhart, was with Henry Tauler, associated with the Friends of God, an informal group of German mystics who espoused a spiritual revivalism. For an interesting and brief account of his life and work see James Clark, *The Great German Mystics: Eckhart, Tauler and Suso* (New York: Russell & Russell, 1949) pp. 55–74.

11. Henry Suso, *The Life of the Servant*, James M. Clark (tr.) (London: James Clark, 1952) p. 55.

12. On this point Suso writes, 'Sometimes God ordains grievous sufferings for a man although he is not to blame. In such trials God either

intends to test him, to see how firmly he stands, or what strength he has in himself, as we often read in the Old Testament' (ibid., p. 130).

13.   Donald Evans, 'Mysticism and Morality', *Dialogue*, vol. XXIV (1985) p. 305. Here Donald Evans clarifies this process in terms of Underhill's view. From the mystical perspective, egoism is not just self-centred motivation, but 'fundamentally a defensive self-contraction which resists the flow of loving light through oneself to others'.

14.   Anonymous, *Meditations on the Tarot: A Journey Into Christian Hermeticism*, Robert A. Powell (tr.) (Warwick, NY: Amity House Inc., 1985) p. 9. This book gives a highly provocative account of Christian mysticism within the framework of the Tarot. It is quite a vast and significant work; Thomas Keating refers to it as 'the greatest contribution to date toward the rediscovery and renewal of the Christian contemplative tradition'. I will be referring to it throughout this section on mysticism and theodicy.

15.   Ibid., p. 10.

16.   This latter category of the paranormal is often distinguished from mysticism proper in so far as it involves visual and auditory kinds of experiences of a highly effable nature. At this point I wish to postpone discussion of this realm of mysticism, though I should note that memories of past lives are relevant to theodicy, as we will see in Chapter 10.

17.   This is the view of Donald Evans, a position that I find very plausible.

18.   Anonymous, *Meditations on the Tarot*, p. 166.

19.   Ibid.

20.   W. T. Stace, *Mysticism and Philosophy*, pp. 15–16.

21.   Underhill, *Practical Mysticism*, p. 91.

22.   Donald Evans, 'Christian Spirituality and Social Action', in Stanley Fefferman (ed.), *Awakened Heart: Buddhist–Christian Dialogue in Canada* (Toronto: United Church House, 1985) p. 122. In this paper Evans proposes a reconciliatory approach to these contemplative and social activist modes.

23.   Underhill considers this experience to be depicted in words of immanence or in terms of transcendence, depending on the disposition of the mystic. However, this distinction is rather awkward and obscure. For instance, transcendence suggests the experience of something external to the mystic when such is not the case. Further, it implies a similarity with an outward-looking experience of the divine presence. Because of these problems I prefer to contrast these descriptions in terms of a cataphatic–apophatic distinction.

24.   Underhill, *Practical Mysticism*, p. 122.

25.   Nicolas Berdyaev, *The Destiny of Man*, Nataliia Duddington (tr.) (London: G. Bles, 1937) pp. 25, 34.

26.   Underhill, *Practical Mysticism*, p, 130.

27.   Ibid., p. 129

28.   Ibid., p. 131.

29.   Ibid., p. 135.

30. Ninian Smart would agree with Underhill on the view that these experiences differ only in terms of how they are interpreted. He suggests that experiential accounts are 'ramified' according to the interpretive doctrine of the mystic's religious tradition. See Smart, 'Interpretation and Mystical Experience', *Religious Studies* vol. I (1965) no. 1, pp. 75–87 where Smart argues against Zaehner in this regard.
31. Zaehner, *Mysticism Sacred and Profane.*
32. Anonymous, *Meditations on the Tarot*, p. 167.
33. Ibid., p. 36.
34. Ibid.
35. Ibid.
36. Ibid.
37. Louis Dupré, 'The Christian Experience of Mystical Union', *The Journal of Religion*, vol. LXIX (January 1989) no. 1, p. 9.
38. Ibid., p. 10.
39. Ibid., p. 9.

7   Theodical Evidence in Meister Echhart

1. Evelyn Underhill, *Mysticism*, p. 463.
2. Matthew Fox (ed. and comm.), *Breakthrough: Meister Eckhart's Creation Spirituality in New Translation* (Garden City, NY: Image Books, 1980). See pp. 1–4 where Fox provides an extensive account of the great influence of Eckhart.
3. Matthew Fox's copious notes attest to this trend; also Richard Woods, *Eckhart's Way* (Wilmington, Delaware: Michael Glazier, 1986) pp. 222–33, provides an extensive bibliography confirming this renewed interest in Eckhart.
4. Immanuel Kant, 'On the Failure of all Philosophical Theodicies', in M. Despland (tr.), *Kant on History and Religion* (Montreal: McGill-Queen's University Press, 1973) p. 292.
5. Anonymous, *Meditations on the Tarot*, Robert A. Powell (tr.), pp. 536–7.
6. Ibid., p. 543.
7. Ibid.
8. It is important to note that John Hick maintains this position. In his most recent work he says 'all cognitive awareness is a mode of experiencing-as in terms of concepts and patterns of meaning' (*An Interpretation of Religion: Human Responses to the Transcendent*, [New Haven, Conn.: Yale University Press, 1989] p. 294). Hick proposes culturally relative categories of religious experience analogous to Kant's framework of categories, concepts *by which* 'the environing divine reality is brought to consciousness' (p. 245). Human beings relate to the Real only in terms of modes of awareness. Primary categories are personal God and non-personal Absolute, but these are culturally particularised, leading to the great plurality of religious beliefs, practices and attitudes. Hick, then, concurs with Steven Katz who argues that mystical experience is 'over-determined' by

and dependent upon the mystic's interpretive modes, and that there can be no linguistically and conceptually unmediated experiences. As I have mentioned in Chapter 6, n6, I consider this view of mystical experience/interpretation to be mistaken.

9. William James, *The Varieties of Religious Experience* (New York: The New American Library, 1958) p. 307. James cites this as a description of cosmic consciousness.

10. Louis Dupré, 'The Christian Experience', p. 5.

11. Ibid., p. 6.

12. Ibid.

13. Ibid., p. 6–7.

14. Ibid., p. 7.

15. Ibid., p. 9.

16. James Clark, *Meister Eckhart: an introduction to the study of his works with an anthology* (London: Thomas Nelson, 1957) p. 52.

17. Ibid., p. 50.

18. In this chapter quotations of Eckhart from Fox's *Breakthrough* are cited in the text.

19. Regarding Eckhart's view of the peak of the soul as intellect, Richard Woods says: 'It is clear in many references that Eckhart has in mind the intellect or understanding itself, the highest power of the soul which in high scholasticism was called the *ratio superior*, the mind as turned toward God' (Woods, *Eckhart's Way*, p. 59).

20. Bernard McGinn (ed.), *Meister Eckhart: Teacher and Preacher* (Toronto: Paulist Press, 1968) p. 152.

21. I realise that Eckhart's characterisation of evil here raises issues regarding its reality and negative force. We will be examining Eckhart's view of the nature of evil in much greater detail in Chapter 8, as it is relevant to the issues surrounding positive/affirmative theodicy.

22. James Clark and John V. Skinner (eds and trs), *Meister Eckhart: Selected Treatises and Sermons Translated from Latin and German with an Introduction and Notes*, (New York: Harper & Row, 1958) p. 196.

23. Donald Evans, *On Being Completely Human*, (unpublished manuscript) Chapter 5.

24. Ibid.

25. Ibid.

26. Underhill, *Mysticism*, p. 73.

27. Underhill, *Practical Mysticism*, p. 20.

8 The Consolatory Power of Mystical Experience

1. Zaehner, *Our Savage God*, p. 65.

2. Ibid., pp. 65, 67.

3. From a theistic theodical perspective, amoral and immoral mysticism will be associated with egocentric or perhaps demonic experiences, or with lower level experiences which the mystic ought to subordinate to the dynamic and creative theistic consolatory experiences.

4. Underhill, *Mysticism*, p. 224.

5. Bernard McGinn (ed.), *Meister Eckhart* (Toronto: Paulist Press, 1968) p. 152.

6. 'The Bull *"In agro dominico"'*, in Edmund Colledge and Bernard McGinn (eds and trs), *Meister Eckhart: The Essential Sermons, Commentaries, Treatises, and Defense* (New York: Paulist Press, 1981) p. 78. For an insightful discussion of the controversies surrounding Eckhart's trial and condemnation, as well as an account of the decline and resurgence of interest in Eckhart, see James M. Clark, *The Great German Mystics*, pp. 7–35.

7. Zaehner, *Our Savage God*, p. 56.

8. John Macquarrie, *In Search of Deity* (London: SCM Press, 1984), p. 61.

9. Plotinus says in this regard: 'All knowing comes by likeness. The Intellectual-Principle and the Soul, being Ideal-Forms, would know Ideal-Forms and would have a natural tendency towards them; but who could imagine Evil to be an Ideal-Form, seeing that it manifests itself as the very absence of Good?'. Plotinus, *The Enneads*, Stephen MacKenna (tr.) 2nd edn rev. (London: Faber & Faber, 1956) 1.8.1, p. 66.

10. Ibid., 1.8.3, p. 68.

11. B. A. G. Fuller argues that 'Logically for Plotinus, Evil should occur as the beginning of the emanatory process', at the moment of existence of that which is other than the One. Fuller says, the emanatory process, then, would be 'birth-marked with Evil'. Fuller, *The Problem of Evil in Plotinus* (Cambridge University Press, 1912) p. 83. However, I think this suggestion would only be accurate if the emanation process were regarded as an error or a mistake, more in a gnostic sense of creation than in the idea of an overflowing of the One, which is the view of Plotinus. In any case, Plotinus insists, as Fuller points out, that evil appears 'not in the first, but in the last stage of emanation' (p. 83).

12. Plotinus, *The Enneads*, 1.8.3, p. 68.

13. Macquarrie, *In Search of Deity*, p. 71.

14. Plotinus, *The Enneads*, 1.8.4, p. 69. In this regard Fuller comments: 'Evil, then, is not a modification of Matter by Form, but a modification of Form by Matter. It may lie in a disposition of the body, but the disposition is evil only in so far as it represents a partial disintegration of form and measure into formlessness and lack of measure, due to the material admixture'. Fuller, *The Problem of Evil in Plotinus*, p. 234.

15. Besides the obvious influence of the more 'non-mystical' scholastic philosophy upon Eckhart, Clark also refers to both Plotinus and the Pseudo-Dionysius, along with Augustine, as Eckhart's 'teachers'. See Clark, *The Great German Mystics*, p. 18.

16. Pseudo-Dionysius, *The Divine Names*, in Colm Luibheid (tr.), *The Complete Works* (New York: Paulist Press, 1987) 708B, p. 79.

17. Ibid., 704B, p. 77.

18. Ibid., 716B, p. 84.

19. Ibid., 716A, p. 84.

20. Ibid., 716D, p. 85.
21. Ibid., 717A, p. 85.
22. Ibid., 720A, p. 86.
23. Ibid., 717B, pp. 85–6.
24. Ibid., 717B–C, p. 86.
25. Ibid., 720B, p. 87.
26. Ibid., 729B, p. 93.
27. Ibid., 732C–D, p. 94.
28. Ibid., 725C, p. 91.
29. Ibid., 720C, p. 87.
30. Dionysius says, 'it seems to me that those who have been purified should in fact be perfectly uncontaminated, that they should be free of all dissimilar blemish . . . [they] should receive the divine light in full'. Pseudo-Dionysius, *The Celestial Hierarchy*, in Colm Luibheid (tr), *The Complete Works*, 165D, p. 155.
31. Macquarrie, *In Search of Deity*, p. 74. Macquarrie also comments: 'The very notion of hierarchy implies both receiving and giving. Those who are purified help to purify others; those who are illumined give illumination to others; those who have attained to communion with the divine bring others to the same relation. Human beings are unified with each other as they seek union with God' (p. 83).
32. Pseudo-Dionysius, *The Celestial Hierarchy*, 165A, p. 154.
33. Macquarrie, *In Search of Deity*, p. 84.
34. Pseudo-Dionysius, *The Celestial Hierarchy*, 165A, p. 154.
35. Fox, *Breakthrough*, p. 276.
36. Ibid., p. 329.
37. Clark and Skinner, *Meister Eckhart: Selected Treatises*, pp. 115, 120, 137, 138, 140, 142.
38. Fox, *Breakthrough*, pp. 484–5.
39. See Chapter 7.
40. Dupré, 'The Christian Experience', p. 7.
41. Fox, *Breakthrough*, p. 135.
42. This point is made by Clark and Skinner in *Meister Eckhart: Selected Treatises* in reference to the commentary of Josef Quint (p. 142).
43. Macquarrie, *In Search of Deity*, p. 180.
44. Ibid., p. 181.
45. Ronald Goetz, 'The Suffering God: The Rise of a New Orthodoxy', *The Christian Century* (April 16, 1986) pp. 385–9. In this essay Goetz cites Barth, Berdyaev, Bonhoeffer, Brunner, Cobb, Cone, Kung, Moltmann, Niebuhr, Pannenberg, Reuhter, Temple, Teilhard and Unamuno as modern theopaschite thinkers, and gives an interesting but general discussion of some of the issues and significances of this line of thought.
46. Ibid., p. 389.
47. Fox, *Breakthrough*, p. 235.
48. Ibid., p. 234.
49. This analogy comes out of discussion with Donald Evans.
50. 'Counsels on Discernment', in Colledge and McGinn, *Meister Eckhart*, p. 265.

51. Fyodor Dostoevsky, *The Brothers Karamazov: The Constance Garnett Translation revised*, Ralph E. Matlaw (ed.) (New York: Norton, 1976). In this chapter all quotations from this edition are cited in the text.

52. Robert V. Wharton argues in 'Evil in an Earthly Paradise: Dostoevsky's Theodicy' , *The Thomist*, vol. XXXXI (1977) pp. 567–84, that Zosima's theodicy is of an 'essentially rationalistic nature' (p. 583). Wharton suggests that Zosima's theodicy rests in his realisation that life 'is in truth paradise' (p. 581). But this realisation, Wharton insists, derives from a non-mystical experience of reason. Moreover, Wharton argues that this non-mystical experience places the responsibility of the despoilment and non-recognition of this paradise firmly upon human beings, not God. However, it will become clear from the excerpts I quote that Zosima's theodicy *is* based on mystical experience, and that, in any case, his theodicy *does not* provide a rational response to Ivan's problem of innocent-suffering, as we developed it in Chapter 2.

53. Peace, *Dostoyevsky*, p. 294.

54. My emphasis.

55. Purgatory is also a possible move to save theodicy, but I will argue in Chapter 10 that this move is not as effective or plausible as reincarnation.

9 The Origin of Evil in Human Nature: Jacob Boehme's *Ungrund*

1. For example, besides Dostoevsky, Hick and Kant, who have been mentioned already, Martin Buber, Gabriel Marcel and Nicolas Berdyaev all propound this kind of a fundamental moral structure in their ethical theories.

2. Evelyn Underhill refers to him as 'one of the giants of mysticism' and both William Law and Nicolas Berdyaev speak of him as 'one of the greatest mystics of all time'. See Underhill, *Mysticism*, p. 469; and Stephen Hobhouse's observations in H. L. Martensen, *Jacob Boehme*, T. Rhys Evans (tr.) (London: Rocklift, Salisbury Square, 1949) p. xi.

3. Boehme had a significant influence upon certain major figures of western philosophy. Paul Tillich notes that Boehme's thought had a major impact upon Schelling, Hegel, Schopenhauer, Nietzsche, Hartmann, Bergson and Heidegger. See the foreword of Joseph Stoudt's *Jacob Boehme: His Life and Thought* (New York: The Seabury Press, 1968) p. 7.

4. In this regard Alexander Koyré writes: 'Le grand problème qui domine toute sa pensèe est le double problème traditionnel du mal et des rapports entre Dieu et le monde' (The principle problem which dominates all of his thought is the twofold traditional problem of evil and of the relations between God and the world). Koyré, *La Philosophie De Jacob Boehme* (Paris: Librarie Philosophique J. Vrin, 1929) p. 72. My translation.

5. Koyré considers the theme of evil to be 'Le problème essentiel du livre' (Ibid., p. 179).

6. Jacob Boehme, *Epistles* (1730) ch. 12, para. 67, as quoted in Stoudt,

Jacob Boehme, p. 108. Also, the 'Preface to the Reader' in *The Three Principles* refers to the book as 'the A, B, C to all his Writings; and those who read it carefully, will find it, though hard at first, easy at last, and then all his other Books easy, and full of deep Understanding' (see Jacob Boehme, *The Three Principles of the Divine Essence*, John Sparrow [tr][1648 translation], in *The Works of Jacob Behmen, The Teutonic Theosopher*, Vol. 1 [London: Pater-noster Row, 1764]). Though some of the more alchemist sections of the text still remain very obscure to me, my reading of Boehme confirms this perspective. Thus I am surprised that the secondary sources do not refer to this book more frequently. Koyré, however, does recognise the significance of this book and he provides a very astute commentary on it in *La Philosophie De Jacob Boehme* (see pp. 169–236).

7.   Koyré considers this text to be one of the more obscure and confusing of Boehme's works. The book was written several years after *Aurora*, following a period where Boehme immersed himself in the work of sixteenth-century spiritualists, Schwenkfeld, Weigel, Pseudo-Weigel, Fall and Resurrection literature, and Paracelsus and his followers. The influence of the alchemy of Paracelsus is quite pronounced in this book, which in some sections, in Koyré's words, 'produit une confusion indescriptible'. See Koyré, *La Philosophie De Jacob Boehme*, pp. 170, 174–6.

8.   Koyré situates *The Three Principles* in the middle of a three-stage evolution of Boehme's thought. This evolution is characterised by a 'différence de ton, de manière, de style de ces écrits' (difference of tone, of method, of style of the writings) (p. 70). My translation. *High and Deep Grounding of Six Theosophic Points* is a more refined work of the third stage, less given to alchemist imagery. It is thought by Koyré to be more profound, conscientious and philosophical (*La Philosophie de Jacob Boehme*, p. 70). It is, however, also much more terse, and does not contain the background detail present in *The Three Principles*. I will refer to John Rolleston Earle's translation of Jacob Boehme, *High and Deep Grounding of Six Theosophic Points*, in *Six Theosophic Points and Other Writings*, (Ann Arbor: University of Michigan Press, 1958).

9.   Boehme, *Epistles*, ch. 12, para. 71, as quoted in Stoudt, *Jacob Boehme*, p. 117.

10.   Jacob Boehme, *The Three Principles of the Divine Essence*. Citations from this work appear as chapter and paragraph numbers in the text.

11.   These categories of SULPHUR and MERCURIUS are very important symbols in Boehme's presentation. H. L. Martensen states that these categories are to be understood as the spirit behind substance, and are derived from the Swiss physician Paracelsus (1493–1541) (See Martensen, *Jacob Boehme*, pp. 23–4).

12.   In *A Fundamental Statement Concerning the Earthly and Heavenly Mystery* (Boehme, *Six Theosophic Points*, pp. 139–62), Boehme describes the magical nature of this craving in much more detail. In the first text he says: 'But as there is nothing that can give anything,

accordingly the craving itself is the giving of, which yet also is a nothing, or merely a desirous seeking. And this is the eternal origin of Magic'. Also see *A Short Explanation of Six Mystical Points*, in Boehme, *Six Theosophic Points*, especially the fifth point, pp. 131–5.

13. Boehme, *Six Theosophic Points*, Part I, ch. 1, para. 38.
14. Ibid., para. 10.
15. Ibid., para. 11.
16. Ibid., para. 12.
17. Ibid., para. 16.
18. Ibid., para. 18.
19. Ibid., para. 3.
20. Ibid., para. 1.
21. Ibid., ch. 2, para. 11.
22. Koyré concurs on this important interpretive point of Boehme. He says: 'En effet, le second principe de la nature divine nous était apparu comme surajouté en quelque sorte au premier qui en forme la base et l'engendre. Mais c'est une erreur d'optique; le second principe n'est pas seulement tout aussi nécessaire à la formation de la vie divine que le premier, mais, en un certain sens, le premier principe n'existe que pour pouvoir engendrer le second: bien plus, au fond cet engendrement n'est pas unilatéral, mais mutuel. Le premier et le second principe s'engendrent et se conditionnent corrélativement, et le premier n'aurait pas davantage pu subsister sans le second, que le second n'aurait pu être sans le premier. Ils naissent à la fois, "avant" leur naissance Dieu n'est qu'un esprit absolument indéterminé, et "comme un rien"'. (In effect, we have seen the second principle of the divine nature as superadded, so to speak, upon the first, which forms its basis and produces it. But this is an optical illusion; the second principle is not only as necessary to the formation of the divine life as the first, but, in a certain sense, the first principle exists for no other reason than to produce the second. Moreover, in reality this production is not unilateral, but mutual. The first and the second principles produce and condition themselves correlatively, and the first would no more have been able to exist without the second, than the second would have been able to be without the first. They are born at the same time; "before" their birth God is nothing but an absolutely indeterminate spirit, and "like a nothing".) Koyré, *La Philosophie De Jacob Boehme*, pp. 207–8. My translation.

Though the first principle is the creative power, in a sense, of God and the world, it is really nothing apart from the second principle. The second principle is as necessary to the creative process as the first (indeed, Boehme ascribes 'wisdom', 'understanding' and 'omnipotence' to it (5.14)), and the first only exists in the context of the second. Boehme obviously does not consider the *Ungrund* as the absolute origin of God and the world (see also Koyré, p. 193). Rather it is to be understood as the primordial potential energy, that force which is actualised only in association with the second principle, giving vitality to the divine life. Indeed, the mutual interdependence of these two principles in the divine life is highlighted in the fact that neither principle can, in itself, be characterised as the material, formal, efficient or final cause of God and human beings. This fact will become clearer when we turn directly to the second principle.

23. Boehme, *Six Theosophic Points*, Part II, ch. 3, para. 6.
24. Ibid., Part V, ch. 7, para. 3.
25. Ibid., para. 5.
26. As Koyré says, Boehme stresses that 'En Dieu tout est un et ne comporte pas de distinctions' (Koyré, *La Philosophie de Jacob Boehme*, p. 187).
27. Nicolas Berdyaev, *Spirit and Reality*, George Reavey (tr.) (London: G. Bles, 1939) p. 139. This view of Berdyaev comes to me via James McLachlan's 'Existentialist Interpretations of the Desire to be God: Radical Freedom in Sartre and Berdyaev', unpublished PhD Thesis, University of Toronto, 1989 (see especially pp. 159–69). As we have seen, the supposed similarity between the *Ungrund* and Eckhart's Godhead is not fully evidenced in *The Three Principles*. Though Boehme refers to the first principle as a nothingness in itself, he characterises it in rather positive and dynamic terms. In contrast with this we will later see that the second principle is depicted as in itself but a passive unity and thus perhaps more closely resembles Eckhart's Godhead in one respect. Still, perhaps the first and second Principles can independently *both* be thought to constitute what Eckhart considers the Godhead; this seems likely given Eckhart's depiction of the essential creativeness that arises from this negative source, a feature that requires in Boehme's conception both the first and second principles.
28. Berdyaev, *Spirit and Reality*, p. 141.
29. Koyré, *La Philosophie De Jacob Boehme*, p. 196. See Chapters 6–9 of *The Three Principles*.
30. For example, though Boehme insists that God is solely good and merciful he speaks of God as 'cursing the earth'. Also, God created Adam and Eve in paradise and tempted them knowing full well that the fall was inevitable, and Adam, though androgynous in paradise, nevertheless falls in lust before the temptation, whereby God forms Eve from Adam's essence. Indeed, Boehme's view here is not easily expressed in terms of the Biblical creation story and fall, and it is highly obscured in certain sections by his alchemist imagery. Still, his interpretation is original and provocative. See especially Chapters 10–17 of *The Three Principles*.
31. Boehme gives a practical example of the processes of this threefold similitude in an account of the role of reason in spiritual transformation. Likened to the first principle (Father), reason does not experience God and it speaks against His existence. Human reason recognises the weaknesses of human nature and its mortality, the strain of evil inherent to it, and it sees the absence of temporal justice. Such observations, argues Boehme, lead to the denial of the existence of God (*The Highly Precious Gate of the Divine Intuition*, (1.1) in

Six Theosophic Points). Yet, on the other hand, this scepticism plays upon itself; in their doubts the sceptics might 'begin to hate the frail, foolish life, and to die with Reason, and to give up the will to God' (1.37). In this hard scepticism reason desires the higher ground (light of the Word) that will release it from its tormented state, it desires 'to die to suffering' (1.4). So reason can self-destruct in its scepticism, breaking apart in its nihilism, and the will behind it transforms itself into the higher will of God (direction of the Holy Spirit), into the experience of 'the supersensible, superfathomable, eternal One' (2.18).

32. Hick, *Evil and the God of Love*, p. 291.
33. Hick says '[Man] did not fall into this from a prior state of holiness but was brought into being in this way as a creature capable of eventually attaining holiness'. *Evil and the God of Love*, p. 323.
34. In this view of the role and the influence of the *Ungrund* Boehme's theodicy shows similarity to Carl Jung's view of the dark side of God as he presents it in *Answer to Job*, R. F. C. Hill, (tr.), (Princeton University Press, 1973). Jung observes a dark side of the human unconscious, a negative unconsciousness that must be experienced and overcome in the context of an autonomous movement to divine consciousness. Like Boehme, Jung locates this source in the dark side of God, considers it necessary to the dynamism of God and the natural world, and recognises the grave danger of the unconscious remaining within itself, self-isolated from the light of the higher consciousness. However, Jung explains the origin of this impulse to evil in terms of an unconscious God who Himself is undergoing an historical process to consciousness. Though Boehme recognises the significance of human beings in fulfilling the Divine Essence, he does not consider God's moral consciousness to depend upon the historical human–Divine encounter. And, whereas Jung attempts to explain evil through an unconscious God in process to consciousness, Boehme justifies evil in terms of the first and second principles of the Divine Essence. So Boehme's theodicy is consistent with the dichotomy and teleology that Jung observes in the human psyche while at the same time defending a morally conscious and good God as the source of human life. And it is significant that though Boehme's theology does not consider God to be amoral or wicked, it nevertheless maintains a strong sense of the tragic in the human condition.
35. For example, in *The Three Principles* Boehme says 'there is a constant Will to generate and work, and the whole Nature stands in a great Longing and Anguish, willing continually to generate the divine Virtue, God and Paradise being hidden therein, but it generates after its Kind, according to its Ability' (7.27). He also says 'the (outward Body) is but a misty, (excrementitious, dusky, opaque Procreation) or Out-Birth in the third Principle, wherein the Soul lies captive, as in a dark Dungeon' (7.23).
36. Boehme, *Highly Precious Gate*, 1.15.
37. Boehme, *Six Mystical Points*, 3.25.

214 *Evil and the Mystics' God*

38. Boehme, *Highly Precious Gate*, 2.26.
39. McLachlan, *Existentialist Interpretations*, p. 155.
40. Dostoevsky, *The Brothers Karamazov*, p. 614.
41. Ibid., p. 615.

10 Dysteleological Evil and Rebirth

1. Fyodor Dostoevsky, *The Borthers Karamazov: The Constance Garnett Translation revised*, Ralph E. Matlaw (ed.), p. 219.
2. Ibid., p. 219.
3. Hick, *Evil and the God of Love*, p. 376.
4. John Hick, *Death and Eternal Life* (Glasgow: William Collins Sons, 1976) p. 456.
5. E. H. Plumptre, *The Spirits in Prison and Other Studies on the Life After Death* (London: Wm. Isbister Limited, 1885) p. 298.
6. Ibid., p. 136. Such speculation led to the condemnation of the eschatology of Origen at the Council of Constantinople (696 CE), where certain thinkers are accused of 'inventing a mythology . . . after the manner of the Greeks, and inventing changes and mitigations of our souls and bodies, and impiously uttering drunken ravings . . . as to the future life of the dead' (p. 142).
7. Ibid., p. 132.
8. See the entries for 'Purgatory' in F. L. Cross and E. A. Livingstone (eds), *Oxford Dictionary of the Christian Church* (Oxford University Press, 1983) pp. 1144–5; and in Vergilius Ferm (ed.), *An Encyclopedia of Religion* (New York: The Philosophical Library, 1945), p. 628.
9. Terence Penelhum, *Butler* (London: Routledge & Kegan Paul, 1985) p. 163.
10. Joseph Butler, *Analogy of Religion* (London: Society for Promoting Christian Knowledge, 1909), Part I, ch. 3, p. 56.
11. Penelhum, *Butler*, p. 169.
12. For example, Hick describes the many lives and worlds of his paraeschatological conception as follows: 'It will be a real spatio-temporal environment, functioning in accordance with its own laws, within which there will be real personal life – a world with its own concrete character, its own history, its own absorbing and urgent concerns, its own crises, perils, achievements, sacrifices, and its own terminus giving shape and meaning to existence within it' (Hick, *Death and Eternal Life*, p. 218). Hick describes future life in terms of this world, though emphasising, of course, the *unique* orientating terminus that distinguishes it from this world. However, our cases of dysteleological evils blur the connecting relationship between this world's terminus and those of other realms. What is the point of *this* life for those who are so prematurely excluded from participation in this world, and what is the criteria of their exclusion?
13. Swami Nikhilananda, *Self-Knowledge of Sri Sankaracharya* (Mylapore, Madras: Sri Ramakrishna Math, 1970) p. 94.
14. Ibid., p. 35.

15. Ibid., p. 34.
16. G. C. Nayak, *Evil, Karma and Reincarnation* (Santiniketan, West Bengal: Centre of Advanced Study in Philosophy, Visva-Bharati, 1973), p. 55.
17. Śaṅkara, *The Vedānta Sutras*, G. Thibaut (tr.), in F. Max Müller (ed.), *The Sacred Books of the East*, Vol. 34, Part I (New Delhi: Motilal Banardisass, 1973) section 2, ch. 1, no. 34, pp. 358–9.
18. Ibid., no. 35, p. 360.
19. Ibid.
20. For an intelligible and simplified account of this rather complex cosmic scenario see David R. Kinsley, *Hinduism* (Englewood Cliffs, N.J.: Prentice-Hall, 1982) p. 86.
21. Hick criticises Śaṅkara's argument, pointing out that this solution to the inequalities of life 'has not been produced but only postponed to infinity'. He says, 'One can affirm the beginningless character of the soul's existence in this way; but one cannot then claim that it renders either intelligible or morally acceptable the inequalities of our present lot' (Hick, *Death and Eternal Life*, p. 309). I get the impression that Hick is looking for a solution that Śaṅkara refuses to give: a full and complete account of the inequalities of life. Śaṅkara, however, argues that there is no full and complete account for this or that particular inequality. Though evil cannot be made fully intelligible in this sense, it seems to me that Śaṅkara's *view* is intelligible. Nevertheless, I agree with Hick that Śaṅkara's solution is morally unacceptable, but not because it cannot give a full and complete account of the inequalities of life. My reasons will become clear in a moment.
22. Nikhilananda, *Self-Knowledge*, pp. 86–7.
23. From the introduction of Thibaut's translation of Śaṅkara *The Vedānta Sutras*, p. xxv.
24. In this regard Śaṅkara comments: 'We see in every-day life that certain doings of princes or other men of high positions who have no unfulfilled desires left have no reference to any extraneous purpose, but proceed from mere sportfulness, as, for instance, their recreations in places of amusement. We further see that the process of inhalation and exhalation is going on without reference to any extraneous purpose, merely following the law of its own nature. Analogously, the activity of the Lord also may be supposed to be mere sport, proceeding from his own nature, without reference to any purpose'. (Śaṅkara, *The Vedānta Sutras*, section 2, ch. 1, section 34, pp. 356–7).
25. Nayak, *Evil, Karma and Reincarnation*, p. 62.
26. Ibid., p. 64.
27. Ibid.
28. Ibid., p. 63.
29. I develop these problems of personal identity for retributive rebirth in more detail in Stoeber, 'Personal Identity and Rebirth', *Religious Studies*, vol. XXVI (1990) pp. 493–500. The paper argues that retributive rebirth involves serious problems given the ambiguousness of

personal identity in the conception, problems which soul-making rebirth overrides.

30.   Sri Aurobindo, *The Problem of Rebirth*, from *Sri Aurobindo Birth Centenary Library* (Pondicherry, India: Sri Aurobindo Ashram Trust, 1971) Vol. 16, p. 87.
31.   Ibid., p. 118.
32.   Ibid.
33.   Ibid., p. 153.
34.   Ibid., p. 121.
35.   Sri Aurobindo, *Letters on Yoga*, in *Birth Centenary Library*, Vol. 22, p. 451.
36.   For Aurobindo this spiritual evolution is quite complex, involving what he calls a triple transformation. The mystical movement begins with the evolution of Mind out of inconscient Matter (psychic transformation), through levels of Mind (Higher, Illumined and Intuitive Mind) to Overmind (spiritual transformation), and culminating in a descension of Supermind which transforms matter spiritually, establishing a divinised community on earth (supramental transformation). For good descriptions of these stages see Robert Minor, *Sri Aurobindo: The Perfect and the Good*, (Calcutta: Minerva, Pvt., 1978) pp. 108–15; and L. Thomas O'Neil, *Towards the Life Divine* (New Delhi: Manohar, 1979), pp. 46–79, 97–9. However, for our purposes we need only be concerned with the theodical implications of his interpretation of rebirth.
37.   Again, I direct the reader to my 'Personal Identity and Rebirth', where these issues are developed in more detail.
38.   Hick, *Evil and the God of Love*, p. 399.
39.   Anonymous, *Meditations on the Tarot*, Robert A. Powell (tr.), p. 93.
40.   Ibid., p. 92.
41.   Ibid., p. 376.
42.   Ibid., p. 93.
43.   Ibid. p. 360–62.
44.   For example, Aurobindo says, the being 'goes out in the subtle body and goes to different planes of existence for a short time until it has gone through certain experiences which are the result of its earthly existence. Afterwards it reaches the psychic world where it rests in a kind of sleep, until it is time for it to start a new life on earth' (Aurobindo, *Birth Centenary Library*, Vol. 22, p. 435.
45.   Hick, *Evil and the God of Love*, p. 366.

Bibliography

Anonymous, *Meditations on the Tarot: A Journey into Christian Hermeticism*, Robert A Powell (tr.) (Warwick, NY: Amity House, 1985).

Aurobindo, Sri, *Sri Aurobindo Birth Centenary Library*, Vols 16, 22 (Pondicherry, India: Sri Aurobindo Ashram Trust, 1971).

Basham, A. L., *The Wonder that was India* (Calcutta: Rupa, 1967).

Belknap, Robert, *The Structure of the Brothers Karamazov* (Paris: Mouton, The Hague, 1967).

Berdyaev, Nicolas, *The Destiny of Man*, Nataliia Duddington (tr.) (London: G. Bles, 1937).

Berdyaev, Nicolas, *Dostoievsky*, Donald Attwater (tr.) (London: Sheed & Ward, 1934).

Berdyaev, Nicolas, *Spirit and Reality*, George Reavey (tr.) (London: G. Bles, 1939).

Boehme, Jacob, *Six Theosophic Points and Other Writings*, John Rolleston Earle (tr.) (Ann Arbor, Michigan: University of Michigan Press, 1958).

Boehme, Jacob, *The Three Principles of the Divine Essence*, John Sparrow, (tr.) (1648 translation), from *The Works of Jacob Behmen, The Teutonic Theosopher*, Vol. 1 (London: Pater-noster Row, 1764).

Butler, Joseph, *Analogy of Religion* (London: Society for Promoting Christian Knowledge, 1909).

Clark, James, *The Great German Mystics: Eckhart, Tauler and Suso* (New York: Russell & Russell, 1949).

Clark, James, *Meister Eckhart: An Introduction to the Study of his Works with an Anthology* (London: Thomas Nelson, 1957).

Clark, James, and Skinner, John V. (eds and trs), *Meister Eckhart: Selected Treatises and Sermons Translated from Latin and German with an Introduction and Notes* (New York: Harper & Row, 1958).

Colledge, Edmund, O. S. A., and McGinn, Bernard (eds and trs), *Meister Eckhart: The Essential Sermons, Commentaries, Treatises, and Defense* (New York: Paulist Press, 1981).

Cross, F. L. and Livingstone, F. A. (eds), *Oxford Dictionary of the Christian Church* (Oxford University Press, 1983).

Dasgupta, Surendranath, *Hindu Mysticism* (New York: Frederick Unger, 1927).

Doniger O'Flaherty, Wendy, *The Origins of Evil in Hindu Mythology* (Berkeley: University of California Press, 1976).

Dostoevsky, Fyodor, *The Brothers Karamazov: The Constance Garnett Translation revised by Ralph E. Matlaw – backgrounds and sources, essays in criticism*, Ralph E. Matlaw (ed.) (New York: Norton, 1976).

Dostoevsky, Fyodor, *Crime and Punishment*, Constance Garnett (tr.) (New York: Random House, 1956.

Dostoevsky, Fyodor, *The Devils*, David Magarshack (tr.) (Middlesex, England: Penguin, 1968).

Dostoevsky, Fyodor, *The Idiot*, John W. Strahan (tr.) (New York: Washington Square, 1965).

Dupré, Louis, 'The Christian Experience of Mystical Union', *The Journal of Religion*, vol. LIX (January, 1989) no. 1, pp. 1–13.

Evans, Donald D., 'Can Philosophers Limit What Mystics Can Do?', *Religious Studies*, vol. XXV (1989) no. 3, pp. 53–60.

Evans, Donald D., 'Christian Spirituality and Social Action', in Stanley Fefferman (ed.), *Awakened Heart: Buddhist–Christian Dialogue in Canada* (Toronto: United Church House, 1985) pp. 117–29).

Evans, Donald D., 'Mysticism and Morality', *Dialogue*, vol. XXIV (1985), pp. 297–307.

Evans, Donald D., *On Being Completely Human*, unpublished manuscript.

Ferm, Vergilius (ed.), *An Encyclopedia of Religion* (New York: The Philosophical Library, 1945).

Fox, Matthew (ed. and comm.), *Breakthrough: Meister Eckhart's Creation Spirituality in New Translation* (Garden City, NY: Image Books, 1980).

Friedman, R. Z., 'Evil and moral agency', *Philosophy of Religion*, vol. XXIV (1988) pp. 3–20.

Fuller, B. A. G., *The Problem of Evil in Plotinus* (Cambridge University Press, 1912).

Goetz, Ronald, 'The Suffering God: The Rise of the New Orthodoxy', *The Christian Century* (16 April 1986) pp. 385–9.

Gooch, Paul W., 'On Rivalry in Theodicy: Irenaeus, Augustine, and John Hick', unpublished.

Hart, H. L. A., *Punishment and Responsibility* (Oxford: Clarendon Press, 1968).

Herman, Arthur L., *The Problem of Evil in Indian Thought* (Delhi: Motilal Banarsidass, 1976).

Hick, John, *Death and Eternal Life* (Glasgow: William Collins, 1976).

Hick, John, *Evil and the God of Love* (London: Macmillan, 1966).

Hick, John, *An Interpretation of Religion: Human Responses to The Transcendent* (New Haven: Yale University Press, 1989).

Hick, John, *Problems Of Religious Pluralism* (London: Macmillan, 1985).

Hick, John, 'The Problem of Evil', in Paul Edwards (ed.), *The Encyclopedia of Philosophy* (New York: Macmillan, 1967).

Horne, James, *The Moral Mystic* (Waterloo, Ont.: Wilfred Laurier University Press, 1983).

Hume, David, *Dialogues Concerning Natural Religion*, Henry D. Aiken (ed.) (New York: Hafner, 1948).

Irenaeus, *Adversus Haereses*, W. W. Harvey (ed. and tr.) (Cambridge: n.p., 1857).

Irenaeus, *Apostolic Preaching*, in H. Bettenson (ed. and tr.), *The Early Christian Fathers: a Selection from the Writings of the Fathers from*

St Clement of Rome to St Athanasius (New York: Oxford University Press, 1969).

James, William, *The Varieties of Religious Experience* (New York: The New American Library, 1958).

Jung, C. G., *Answer to Job*, R. F. C. Hill (tr.) (Princeton University Press, 1973).

Kant, Immanuel, *Critique of Judgement*, J. H. Bernard (tr.) (New York: Hefner, 1951).

Kant, Immanuel, *Critique of Judgement*, J. C. Meredith (tr.) (Oxford: Clarendon Press, 1951).

Kant, Immanuel, *Critique of Practical Reason*, Lewis White Beck (tr.), (Indianapolis: Bobbs-Merrill, 1956).

Kant, Immanuel, 'On the Failure of All Attempted Philosophical Theodicies', in M. Despland (tr.) *Kant on History and Religion* (Montreal: McGill–Queen's University Press, 1973).

Kant, Immanuel, *Religion Within the Limits of Reason Alone*, T. M. Greene and H. H. Hudson (trs.), (Chicago: Open Court, 1934).

Katz, Steven (ed.), *Mysticism and Philosophical Analysis* (London: Sheldon Press, 1978).

Katz, Steven (ed.), *Mysticism and Religious Traditions* (Oxford University Press, 1983).

Kinsley, David, *Hinduism* (Englewood Cliffs, NJ: Prentice-Hall, 1982).

Koyré, Alexander, *La Philosophie De Jacob Boehme* (Paris: Librarie Philosophique J. Vrin, 1929).

Lawrence, D. H., 'Preface to Dostoevsky's *The Grand Inquisitor*', in René Wellek (ed.), *Dostoevsky* (Englewood Cliffs, NJ: Prentice-Hall, 1962).

Leibniz, G. W., *Theodicy*, E. M. Huggard (tr.) (London: Routledge & Kegan Paul, 1951).

Loades, Anne, 'Kant and Job's Comforters', in S. Sykes and D. Holmes (eds), *New Studies in Theology*, Vol. 1 (London: Gerald Duckworth, 1980).

Macquarrie, John, *In Search of Deity* (London: SCM Press, 1984).

Martensen, H. L. *Jacob Boehme*, T. Rhys Evans (tr.) (London: Rocklift, Salisbury Square, 1949).

McGinn, Bernard, (ed.), *Meister Eckhart: Teacher and Preacher* (Toronto: Paulist Press, 1968).

McLachlan, James, 'Existentialist Interpretations of the Desire to be God: Radical Freedom in Sartre and Berdyaev', unpublished PhD Thesis, University of Toronto, 1989.

Minor, Robert, *Sri Aurobindo: The Perfect and the Good* (Calcutta: Minerva Associates, Pvt., 1978).

Nayak, G.C., *Evil, Karma and Reincarnation* (Santiniketan, West Bengal: Centre of Advanced Study in Philosophy, Visva-Bharati, 1973).

Nikhilananda, Swami, *Self-Knowledge in Sri Sankaracharya* (Mylapore, Madras: Sri Ramakrishna Math, 1970).

O'Neil, L. Thomas, *Towards the Life Divine* (New Delhi: Manohar, 1979).

Otto, Rudolf, *Mysticism East and West*, B. L. Bracey and R. C. Payne (trs), (New York: Macmillan, 1972).

Peace, Richard, *Dostoyevsky* (Cambridge University Press, 1971).

220 Evil and the Mystics' God

Penelhum, Terence, *Butler* (London: Routledge & Kegan Paul, 1985).
Penelhum, Terence, *Religion and Rationality* (New York: Random House, 1971.
Plantinga, Alvin, *God, Freedom and Evil* (New York: Harper & Row, 1974).
Plotinus, *The Enneads*, Stephen MacKenna (tr.), 2nd edn rev. (London: Faber & Faber, 1956).
Plumptre, E. H., *The Spirits in Prison and Other Studies on the Life After Death* (London: Isbister, 1885).
Popkin, Richard H., 'Fideism', in Paul Edwards (ed.), *The Encyclopedia of Philosophy* (New York: Macmillan, 1972).
Popkin, Richard H., 'Pierre Bayle', in Paul Edwards (ed.), *The Encyclopedia of Philosophy* (New York: Macmillan, 1972).
Pseudo-Dionysius, *The Complete Works*, Colm Luibheid (tr.) (New York: Paulist Press, 1987).
Ricoeur, Paul, 'Evil, A Challenge to Philosophy and Theology', David Pellauer (tr.), *Journal of the American Academy of Religion*, vol. LIII (December, 1985) no. 4, pp. 635–48.
Śaṅkara, *The Vedānta Sutras*, George Thibaut (tr.), in F. Max Müller (ed.), *The Sacred Books of the East*, Vol. 34, part I (New Delhi: Motilal Banarsidass, 1973).
Schopenhauer, Arthur, *Essays and Aphorisms*, R. J. Hollingdale (tr.) (Markham, Ontario: Penguin, 1981).
Smart, Ninian, 'History of Mysticism', in Paul Edwards (ed.), *The Encyclopedia of Philosophy* (New York: Macmillan, 1974).
Smart, Ninian, 'Interpretation and Mystical Experience', *Religious Studies*, vol. I (1965) no. 1, pp. 75–87.
Smart, Ninian, 'Jakob Boehme', in Paul Edwards (ed.), *The Encyclopedia of Philosophy* (New York: Macmillan, 1974).
Smart, Ninian, *Reasons and Faiths* (London: Routledge & Kegan Paul, 1958).
Smart, Ninian, 'Reincarnation', in Paul Edwards (ed.), *The Encyclopedia of Philosophy* (New York: Macmillan, 1967).
St. Thomas Aquinas, *Summa Theologica*, Fathers of the English Dominican Province (tr.) (New York: Benziger Brothers, 1948).
St. Thomas Aquinas, *Truth*, Robert W. Schmidt, S. J. (tr.) (Chicago: Henry Regnery, 1954).
Stace, W. T., *Mysticism and Philosophy* (Philadelphia: Lippincott, 1960).
Stoeber, Michael, 'Personal Identity and Rebirth', *Religious Studies*, vol. XXVI (1990) pp. 493–500.
Stoudt, Joseph, *Jacob Boehme: His Life and Thought* (New York: Seabury, 1968).
Suso, Henry, *The Life of the Servant*, James M. Clark (tr.) (London: James Clark, 1952).
Terras, Victor, *A Karamazov Companion* (Madison, Wisconsin: The University of Wisconsin Press, 1981).
Traversi, D. A., 'Dostoevsky', in René Wellek (ed.), *Dostoevsky* (Englewood Cliffs, NJ: Prentice-Hall, 1962).
Troyat, Henry, *Firebrand*, Norbert Guterman (tr.) (New York: Roy, 1946).
Underhill, Evelyn, *Mysticism* (New York: New American Library, 1974).

Underhill, Evelyn, *Practical Mysticism* (New York: Dutton, 1943).

Voltaire, *Candide*, in Edmund Fuller (ed.), *Voltaire* (New York: Dell, 1959).

Wharton, Robert, 'Evil in an Earthly Paradise: Dostoevsky's Theodicy', *The Thomist*, vol. XXXXI (1977) pp. 567–84.

Woods, Richard, *Eckhart's Way* (Wilmington, Delaware: Michael Glazier, 1986).

Zaehner, R. C., *Mysticism Sacred and Profane* (Oxford University Press, 1957).

Zaehner, R. C., *Our Savage God* (New York: Sheed & Ward, 1974).

Zenkovsky, V. V., 'Dostoevsky's Religious and Philosophical Views', in René Wellek (ed.), *Dostoevsky* (Englewood Cliffs, NJ: Prentice-Hall, 1962).

Index

Voltaire   9, 35, 38, 44–9
Wharton, R.   197n2, 209n52
Woods, R.   205n3, 206n19

Zaehner, R. C.   95–6, 122, 202n1, 202n2
Zenkovsky, V.   32, 33, 197n1